THERE
ARE
STILL
KINGS

THERE
ARE
STILL
KINGS

◆ ◆ ◆

THE TEN ROYAL FAMILIES
OF EUROPE

◆ ◆ ◆

Laure Boulay
and Françoise Jaudel

◆ ◆ ◆

Translation by Linda Dannenberg

CLARKSON N. POTTER, INC./PUBLISHERS

DISTRIBUTED BY CROWN PUBLISHERS, INC.

NEW YORK

Published by Clarkson N. Potter, Inc., One Park Avenue, New
York, New York 10016, and simultaneously in Canada by General
Publishing Company Ltd.

Manufactured in the United States of America.

This book has been previously published in the French language
under the title *Il est encore des rois*.

The authors wish to thank Shirley Wohl for
her help with this edition.

Designed by Beth Tondreau.

LIBRARY OF CONGRESS CATALOGING IN PUBLICATION DATA
Jaudel, Françoise.
There are still kings.
Translation of: Il est encore des rois.
1. Europe—Kings and rulers—Biography.   2. Royal
houses—Europe—History—20th century.   I. Boulay de la
Meurthe, Laure.   II. Title.
D412.7.J3513   1984   940.55′092′2[B]   83-26893
ISBN 0-517-54838-0

10   9   8   7   6   5   4   3   2   1
First American Edition

CONTENTS

INTRODUCTION

Times have changed. Today, the only people who still live like princes . . . are kings. Theirs are extraordinary lives, steeped in history, tradition, and privilege. They live in magnificent palaces hung with masterpieces gathered over the centuries; for ceremonial occasions they roll out in ornate antique carriages, the kings brilliantly uniformed, the queens in sumptuous gowns and sparkling diadems. Like a chief of state, this rare royal species travels under heavy escort, its every move watched by the public and chronicled by the press.

But once upon a time, there were all kinds of beautiful ladies and handsome men who lived royally. Aristocrats, screen idols, millionaires, and industrial barons, as well as kings, dined in palaces and spent with lavish abandon. Europe was a poorer place then. Those who labored just to earn their daily bread gaped, stupefied, at the doings of these fantasy creatures from another world—the world of happiness, luxury, and perpetual parties. All that has disappeared. Today our screen idols squirrel away their money for the day when they sink into obscurity. Many aristocrats have seen their fortunes dwindle because of inheritance and real estate taxes. And the millionaires—many now billionaires—have grown fearful of political fluctuations, public enmity, and ransom attempts and live quietly behind tightly shut doors, with their fortunes for company. Today, when you are *truly* rich, you must never flaunt it.

Unless you happen to be a king. Ten of Europe's sovereigns have managed to survive all the upheavals of this century and to persevere, though at the expense of their power. They no longer tyrannize; their claws have been clipped, their fangs dulled. Today, in their benign state, their main function is to reinforce what a monarchy perhaps best symbolizes: national unity. A president of a republic personifies its government, a sovereign of a country embodies its soul. When the son of a president marries, it is a family affair; when the son of a king marries, it is the country's affair.

If we are to believe the popular press, all of today's royal families are handsome, intelligent, wise, virtuous, and effective. Admirably pious, formidably athletic, modern yet traditional, the contemporary royal couple should certainly be happy. By taking an inside look at these families, who are often portrayed on pedestals bathed in soft, rosy light, we have attempted to reveal who and what they really are—to strip away the myth and expose the reality. Do they continue to exist only because government has forgotten to abolish an obsolete institution? Or do they indeed still serve some sort of purpose?

The sovereigns remain popular in their countries as long as they continue to respect a few tacit rules. They must always keep themselves above party politics, never taking sides publicly on issues, and they must consistently fulfill their royal duties: presiding over official receptions and inaugurations, bestowing honorary decorations, and overseeing charitable activities. In certain cases they may give their advice on the formation of a new government. They must live a private life that is, if not irreproachable, then at least not publicly reprehensible. And they must accept publicity with grace, recognizing that every royal step falls in the public domain.

Whatever would become of Spain without its king? Juan Carlos has very likely kept his country from embarking on a second civil war. And, ironically, it was the Spanish monarchy that helped restore a democracy after forty years of dictatorship. How dull the Scandinavian countries might be without the trials and tribulations of their royal families. Monaco, a tiny kingdom perched on a rock, has the only absolute monarch in Europe. Prince Rainier wields more real power than the queen of England. He alone governs, while the other sovereigns have no right to political rule. Baudouin, through his discreet influence and effectiveness, has enabled Belgium to avoid serious political schisms. As for the British— even if their empire were reduced to one island on the verge of sinking, the prestige of the royal family would still beam out over the entire world. In spite of the social and economic problems that beset their country, the English still fiercely cherish the pomp and splendor of their monarchy.

For the most part, and in a variety of idiosyncratic ways, the sovereigns of Europe are conscientious and committed. There is not a single unworthy king, even if among their nearest and dearest there may be a few notable eccentrics. They are well aware of their fragile state, realizing that their thrones are hardly essential to the future. And it is quite likely that in the days to come the serious stresses and strains on royal duty will imperil the principle of monarchy itself.

The sovereigns no longer have enough power or prominence to reawaken a once unshakable passion for the crown. While they may no longer be in danger of losing their heads, should disenchantment with monarchy peak, they do face the more common specter of heavier taxes. Ten royal houses have weathered the slings and arrows of fortune up to this point, but the current crop of European kings remains in danger of extinction.

Many crown princes have married commoners, thus diluting their lines. And several monarchs, inspired by an egalitarian trend, have become "bourgeois" kings. The mystique that has surrounded royalty down through the centuries is slowly fading away because of the excess of misalliances and encroaching republicanism. To slow it down, the sovereigns must love and be loved like the most humble of their subjects. Today the strength of their kingdoms lies in their hearts.

ENGLAND

◆

Ruling with Scepter, Sword, and Charisma:
The Superstars of Buckingham Palace

W hen Britain wins a battle, she shouts 'God Save the Queen.' When she loses, she votes down the prime minister." The words are those of Winston Churchill, for nine years the prime minister of England, and a man who, throughout his life, was a staunch admirer of the British monarchy. England stands unique; in no other country on earth do the citizens so readily pay homage to their queen, as if their lives and liberties still depended on her. It is in great part because of this unwavering fealty that, throughout the Western world, for aristocrat and commoner alike, the word "royalty" is synonymous with the queen of England.

GORGEOUSLY SHOWY but aloof, the Court of St. James's has always fascinated onlookers, both local and foreign. Year in and year out, thousands of spectators patiently stand for hours in front of Buckingham Palace waiting to catch a glimpse of a small, blue-eyed woman in her carriage. Her fifty-eight years have left their mark on her porcelain complexion and set her once-gentle features into a permanently severe expression, softened slightly by a well-practiced smile. She is Elizabeth II, forty-second successor to William the Conqueror and the sixth woman to reign over the United Kingdom of Great Britain and Northern Ireland. But as head of the British Commonwealth she has power well beyond the shores of England and Ireland. She reigns over twenty-six countries: four monarchies in addition to her own and twenty-two republics, including India, Bangladesh, Kenya, and Uganda. And if this weren't enough, she is also queen of fifteen other countries, among them Canada, Australia, New Zealand, and Jamaica.

The opening of Parliament, a ceremony that reaffirms the symbiotic relationship between the monarchy and the people, offers England an occasion to flaunt the pomp and riches of the crown. Seated in an Irish carriage of state (acquired by Queen Victoria in Dublin in 1852) drawn by six horses, the queen passes through the great gate of Buckingham Palace. The Master of the Horse prances alongside the carriage followed by the Household Cavalry, a unit comprised of two regiments, the Life Guards, and the Blues and the Royals, who accompany the queen at all official receptions.

As soon as the queen leaves the palace another carriage, no less richly ornamented, pulls out from the Tower of London. Carried within, resting on a large velvet cushion, is the Imperial Crown of State, which the queen will wear to address the combined Houses of Lords and Commons. Awaiting Her Majesty at the door of Parliament at Westminster are the Lord Chancellor, in a black robe embroidered with gold, the Lord Great Chamberlain, and the Earl Marshal of England, who will escort her into a private salon. Here she will don her purple ermine-lined cape and exchange her pearl-and-diamond tiara for the Imperial Crown, whose oak-leaf patterned gold setting is encrusted with three thousand diamonds.

Two pages of honor carry her train as the queen, accompanied by Philip, the prince consort, and followed by her ladies-in-waiting, begins the long procession to the House of Lords. There she will give an address from the throne outlining the legislative program of Great Britain for the next session of Parliament. The Lord Chamberlain, kneeling before her, removes the royal address from an embroidered bag and hands it to the queen. It has, in fact, been drafted by the prime minister, and she does not have the right to change a single word.

———

A STRANGE and illogical institution. According to the law, according to tradition, the queen is the supreme head of state and she holds absolute power. She is the source of justice, which is rendered in her name; she is the commander-in-chief of the armed forces, and she is the head of the Church of England. The prime minister and the members of government are ostensibly her servants.

The venerable Winston Churchill, a descendant of the Marlboroughs, one of the most illustrious of England's aristocratic families, was the first prime minister to be accorded the honor of having a sovereign dine in his home. He was eighty-five years old at the time and had dressed for the occasion in black silk breeches and white stockings. At the end of the evening, after escorting the royal party to the door, he bowed almost to the waist to the thirty-three-year-old woman who was his queen.

The close links between the crown and the government are widely apparent. No document and no official paper has any value unless it carries the royal signature. The royal initials are even engraved on public mail boxes. The nomination of any high official, from the prime minister to the governor of an obscure dominion of the crown, is highlighted by the royal favor—that of kissing the queen's hand. This ceremony dates back to medieval times, when the kissing of hands affirmed the bond between a sovereign and his vassals. Almost every minister who has governed under the reign of Elizabeth II has bowed to this custom, even the uncompromising socialists. Harold Wilson was one of the rare exceptions. Named prime minister, he refused to put on the traditional morning coat, but he did agree to wear the striped pants and black vest. Richard Crossman, a minister from the extreme left of the Socialist party, also caused a few difficulties, but he too finally capitulated and entered into the complex and paradoxical game which reflects the England of today. It is a kingdom where everything—social stratification, politics, even the theater and business—revolves around the crown, where a renowned poet becomes a royal poet, where a prominent menswear shop is proud to announce in its window that it furnishes ties to Prince Philip, and where whiskey producers battle for the privilege of purveying to the royal household. But it is also a kingdom where the queen has absolutely no real power, not even the right to vote.

Walter Bagehot, the greatest writer on English constitutional law, points out in his work *The English Constitution* (1867) that the queen has only "the right to be consulted, the right to encourage, and the right to warn." In spite of these constitutional restrictions, several English monarchs, from Queen Victoria to Elizabeth II herself, have played direct or indirect political roles, leaving their imprint on the government of Great Britain. Queen Victoria openly reproached William Gladstone, her prime minister, whom she detested, and made veiled threats to Lord Palmerston, the minister of foreign affairs. And Elizabeth II played, perhaps involuntarily, a crucial political role in naming Harold Macmillan, and later Sir Alex Douglas-Home, to the post of prime minister.

THREE HISTORIC incidents—or as some historians see it, three tragic events—paved Elizabeth's path to the throne. The first can be traced back to 1820, when the prince-regent, after a particularly dissolute life, became king at the age of fifty-seven, taking the name George IV. Although a bigamist at one point in his life, George IV left no heirs, and the crown passed on to his brother, William IV. William, also childless, was as dissipated as his older brother and spent most of his time surrounded by mistresses. The next in line to the throne was the third brother, Edward, the duke of Kent, whose bachelor life was hardly more exemplary. He had reached his fifties when, panic-stricken by the idea that the royal line was about to be extinguished, he decided to get married —to Princess Mary Louise Victoria of Saxe-Coburg. He died before succeeding William IV, but he left a daughter, the sole descendant of this family that reveled in drinking, dining, and debauching. She was named Victoria and became queen at the age of eighteen.

The second event occurred later in the nineteenth century and concerns the duke of Clarence, the eldest son of King Edward VII and next in line to the throne. The duke, according to numerous historians, best exemplifies the dissolute tendency of the English royal family. He was, it seems, one of the most faithful clients of the telegraph boys in Cable Street in the East End of London. There he contracted a series of what were then profoundly shameful maladies and died at the age of twenty-six from a combination of infections, leaving to his younger brother—the future King George V (Elizabeth II's grandfather)—his fiancée, Mary of Teck, and the crown.

The third event that paved the way for the reign of Elizabeth II happened almost fifty years ago. Her father's older brother, the charming and seductive David, became king of England under the name of Edward VIII. Within a year he abdicated in favor of his younger brother Albert, the duke of York, who on his coronation took the name of George VI.

Bertie, as he was called, stuttered from the time he was five years old, when, naturally left-handed, he was forced to write with his right hand. Like his father, King George V, Bertie was pale and withdrawn, but given to abrupt bursts of anger during which he would shout and on occasion break anything within reach. Also like his father, he had problems with his handwriting. David Lloyd George, the great English statesman, imparted to friends one day, "In my whole life, I have never seen anyone write as slowly as the king." Bertie's private journal was full of writing mistakes, and he never even knew how to spell the name of Shakespeare. All of this was of slight significance, however, since Albert was only the younger son and it would be the elder David who would mount the throne.

Albert inherited from his father a great sense of order and a meticulousness in the accomplishment of any task. Another legacy was a stubborn resistance to any intellectual pursuit. George V, it was said at court, had never read a single book. He loved the operetta *Rose Marie,* which he went to see regularly with the queen; each time he was captivated by the music and the plot. When the well-known historian Harold Nicolson was writing the king's biography, he confided to his wife that it was terribly difficult to make his subject attractive.

> He is all right as a gay young midshipman. He may be all right as a wise old king. But in the intervening period when he was duke of York, he did nothing at all but kill animals and stick in stamps.

Bertie was a chip off the royal block. Due in large part to his sense of order and his perseverance, he entered the Royal Naval College, was graduated sixty-third out of a class of sixty-seven, and was made a second lieutenant. At a ball shortly thereafter he met the young and beautiful Elizabeth Angela Marguerite Bowes-Lyon, daughter of the count of Strathmore and Kinghorne. She was effervescent, amusing, and extremely rich—and hardly enchanted by the attentions of the king's son. Albert, duke of York, persisted. His first offer of marriage was rejected by the girl and her parents. As a means of consolation, George V smilingly told his son: "You'll be a lucky fellow if she accepts you." According to gossip at the time, Elizabeth Bowes-Lyon went on to have an unhappy love affair, while Albert waited in the wings. But his lucky day eventually arrived, and in 1923 Elizabeth became his wife. She made her mark in the history of English royalty as a woman who knew how to give her husband the confidence, the vitality, and the dynamism that he lacked. And she became one of the most popular queens England has ever known.

Albert was deeply smitten with the beautiful Elizabeth while she grew to love him, and it was thus into a very happy and united family that the current queen was born on April 21, 1926. She came into the world through a Cesarean delivery at the home of her maternal grandparents, at 17 Bruton Street. Her paternal grandparents, King George V and Queen Mary, were informed of the birth at 2:40 A.M. at Windsor Castle, and came to London the next day to see the infant, later baptized Elizabeth Alexandra Mary.

From the very beginning, King George V exerted a profound influence on his granddaughter. She was the only person to whom he ever demonstrated any affection. She spent hours with the old king, who perhaps endowed her with the sense of discipline, duty, and work that is her hallmark and that was strikingly obvious even during her childhood. When she was only ten, she would get out of bed in the middle of the night to make sure that her clothes were neatly folded and that her shoes were perfectly aligned. One day when she had a bad case of the flu her doctor ordered her immediately to bed, but she refused to miss any of her classes.

She was four years old when her mother gave birth to a second daughter, Margaret Rose. This little creature was the complete opposite of her older sister, who took her seriously in hand. The young Elizabeth instructed her in comportment, giving her little elbow pokes during official ceremonies and whispering to her to stand up straight, to stay still, to not move her feet.

Margaret's birth marked another kind of beginning as well, that of a profound affection between the future queen and "Bobo," a young woman who was to become a lifelong friend. Since the princesses' nanny, Mrs. Knight (who had formerly raised their mother), had to devote all her attention to the baby, she hired Margaret MacDonald, a coachman's daughter, to assist her as "Jill-of-all-trades" in the nursery. Between little Elizabeth and young Margaret MacDonald (whom Elizabeth nicknamed Bobo) a bond formed that endures today. Bobo lives at Buckingham Palace, where she is the queen's wardrobe mistress, responsible for her vast collection of clothes and jewels.

Elizabeth was ten years old when she learned she would one day be queen of England and empress of a territory inhabited by hundreds of millions of people. On Friday, December 11, 1936, her uncle Edward VIII, who wanted to marry an American divorcée, abdicated. In his radio statement to the people, Edward declared: "You must believe me when I tell you that I have found it impossible . . . to discharge my duty as king as I would wish to do without the help and support of the woman I love."

In an ominous atmosphere, Bertie succeeded to the throne under the name of George VI, and Elizabeth became the crown princess. England was in the throes of economic problems and the world was in a state of ferment: Spain was in the middle of a civil war, Mussolini was on a colonial rampage, and in the heart of Europe Nazi Germany, under the direction of the Führer, was arming itself with its eye fixed on Austria, and imperiling the entire world. At this moment of domestic and international tension, England needed a king, perhaps one less dramatic than the handsome Edward VIII but certainly one more stable and ready to respect the constitution and its customs. Bertie, or rather His Majesty King George VI, appeared to fulfill these requirements. He and his family, Queen Elizabeth, Elizabeth and Margaret, were the incarnation of the virtues so dear to England—discretion, moderation, and stability.

The new, anti-intellectual king was in a way reassuring to the middle classes—sort of a common man. On the other hand, he was the more menaced by and violently opposed to the "red" intellectuals who were agitating at Oxford and London. The value of the pound had fallen and unemployment had risen when the royal family settled in "above the store" (as Prince Philip would later put it)—Buckingham Palace.

The little princesses were overjoyed to discover an immense park surrounding their new home, with a little hill and a lake into which Prince Albert, consort to Queen Victoria, had once fallen. They saw their parents almost every day when the family was in London. Vacations were spent in the family chateaux—Balmoral in August, Sandringham for the Christmas holidays, and Windsor in June. They were picturesque residences, the most modest of which had three to four hundred rooms.

IN THESE early days of their father's reign, a new relationship sprang up between the two sisters. Elizabeth, nicknamed Lilibet, had always been the more serious, the more applied, the more disciplined, while Margaret always played on her charm, her mischievousness, and her talent as a clown. But they got along well, playing together, learning together, simply being two little girls together. Suddenly one day, everything changed. Margaret was still the amusing little princess, but her older sister was now crown princess, heir to the throne of England. Government officials who came for an audience with the king acknowledged Elizabeth ceremoniously when they passed her in the palace hallways. The ladies of the highest society held her in great reverence, and the judges, topped by their great white wigs, paid her homage.

Meanwhile World War II loomed on the horizon, and across the country tension mounted. Many families, fearing bombardment or even a full-scale invasion, sent their children out of the country, mostly to Canada. But the royal family decided to set an example of courage and optimism by sending the princesses to Windsor Castle, only half an hour from London, for the duration of the war.

On October 13, 1940, sensing that the morale of the country was wavering, the government requested at court that the crown princess speak over the radio to boost British spirits. Unlike her father, who four years after his coronation was still ill at ease speaking in public, Elizabeth showed no trepidation. In a sweet, clear voice she addressed the British empire in the four corners of the world: "I can truthfully say to you all that we children at home are full of cheerfulness and courage. . . . We know, every one of us, that in the end all will be well." Margaret was seated at her sister's side in front of the microphone, and at the end of Elizabeth's address, millions of listeners across the empire heard: "Come on, Margaret, say your sentence." And little Margaret joyously shouted, "Good night, children."

Above: The little princesses—Elizabeth and Margaret Rose—on the balcony of Buckingham Palace following the coronation of their father. (British Information Services)

Elizabeth and Philip in full regalia of the most prestigious Royal Order of the Garter. (British Information Services)

It was during the war that Elizabeth was to meet the man who would become her husband. They saw each other for the first time on July 22, 1939, when the royal family made an official visit to Dartmouth Naval College. By coincidence—some say by design —one of their relatives, Lord Louis Mountbatten, a marine officer, was present when the royal yacht *Victoria and Albert* moored. Because of an epidemic of chicken pox and mumps, the princesses were forbidden to visit the school and mingle with the officers-in-training. Nevertheless, Lord Mountbatten chose one of the young officers, Philip, to represent his fellows and keep the princesses company. Philip, eighteen years old and resplendent in his white uniform, presented himself at the home of the school's commanding officer, Admiral Sir Frederick Dalrymple-Hamilton. Crawfie, the girls' ever-present governess who had succeeded Mrs. Knight, described him later in her scandal-causing book: "A good-looking, fair-haired boy, rather like a Viking, with a sharp face and piercing blue eyes." The three young people played with an electric train and shared lemonade and cookies. At the end of the afternoon, to show off his prowess, Philip led the girls and Crawfie to the tennis court, where he proceeded to leap over the net several times. Thirteen-year-old Elizabeth was dazzled. "How good he is, Crawfie. How high he can jump!"

Evidently, Philip made a huge impression on the princess. The next day, the king invited the officers from the base to lunch aboard his yacht. At the request of Elizabeth, Philip was among them. What they said to each other during this day is not a matter of record, but that night, when the yacht cast off its moorings to set sail, the officers gave it a cheer and accompanied it out of port in rowboats. At the end of the bay they halted, except for one boat that continued to follow the royal yacht. The sole occupant put down his oars from time to time to wave farewell to a girl leaning over the bulwarks. It was, of course, Philip, ignoring the royal orders to go back, while Princess Elizabeth watched him fondly through an enormous pair of binoculars.

The young officer and the princess saw each other throughout the war years. Philip was often invited to spend his leaves at Windsor Castle. In 1943 rumors were already circulating of a possible marriage, for Philip was one of the rare outsiders invited to spend Christmas with the royal family. There were in all just nine around the holiday table at Windsor Castle—the king, the queen, the two princesses, four close family relatives, and Philip. The girls gave a little pantomime performance of *Aladdin's Magic Lamp,* and later everyone played charades. The next day other guests arrived and that evening the gramophone was turned on for dancing. Philip, tenderly entwined with Elizabeth, led her in a foxtrot and tango.

There is no doubt that everyone saw in this young man a serious candidate for marrying the future queen. It was also obvious that the couple were seriously taken with each other. However, Philip didn't have a cent. He wasn't English, and he was serving in the navy as a foreigner. Nevertheless, what he did have going for him was the fact that he could count a good two dozen kings and princes among his brothers-in-law, cousins, and uncles, that he was handsome and—it was thought—submissive, and that he belonged to none of the aristocratic English clans, a positive factor since the clans were extremely jealous of one another. His uncle, "Dickie" Mountbatten (who was assassinated in 1979 in an IRA attack), was a close relative of the king and queen and one of the king's most influential advisers. Dickie was the son of one of Queen Victoria's granddaughters and the German prince Louis of Battenberg, who had Anglicized his name at the beginning of World War I, when he served as First Lord of the Admiralty. (This act of loyalism proved useless when the wave of Germanophobia that later broke over England forced him to resign his commission.)

Philip was not unfamiliar with misery. As a child, he used to stay indoors at school all day when it rained because he didn't have a raincoat. His mother, Alice of Battenberg, sister of Uncle Dickie, lived in Paris, where she immersed herself in Greek Orthodox religious mysticism. His father, Prince André, lived by his wits alone, shuttling between Paris and Monte Carlo, where he was an habitué of the casinos. The young Philip was the fruit of a very recent chapter in European history. To understand the man who is today the husband of Queen Elizabeth II, probably the only man she regularly listens to or consults, and a man who has helped mold the modern image of England, it is necessary to jump several decades back in history and slightly to the east geographically.

AT THE SOUTHEAST POINT of Europe lies Greece, which for three centuries submitted to Ottoman occupation. When it finally achieved independence at the beginning of the nineteenth century, the country needed a king capable of reuniting a people torn apart by internal quarrels. Otton, the son of the king of Bavaria, became king of the Greeks. He built a small German-style palace in Athens and managed to hold on to his throne for thirty years before he was forced to pack up his bags and flee. Greece was again in the throes of civil war. A new king was needed. France and Russia each proposed a candidate, but the Greeks believed they would be better protected if they went to Great Britain. Queen Victoria didn't want to send one of her sons to what she considered a precarious and dangerous throne. But she did recommend Prince Wilhelm of Schleswig-Holstein-Sonderburg-Glücksburg, the seventeen-year-old grandson of King Frederic VII of Denmark and a cadet at the Naval College in Copenhagen. Young Willy was acceptable to the Russians, since his family was vaguely related to the Romanovs, and satisfactory to the French, since Napoleon III was confident that he would succeed in recruiting into his camp an inexperienced and, reputedly, easily influenced young man. On October 30, 1863, Willy arrived in Piraeus and took the title of George I, King of the Hellenes. After a long and difficult reign he was assassinated in 1913. The oldest of his seven children, Constantin I, succeeded him.

Willy's second oldest son, Prince André—future father of Prince Philip—served in the army during the Greco-Turkish war of 1922. Arrested for desertion and high treason, he narrowly escaped execution by firing squad—thanks only to the intervention of George V of England—and was subsequently expelled from Greece with his wife and children.

Prince André and his family went into exile under the worst possible conditions. They had no house to go to and no money, and the Greek government had even stripped the family of their nationality and their name. The king of Denmark used his royal prerogative to bestow on them Danish citizenship, and the prince and his family installed themselves as well as they could in Paris. Other family members were able to give them substantial aid, especially George, Prince André's brother. Prince Philip was sent to Monsieur MacJannet's nursery school in Saint-Cloud, *the* place for children of rich Americans living in Paris. His education was paid for by an American heiress who had married his uncle Christopher, but he was still the poorest student in the school. His uncle, the king of Sweden, sent him some pocket money, but the sum was fixed every year and very modest; for Christmas he received one pound.

Relations between Philip's parents, who at one time had been very much in love, were steadily growing worse. Princess Alice, Philip's mother, was involved with Hellas, a Parisian boutique that sold Greek-made products as well as paintings, including works by her brother-in-law, who signed his canvases "Nicolas the Prince." Philip's father, Prince André, a born-again playboy, became more and more exasperated by his wife's growing infatuation with mysticism. For several years the couple lived together in the same apartment, where their quarrels became increasingly violent. Eventually they separated. At the age of eight, Philip went to join his mother's two brothers in London because the whole family agreed on one point: "England is the safest place for royalty." Philip was sent to Salem, the famous German boarding school on the edge of Lake Constance, run by the celebrated educator Kurt Hahn. After Hahn fled the Nazis and opened the Gordonstoun school in Scotland, Philip was transferred there—where he was doubtless the only child without pocket money, without close relatives with whom he could spend school holidays, and without any kind of normal family affection.

WHEN, after years of war and political upheaval, the Greek monarchy was once again restored, Philip went off to Athens to attend the engagement party of Prince Paul, the future Paul I of Greece, and Princess Frederika of Brunswick. At the festivities he chanced upon his father, and over the next few days father and son had several long conversations. According to their intimates, Prince André, whose life was so full of adventures, deception, and trauma, gave his son two bits of advice: Stay in England, because it's the safest place for people like us, and make a good marriage, because you'll never have a penny.

Shortly thereafter, Philip returned to England to prepare for the entrance exam to the Royal Naval College at Dartmouth. In spite of being a foreigner, he was eligible, thanks to the recommendations of his uncle Dickie. In May 1939, he was accepted, scoring sixteenth among thirty-four candidates. It was two months later that he met Princess Elizabeth, the girl who inspired him to leap over the net on the tennis court.

Such was the man who was invited to spend the Christmas holidays of 1943 with the royal family.

THROUGHOUT the war, Elizabeth and Philip wrote each other regularly, and most of the court already considered the young prince a semiofficial suitor of the future queen. Philip's photograph took the place of honor on the mantelpiece in her room, and when her father told her it was a mistake to so openly flaunt her affections, she merely replaced that picture with another one of Philip, bearded, and answered, "This way no one will recognize him." (He had let his beard grow while he served on a frigate in the Mediterranean.)

Philip had no future; as a foreigner, his career in the British navy would be severely limited. And yet this foreigner-without-a-future aspired to the hand of the crown princess of England. He begged his cousin, King George of Greece, to officially ask for the hand of Elizabeth on his behalf. Her father, although not necessarily against such an arrangement, answered, "She is too young for that now." He encouraged his daughter to go out, to see other young people. At the age of eighteen Elizabeth enlisted as second lieutenant in a transport division, where she learned truck and automobile maintenance, and even how to drive a jeep. Her parents presented her with her first car—a Daimler, the royal family's favorite make.

The war was over. Dances were organized at Buckingham Palace to which the young officers of the Royal Guard, stationed a few hundred yards from the palace, were invited. Elizabeth smiled, danced from time to time, but hardly seemed to enjoy herself during these evenings when a regimental orchestra played the latest hits from American musical comedies. On the other hand, her sister Margaret was almost deliriously happy at these festivities. She flirted, she sang, she danced—always the life of the parties at Buckingham. And yet her heart already beat a bit faster for the king's new equerry, a certain Group Captain Peter Townsend.

Philip rarely saw Elizabeth and this troubled him. He was trying to become a naturalized English citizen. His uncle Dickie intervened in his favor, but the government, particularly the foreign office, turned a deaf ear to his case, since Greece was floundering in the midst of a bitter civil war between Communist and Royalist factions. To accord naturalization to a former Greek prince would have been interpreted either as support for one of the sides or, more seriously, as a sign that the British considered the Royalists' cause lost and were according political asylum to one of its representatives.

Nevertheless, Philip and Elizabeth did see each other occasionally, chaperoned almost continually of course, although they somehow managed to negotiate a few tête-à-têtes. In the summer of 1946, without going through any of the formalities normally expected in a middle-class household, let alone the intricate protocol of a royal family, Philip asked Elizabeth to marry him. Without consulting either her father or her mother, or posing the question to the Privy Council or to the government, Elizabeth promptly answered yes. Several years later, when for state reasons she forbade her sister Margaret to marry the man she loved, there were grumbled recollections among her subjects that the queen had married the man *she* loved in spite of the state.

Facing a fait accompli, George VI gave his consent but asked that the engagement not be announced until after Elizabeth's twenty-first birthday. From that point on, the formalities were quickly disposed of. At the beginning of 1947 Philip became an English citizen, residing in London. The only remaining problem was that of a name for him. The war helped a little in the search for a solution. London was still partially in ruins and the city of Coventry, which had suffered the most intense bombing from German planes, had barely started reconstruction. The English public would hardly be in favor of a fiancé, a husband, and finally, a prince consort called Schleswig-Holstein-Sondenburg-Glücksburg. Royal heraldic experts studied the princely problem for weeks before finally discovering that the grandmother of his grandfather had carried the title of the Countess of Oldenburg, having sold off her more illustrious titles. They suggested Anglicizing the name and making Philip the count of Oldcastle. Nobody in the royal family was particularly enchanted with this idea. It was finally the newly-elected Labor government, under the leadership of Clement Attlee, that came up with the solution: Wouldn't it be simpler if he took the name of his mother, Battenberg, already Anglicized into Mountbatten by his grandfather Louis in 1914? The idea was taken up, but the British still could not be swayed. Public opinion polls showed that almost half of the English people were against this marriage to a man of uncertain nationality—Greek,

German, Danish—whose father passed the better part of his time gambling at the green felt tables of Monte Carlo or dining at Maxim's, and whose mother was a sackcloth-clad mystic with an enormous crucifix on her chest.

But England longed for rebirth after the ordeal of war, and this young and handsome couple seemed to augur a happy future. So on November 20, 1947, the marriage was celebrated. All the pomp in the United Kingdom could not mask the humiliation inflicted on the poor bridegroom: none of his four sisters, all married to Germans, had been invited—not even Theodora, the eldest, who had cared for him during his childhood. His parents had declined their invitations, which were sent to them on the express condition, it is rumored, that they not show up.

The princess was radiant in her ivory satin gown, completely embroidered with the roses of the House of York, designed by the official court couturier, Norman Hartnell. The English, during this period of economic austerity, had to use coupons to buy even a yard of the most ordinary fabric. But England, though it may insult its governments, loves its royalty.

Parliament had not succeeded in filling all the requests for lodging from millions of English people made homeless by the war. Yet, faithful to tradition, it voted the young couple—who had taken up temporary residence at Buckingham Palace—a sum of 50,000 pounds (then worth over $150,000) to modernize Clarence House, their future home. The princess was allotted an annual income of 50,000 pounds and Philip finally received a steady income of his own—10,000 pounds a year, more than his entire family possessed since its flight from Greece. He lost his title of prince, which came from the royal house of Athens (but which would be returned to him by his wife, the queen, in 1957) and was named Baron Greenwich, Count of Merioneth and Duke of Edinburgh, by King George VI.

TWO YEARS after their marriage Elizabeth and Philip, now the parents of eight-month-old Prince Charles, moved from Buckingham Palace into the refurbished Clarence House, a sumptuous residence where they found, for the first time, a certain privacy. Elizabeth and Philip had separate bedrooms. The duke's was more like a study, simply and soberly furnished. The princess's was much more elaborate, complete with a canopy bed detailed with an engraved crown at the head. Husband and wife resumed separate careers; Philip, the model naval officer, reported every morning to the admiralty, only a short stroll away; Elizabeth went back to her inaugurations, official visits, and audiences. On August 15, 1950, she gave birth to their second child, Princess Anne.

The duke and the princess often left Clarence House to travel abroad. During their first visit to Washington, D.C., they stayed at Blair House with President Truman and his family, who were in residence there while the White House underwent repairs. One day Truman led the royal couple up to the top floor to meet his bedridden mother-in-law, Mrs. Wallace. When he explained who her visitors were, the eighty-six-year-old woman grasped Elizabeth's hand and exclaimed, "I'm so glad that your father's been re-elected!"

It was during a trip to Kenya in February 1952 that the princess became the queen. On February 5, Elizabeth and some of her entourage—Philip; Martin Charteris, her private secretary; Mike Parker, a member of Philip's personal staff; and Bobo—spent the evening at the Treetops Hotel, which was situated in the upper branches of an enormous tree and overlooked a large watering hole for the jungle animals. They watched the elephants, rhinoceroses, and gazelles quench their thirst in the moonlight. On the afternoon of the sixth, Martin Charteris was called to the telephone: "The king is dead," the palace informed him. At 7:30 that morning, King George's personal valet had gone to awaken his master as usual with a cup of tea. The king didn't stir. Already afflicted with cancer, he had died from a heart attack during the night. Charteris returned to the hotel, where he first informed Lady Pamela Mountbatten, Elizabeth's lady-in-waiting, who in turn informed the duke. It was he who broke the news to Elizabeth that her father was dead and she was queen.

Parker later related that Philip was deeply moved by the news, but that the queen remained calm and betrayed no signs of sadness. With her characteristic foresight—which at times seems uncanny —she had carried with her a black mourning outfit, even though her father had appeared fit and in good spirits when she had left him a few days earlier. With remarkable composure Elizabeth sat down at a table to write letters of apology to the governments of Australia and New Zealand, her next scheduled stops. Accompanied by her retinue, she set off for the closest airport, at Entebbe, and left for London the next day. Awaiting her arrival at the London airport were Prime Minister Winston Churchill, former Prime Minister Clement Attlee, and Minister of Foreign Affairs Anthony Eden, as well as her uncle, the duke of Gloucester. All four greeted her with a deep bow. The new queen of the British Commonwealth was twenty-five years old.

The next day, accompanied by the duke of Gloucester, Elizabeth went to the throne room of St. James's Palace to read her declaration of accession to the throne before an assembly that included the extended royal family, Churchill and other senior government officials, and the top representatives of the Church of England. The first person to come pay her homage was her grandmother, Queen Mary. "Her old granny and subject must be the first to kiss her hand," she said. Queen Mary was then eighty-five years old. She was to die a year later after having known the reign of six monarchs and the death of three of her own sons.

For sixteen months the queen prepared for her coronation. She reorganized the court, received most of her private counselors, and began to meet weekly with members of the government. She inherited as prime minister the old English bulldog Winston Churchill, the man who had won the war and had deep ties to King George VI. Upon learning of the king's death, Churchill had been deeply moved. In the eyes of the old statesman, the late king represented, partially because of his weaknesses, the essence of the British character. Churchill was skeptical of the capacities of this "small young woman." Would she know how to quickly and effectively replace the departed king at a particularly difficult time for England? Elizabeth showed well, and Churchill's confidence was restored. The old prime minister was among the first to demonstrate his admiration and devotion to the new queen.

For three months prior to the coronation ceremony the queen rehearsed her moves, first in a small salon, then in the large throne room of Buckingham Palace, to the accompaniment of records reproducing the events of her father's coronation. She wondered if she would be able, as protocol required, to descend from the throne in Westminster Abbey and kneel while wearing the enormous and heavy traditional Crown of St. Edward. And, returning from Westminster Abbey to Buckingham Palace, would she be able to bear, for a much longer period, the Imperial Crown of State, somewhat lighter but still a substantial burden? To get used to the latter crown she wore it constantly in the palace, even while having tea or taking care of her dogs.

On June 2, 1953, the day of the coronation, London was full to bursting with millions of Englishmen and tourists, as well as thousands of cameramen and journalists from the world media. It was raining heavily, but nothing could discourage the hundreds of thousands of curious onlookers massed along the sidewalks.

The procession to Westminster Abbey began at eight in the morning, led by the lord mayor of London in his carriage drawn by six gray horses and escorted by his personal guard. Next came the members of the royal family, followed by lords and ladies-in-waiting, the Lord Great Chamberlain and the Master of the Horse, the high English aristocracy and foreign guests—all the kings and queens, princes and princesses, and presidents of Europe and beyond. The first head of state to arrive at the Abbey was Queen Salote of Tonga, in the South Pacific, sporting a bright red feather in her hat. In all, about 7,600 people assembled in a cathedral designed to hold half that number. The scene was a fairyland of glittering colors and costumes, majestic music, and figures in resplendent uniforms, a vision beyond the wildest dreams of the most flamboyant Hollywood producer.

At one minute to eleven, accompanied by the horsemen of the Household Cavalry, and banners, flags, and trumpet fanfares, the queen's carriage rolled up in front of the cathedral where the archbishops of Canterbury and York were waiting. As the queen mounted the steps, the Westminster Boys' Choir, which, since the coronation of James II in 1685 had the privilege of welcoming sovereigns, sent up the traditional cry: "Vivat Regina Elizabetha."

The ceremony was divided into three parts: the monarch's recognition and acceptance by the assembly, the oath of royal duties, and the anointing and crowning. The archbishop of Canterbury turned to all four corners of the abbey, proclaiming: "Sirs, I here present unto you Queen Elizabeth, your undoubted queen. Wherefore all you who are come this day to do your homage and service, are you willing to do the same?" All assembled answered, "God bless Queen Elizabeth."

Now came the moment for the oath. The queen kneeled before the altar and solemnly pledged to govern the United Kingdom and the countries of the Commonwealth in accordance with their laws and customs, to respect law and justice, and to maintain the Protestant religion. Her right hand resting on the Bible, she proclaimed in a strong, clear voice, "The things that I have before promised I will perform and keep, so help me God."

Four knights of the Order of the Garter then shielded the queen with a large gold sheet. The ladies-in-waiting quickly helped her remove her purple cape, her crown, and her jewels. The archbishop of Canterbury then anointed her hands, her chest, and the top of her head with sacred oil. (Since many monarchs over the years had complained that the oil had a horrible odor—rancid, according to one—this oil had been specially developed, mixing the essences of roses and orange blossoms.)

The queen was now on the throne, and was handed the diamond-encrusted Sword of State, with these words: "By this sword do justice. Stop the growth of iniquity, protect the Holy Church of God, help and defend widows and orphans, punish and reform what is amiss, and confirm what is in good order." Her ankles were touched with the Spurs of St. George, and the golden Bracelets of Sincerity were placed on her wrists. The imperial purple cape was draped over her shoulders again, and she was handed the golden orb with its jeweled cross. The coronation ring was slipped on the fourth finger of her right hand, and finally she was handed the gold scepter.

The archbishop briefly displayed the Crown of St. Edward to the audience, then placed it on the head of the queen, who seemed, for a few seconds, to sway under its weight. In the name of the peers of the realm the archbishop of Canterbury pledged his fidelity. Then Philip kneeled to pay Elizabeth homage, as did the dukes of Gloucester and Kent and other members of the nobility.

THE CEREMONY was over. Accompanied by her attendants, Queen Elizabeth departed for her new residence, Buckingham Palace. While the assembled guests waited at the top of the abbey steps for their carriages and cars, the new regime's first crisis was unfolding. Under the noses of tens of thousands of spectators, and before hundreds of television cameras, the younger sister of the queen was holding onto a man's arm. With a familiar and affectionate gesture she brushed a speck of dust off his jacket. He was Group Captain Peter Townsend, a heroic British pilot during World War II, now

Twenty-six-year-old Elizabeth looking small and solemn amid the splendor of her coronation in 1953. (London Pictures Service)

serving as one of the queen mother's aides-de-camp. Princess Margaret was exuberant, bursting into laughter and fondling the medals that covered the officer's chest. All of England understood with this gesture that there was something going on between the officer and the princess.

Townsend, formerly an equerry of King George VI, was a commoner and divorced to boot. As soon as his liaison with Margaret was known, the English papers unequivocally condemned the alliance, or even a possible flirtation with a royal princess. Winston Churchill was also violently opposed to it. Such a scandal less than a generation after the abdication of Edward VIII, he believed, could undermine the monarchy to its core.

English law permitted Margaret to marry anyone she chose at the age of twenty-five, but if she married a divorced commoner she would have to renounce her rights to succession in the royal hierarchy as well as her yearly allowance. After an imposed year of separation, Margaret met with Peter at Clarence House. It was probably then that she shared her decision with him: she loved him, but she loved even more her link to the crown.

THE ENGLAND of 1955 was still a far cry from the swinging London society that Margaret would help launch several years later. Its rigid customs and moral code had changed little despite the war and six years of socialism under Prime Minister Clement Attlee (1945–1951). When Attlee beat Churchill in the elections, even the London *Times* had mistakenly believed that the Socialist victory would mean a fundamental change in daily English life.

On an economic level many things did change—from the nationalization of industry to the administration of social security and the new redivision of taxes—but on a social level life was unaffected. With the war ended, British society resumed its former way of life, with its impermeable social strata and its impassable walls between gentleman and commoner.

It was perhaps Princess Margaret, with her tumultuous life, her incessant dramas, and even her scandals, who did more than all the parliamentary legislation combined to change the fabric of English society. Margaret, who had always been the enfant terrible of the family, was not content with what she considered a narrow and stuffy life. She longed for other horizons and other pleasures. Historians and commentators in the English press found that she lacked an "inner strength." But Margaret simply desired the more normal life that was led in almost all the other countries of the world, and even in other European royal families.

Later, in the sixties, Margaret's marriage to a young photographer, Antony Armstrong-Jones, effectively turned a page in the daily and social life of Britain. Almost overnight, entertainers, fashion designers, writers, and even hairdressers became part of the new jet-set British society. London really bloomed. The international set adopted it as a reborn, vital, amusing city where the affluent could have a good, chic time. On King's Road in Chelsea, fashion trends were set that would influence world couture. And in the mews, where old stables were converted into small apartments and inhabited by young men and women from the best families, hashish was passed around as casually as vintage port. Tony Armstrong-Jones, whose father married an airline stewardess shortly after his son's engagement and whose mother, the Countess of Rosse, was known as Tugboat Annie, was a representative of this other England, of which conservatives were aware but which they didn't want to acknowledge.

THE MARRIAGE took place on May 6, 1960, and the couple left for the Caribbean on board the royal yacht *Britannia*. The union was off to an auspicious start. Tony accepted the title of Earl of Snowdon, the queen gave them a "small palace" (actually a part of Kensington Palace) as a gift, and Parliament allotted them a very comfortable income. A son was born, Viscount Linley, and then a daughter, Lady Sarah. Lord Snowdon pursued his career as a photographer and signed a long-term contract with one of the large English Sunday newspapers, a move that provoked anger and jealousy from his competitors.

Life at the Snowdons', at least at the beginning, was merry. Margaret loved to meet new faces from other walks of life—models, actors, journalists—and for a time her home was a meeting place for the best and the brightest in London. There was singing —sometimes by the princess herself—and frenetic dancing to the latest music. But despite this new social wave, the little princess never let anyone forget who she was or what traditionally was due her, an attitude that finally exasperated her husband and alienated most of their friends.

In 1976 their divorce, after a long separation, struck a rude blow to British institutions. In 1953, it was inconceivable that the princess could align herself with a divorced man. And here, twenty-four years later, she was divorced—she, the sister of the queen. In the intervening years England had certainly changed.

The only person who had remained true to herself during this turbulent time was the queen—always neat, stable, firm, and proper while imperturbably accomplishing her task. Nevertheless, she remained close to Margaret and, as always, shared intensely the misfortunes of her sister. Following after her father and her grandfather, the queen, under an aloof façade, is actually quite emotional.

MANY OF Britain's sovereigns since the reign of Queen Victoria have overstepped their constitutional rights—the right to be consulted, the right to encourage, and the right to warn—in trying to influence the political life of the country. Victoria's open hostility toward Gladstone, head of the Liberal party, and her friendship with Disraeli, chief of the Conservatives, is part of English history. Elizabeth II has also been accused of being a bit too entangled with active political life on numerous occasions, and, above all, of abusing her power in choosing several prime ministers.

One of the first political crises during Elizabeth's reign took place in 1953. Prime Minister Winston Churchill, then almost eighty years old, was suddenly and violently taken ill. It seemed obvious that he would abandon power within a short time. Anthony Eden, who was Churchill's assistant and protégé for more than twenty years and a perfect reflection of the politics and the spirit of his mentor, was himself hospitalized in the United States following a serious operation. The number-three man in the cabinet was R. A. Butler—"Rab," as most of his colleagues and the English press affectionately called him. He was the natural choice of the government and of the Liberal party to follow Churchill into office.

Meanwhile, in the rundown resort of Blackpool, the Labor members were holding their annual convention to name the head of their party, who would automatically become prime minister if the party won a majority in the elections. This practice is now the rule among the Conservatives, too, but at that time it was not the case.

In a move that surprised almost everyone, the queen approached the marquess of Salisbury, a member of the influential Cecil family, from whose ranks had come an earlier prime minister in the reign of Queen Victoria.

Robert Gascoyne-Cecil, fifth marquess of Salisbury, had always been close to the queen; he had been one of her father's favorite advisers. When the queen met with him, the whole country believed she had chosen him to replace the ailing Winston Churchill. It had been several generations since a member of the House of Lords had occupied the position of prime minister, but as far as many members of the government were concerned, several more generations would still be too soon. The general discontent flowed from Labor in the House of Commons up through the ranks of the Conservatives.

But Churchill, who apparently had a constitution of iron, swiftly pulled through his crisis. One month later, he was back at Buck's Club with a few ministers and friends, and dined lightly: a dozen oysters, a thick soup, chicken pâté, and strawberry-vanilla ice cream, washed down with a few bottles of white wine and a half-dozen cognacs. After his repast he smoked his customary enormous cigar. Dinner and the cigar marked the temporary end of the crisis, but its shadow lingered on. Two years later, in 1955, Churchill decided to abandon power. The queen, appreciative of all he had done for England, wanted him to bow out of political life with as much glory as possible. It was at this juncture that she accorded him the supreme honor of dining with him at 10 Downing Street. There she asked him, "Would you like a dukedom, or something like that?" Churchill, who was a direct descendant of the duke of Marlborough, was extremely tempted. So much so that the queen, to make her offer even more enticing, suggested to him the title of duke of London. But Churchill had been dissuaded from accepting even a seat in the House of Lords by his son Randolph, who harbored his own political aspirations in the House of Commons. Randolph, for whom his father had sacrificed a duchy, tried several times for a seat in Parliament and was always defeated. (It was Randolph's son, also named Winston Churchill, who finally succeeded in gaining the Commons seat that had been so coveted by his father.)

Churchill, having retired from the political scene, was smoothly succeeded by Anthony Eden, his nephew by marriage. Eden's mandate, however, was to be of short duration. In October 1956, he had joined France in backing an Israeli invasion of the Sinai.

French and British troops were landed in the Suez Canal zone but were forced to make a speedy retreat after pressure from the United States and the Soviet Union. His health undermined by the failure of this operation, which provoked an economic crisis and a violent Labor attack on his government, Eden resigned on January 8, 1957. Once more it was necessary to find a successor, and the most obvious choice was again Rab. A commoner married to the daughter of Samuel Courtauld, one of the richest and most powerful industrialists in England, Rab lived relatively modestly and was popular in all sectors of the Conservative party, especially with the members of the House of Commons. All of England was convinced that Rab would finally move into 10 Downing Street.

But the queen once again sent out a call for the marquess of Salisbury to ask his advice: Who should be named to form the new government? The next day, all government members were invited to present themselves one by one at a small office where Salisbury and Lord Kilmuir awaited them. They were asked to choose between Rab and a new candidate, Harold Macmillan. (Macmillan was a classic member of the English establishment—an old-boy graduate from Eton, son-in-law of a ninth duke and son of a seventh baronet.) The ministers received by Salisbury and Kilmuir later related that they had had the impression of being reincarnated schoolboys sent to the headmaster's office.

Selwyn Lloyd, the former minister of foreign affairs, emphatically protested the procedure and the fact that members of the House of Lords led the inquiry—to no avail. The next day Salisbury went to Buckingham Palace to recommend Macmillan. At the interview between Salisbury and the queen, two other people were present—Lord Chandos and Lord Waverley, neither of whom had any official function but both of whom were members of the oldest English aristocracy. The following day Macmillan was invited to the royal palace, and when he left its gates at 11:15 A.M., he was prime minister of the United Kingdom.

SIX YEARS later a new and much more serious crisis shook the Conservative government. For several months the English, who are rather puritanical and yet fascinated by sex scandals, were delighted by the adventures of their defense minister. John Profumo, it seems, had been exceedingly diligent in maintaining his rapport with a network of call girls, specifically with his favorite, Christine Keeler; she, it was revealed, had been sharing her favors between the British minister and the Soviet naval attaché in London. The sensationalist press reveled in accounts of the regular evening orgies at which the gentlemen, out of discretion, arrived with hoods over their heads to administer or receive the whip. From a conventional sex scandal, almost an old British tradition, the affair mushroomed into an ugly political scandal when the principal party, the young and brilliant Profumo, did what no gentleman worthy of the name would ever permit himself to do: he made a false declaration before the House of Commons. With the style of a seasoned movie star, he stated to his incredulous colleagues, "Miss Keeler and I are just good friends." The scandal was further inflated by an ill turn of fate when Prime Minister Macmillan, a dignified and respected old gentleman, fell seriously ill after having parried criticisms that were flying at him from all corners.

Macmillan, who believed himself to be sicker than he actually was, submitted his resignation to the queen on October 18, 1963, and, in the midst of the Profumo affair, once again raised the problem of a successor. And once again the inevitable Rab seemed to be the obvious choice. He had long considered himself to be a sort of vice prime minister, although the queen had stated on several occasions that such a post did not exist. His principal rival for Macmillan's post was the brilliant Chancellor of the Exchequer, Reginald Maudling. Another Conservative minister, Iain Macleod, was also in the running, as was a member of the House of Lords, Lord Hailsham, a former television journalist, who under his former name of Quintin Hogg had long captivated television audiences.

Macmillan, according to members of the queen's inner circle, had cast his lot with a relatively unknown Scottish lord, the fourteenth earl of Home. To become eligible as prime minister, Home renounced his title of lord and his seat in the House of Lords, and took the name Alec Douglas-Home. He had become secretary for foreign affairs in 1960, after having played a relatively minor role as secretary of state for Commonwealth relations. Tall, thin, and very distinguished, Home had attended all the right schools, beginning with Eton. He and Macmillan were of the same world, almost out of the same mold.

The queen, who was later severely criticized by some for her action, apparently made her choice of prime minister solely on the recommendation of Macmillan, without consulting anyone other than her private secretary, Sir Michael Adeane.

The royal choice caused an uproar in the government. Eleven out of the twenty Conservative ministers were against Home, and two of the most influential, Iain Macleod and Reginald Maudling, informed Macmillan on the eve of his resignation that they would refuse to serve under Home. Within the Conservative constituencies—the grass roots from which the party drew its strength—the results were strongly anti-Home: 60 percent wanted Hailsham as prime minister, 40 percent were for R. A. Butler, and virtually none were for Home. Home's backers were in the House of Lords only, where two-thirds of the peers preferred him to any other candidate.

On the day of his resignation, the queen went to see Macmillan in his hospital room. He reiterated his support for Home and later sent her a note, urging her to make a decision quickly to avoid any revolt in the heart of the party. The queen had known Home forever. He was a great friend of her mother, and his family origins were quite likely even older than, and just as aristocratic as, those of the royal family itself. Home was soon called to Buckingham Palace, and he left with the nomination. Many ministers submitted to the choice, but others maintained their refusal to have any part of a government directed by Home. The queen's decision favoring Home, many believe, largely contributed to the Conservatives' defeat in the elections the following year, when the Labor party came to power and Harold Wilson was named prime minister. This time the queen had had no hand in the choice.

On October 16, 1964, Wilson, accompanied by his wife, father, and sister, arrived at the royal palace for his first audience with the queen. Before his departure for Buckingham Palace, he had told his friends that he did not plan to participate in the hand-kissing ceremony. But the queen, who had apparently been informed, did not even bother with the formality and simply asked Wilson if he accepted the task of forming a new government.

Fortunately, their relations rapidly improved. Of the eight prime ministers who have, to this day, served under her reign—Winston Churchill, Anthony Eden, Harold Macmillan, Sir Alec Douglas-Home, Harold Wilson, Edward Heath, James Callaghan, and Margaret Thatcher—it was with Wilson that she maintained the best rapport. He made more of an effort than any of his predecessors and successors to keep her abreast of world affairs, to interest her, and to amuse her. His successor, Edward Heath, was of a completely different stamp—a cold, reserved man who never seemed to make the slightest effort to please his queen. Her relations with Margaret Thatcher, the first British woman to be elected prime minister, are said to be cordial and correct, but without great warmth. The Iron Lady steers her bark alone and spaces her visits to Buckingham Palace and the other royal residences—where other more accommodating prime ministers appeared regularly—as far apart as possible.

BUCKINGHAM PALACE, the setting for most official royal activities, had slowly sprung up on the grounds of a public garden where, at the end of the seventeenth century, men from the capital came to refresh themselves at the little inns and taverns and made or kept assignations with the thousands of streetwalkers who roamed London at the time.

In 1702 the Duke of Buckingham bought the area to construct a mansion, which was later sold to King George III for the relatively modest sum of 21,000 pounds. The king enlarged the structure considerably, and renamed it "the queen's house." The prince regent, the future George IV, undertook the remodeling of what later became Buckingham Palace. To create an English Versailles, he spent millions of pounds, a colossal sum at the time, but he died without completing the work or ever having lived there. His successors abandoned the palace and it was not used again until Queen Victoria, at the age of eighteen, arrived there twenty-three days after her coronation. Victoria and her husband Albert enlarged Buckingham Palace by twelve rooms and an entire additional wing, still known as the "Albert" wing.

But the palace remained austere, "a tomb," in the words of comfort-loving King Edward VII, who modernized it, installing electricity, bathrooms, and even a few bidets. George VI continued the modernization by adding central heating, elevators, and a swimming pool for his daughters Elizabeth and Margaret.

The royal apartments, on the first floor of the north wing, look out on what is called "the king's garden." Today, the queen works in a central salon where a large Chippendale desk, inherited from her father, is the centerpiece. On it sit dozens of photographs, and always a bouquet of carnations, her favorite flower. At the queen's feet, under the furniture, a half-dozen Welsh corgis come and go. A rather ill-tempered and aggressive breed, they have snapped at the ankles of dozens of ladies-in-waiting, high officials, and ministers. But the queen adores them. She takes them from palace to palace, prepares their meals when she can—each dog has a personal silver bowl—and doesn't hesitate to plunge them into their baths herself when they return from a walk covered with mud.

The central salon opens on one side to the private dining room, and on the other side to Elizabeth's bedroom. Down the hall are her dressing room and bathroom, then the dressing room and bedroom of the prince consort. At one end of the hall is the salon where the queen receives the prime minister, and at the other end is Philip's salon, which serves both as his office and as his audience room. It is the lowest room in the palace, since Philip had a false ceiling installed to make the room more intimate. A great lover of gadgets, he also installed all kinds of electronic equipment, a video recorder, an ultrasophisticated stereo, and an extremely powerful, remote-control radio.

The ceremonial rooms are in the west wing, which carries the name of Napoleon III, who lived there during his visit to London in 1855. From the top of a large staircase extends the central gallery, an immense corridor fifty-five yards long, at the end of which are the throne room and the dining room for official dinners. The great banquets, notably those for chiefs of state, take place around an enormous table, eighty-two feet in length. The tableware, in solid gold, weighs 11,000 pounds. Meals are served by pages dressed in black and gold tunics, bouffant black culottes, and white stockings, and by valets in red and gold tunics, red culottes, and white stockings. Until recently, tradition dictated that they powder their hair with a mixture of flour and water. Philip put an end to this practice, which he judged outmoded and ridiculous.

The queen's annual garden parties at Buckingham Palace are a tradition that dates back to the reign of her grandparents, King George V and Queen Mary, who used to invite a modest six or seven hundred guests. Today, there are often as many as nine thousand who throng through the gardens—high officials, members of court, foreign visitors, and commoners of no special merit other than that they knew someone who knew someone. The male guests, wearing morning coats and striped pants rented from Moss Brothers (the largest establishment of its kind in the world), and their wives, in picture hats and three-quarter-length dresses, arrange themselves in many small groups, by affinity, by chance, or by instruction from one of numerous chamberlains who circulate through this curious and flattered crowd. Two divisions of trumpeters from the queen's Grenadiers play military marches. Waitresses circulate with cups of insipid tea and a few cucumber sandwiches from the caterer Lyons, an extremely popular and inexpensive establishment. (At the end of the reception, mediocre ice cream from the same source is served in cardboard cups.)

Half an hour after the beginning of the festivities the queen appears, accompanied by the royal family: Philip, dignified but ready to be chatty, the queen mother, warm and smiling, and Margaret, pouting. The royal personages disperse into the crowd and try to chat with the majority of the guests, a custom that by necessity renders most of their conversations repetitious as well as short.

The queen, who must shake hundreds of hands, has her own personal technique for avoiding overly enthusiastic grips: she extends a slack hand with the thumb held against the palm, which most well-brought-up people will meet with only the lightest touch.

To take their own tea, the royal group leaves the crowd and repairs to a large red and gold tent called the royal pavilion. Shortly thereafter, the trumpeters suddenly blare the British anthem—"God Save the Queen"—the signal for departure. The royal family disappears as if by magic, and lingering guests are informed that the moment has come to liberate the garden.

This odd ceremonial recurs three or four times each summer, permitting some thirty thousand "chosen" to boast for the rest of their lives, "I took tea with the queen."

It is at Buckingham Palace that the queen does most of her work. There she receives the special "boxes"—small chests, covered with green, black, blue, or red leather according to the ministry from which they are sent. The boxes arrive every morning from Whitehall, the broad avenue where all the administrative offices are located, aboard a horse-drawn carriage. They contain hundreds of documents concerning current affairs that the queen must sign. Sometimes other, more important dispatches arrive from the foreign office. In all cases her consent is nothing more than a formality. Queen Elizabeth's advisers assert that she manages to read the hundreds of long technical documents in a very short time. But, in fact, it seems quite obvious that even the most gifted political expert would need several weeks to wade through and absorb the information in the mass of papers that inundate her worktable every morning.

Perfectly adapted to her role, Elizabeth's single-minded, if not mechanical, character easily accommodates a life of routine. Upon waking, she sips a cup of tea carried in by one of her chambermaids. She reads the papers in bed, dresses, and then joins Philip in the dining room at the end of the corridor close to their private apartments. They breakfast alone, serving themselves from a wide range of hot and cold dishes laid out earlier by the staff. Usually they eat scrambled or soft-boiled eggs with bacon, sausage, or kippers, and toast with marmalade. The queen prepares her own Chinese tea, which she takes with milk but no sugar. Philip prefers coffee. Both avoid cereals or porridge in an effort to combat the tendency to overweight that runs in their families. (Witness the portraits of the middle-aged Queen Victoria, and especially those of her overindulging son, Prince Albert.)

This alimentary moderation lasts throughout the day. Neither soup nor appetizers are served at lunch, and there is almost never a dessert. The standard menu consists of a main course, often lamb, accompanied by green vegetables and salads. Crackers and cheese complete the meal. There is no bread on the table, apparently to avoid temptation. The queen drinks orangeade, while Philip has one or two beers. Coffee is always served after every meal but they take it only once or twice a week, the queen adding milk to hers, Philip drinking his black. Except in the case of special banquets, the menu is almost the same at dinner. Philip enjoys one or two glasses of wine with his meal, preferring the white wines of Moselle. If he is particularly hungry a second main dish is served, but again, rarely a dessert.

These intimate meals are revolutionary in the sense that the queen and prince consort do not "dress" for dinner, as is still the custom in many British aristocratic families. They dine in their street clothes. By contrast, even dining alone at Clarence House, the queen mother never fails to put on a long gown.

The queen decides what she's going to wear for the day by checking her engagement calendar before breakfast. She owns several thousand outfits, most of which are stored on the floor above her apartments in three enormous rooms full of closets. Her evening gowns and other dressy clothes always come from Norman Hartnell, the designer of her wedding gown and creator of her "folly"—a splendid evening dress that she wore during an official visit to Paris to show the French that the English also knew how to make clothes. Every so often the queen goes to Hartnell's showroom to see the new collection. She schedules her visits early in the morning, always before nine o'clock. As soon as she decides on an outfit, it is automatically removed from the collection, along with any other styles that even vaguely resemble it. She is not, however, completely true to Hartnell. For the last several years she has committed a few "infidelities," appearing occasionally in the clothes of two former Hartnell colleagues—Hardy Amies and Ian Thomas, who established their own couture house.

The queen has an immense selection of handbags, in general rather large and almost always with a handle—a style designed to keep her hands free. The handbags seem to play a very basic role in her official life. Court intimates aver that wherever she sits, at the head of a banquet table or at her desk, there are hooks where she can hang her bag out of sight. The sudden reappearance of the bag is the imperative signal that the evening or the audience is over.

Every morning the queen's hairdresser arrives to do her hair; he also accompanies her on all official trips. Her hair has always been arranged in a neat conventional style held in place with a touch of spray so that no stray locks—beguiling on a starlet but not on the queen of England—mar the symmetry of the "do." She uses cosmetics sparingly, some pale pink lipstick, some pale powder, and just a touch of mascara. On her nails she wears colorless polish.

The queen's own fashion taste runs to sporty clothes. When her schedule permits visits to Balmoral or Windsor, she likes to slip into a tweed skirt, a sweater, and sturdy walking shoes. She also dressses in her "country clothes" at Buckingham Palace on days when there are no official audiences. The only difference is that in London the queen misses the joys of the countryside's soggy earth and leaden skies. For, unlike most people, she loves to put on a raincoat, tie a scarf over her head, and walk in the rain.

PERHAPS because Buckingham Palace serves as her official headquarters it is at Windsor and Balmoral castles that the queen feels most at home. She stays at Windsor for six weeks in the spring and during the month of June. This residence, thirty-one miles from London, is the largest castle in Europe and is surrounded by an immense park. The queen and Prince Philip treat it as a simple country house and their private quarters are remarkably comfortable and modern. It is at Windsor that the queen and Philip entertain their friends. To amuse thirty or so guests, there are tennis courts and a swimming pool for daytime activities, while the evenings are passed playing charades, watching television, and, if Princess Margaret is present, dancing. It is also at Windsor that the queen can indulge in one of her favorite amusements—horse racing. (Windsor is very close to Ascot, the race course created in 1711 by Queen Anne, who loved to watch horse races but didn't like to travel too far to see one.) The high point of a house party during the Ascot season begins after lunch. The women, most of whom belong to the highest aristocracy, if they are not in fact royal, wear hats and colorful dresses. The men wear striped pants, vests, light gray cutaways, and top hats. The whole troupe travels by car to the King's Walk, where they climb into the famous Ascot carriages drawn by the no less famous Windsor grays. Tradition dictates that the horse-drawn retinue ride along the race track until it reaches the royal box. The queen and Prince Philip lead the procession, accompanied by the Master of the Horse. Following behind are the other members of the royal family and their guests. The queen, who owns a world-renowned racing stable, is unrecognizable whenever one of her horses runs. In the blink of an eye her customary impassiveness disappears. She can be seen pounding her fist if her horse is lagging behind or raising her hands to heaven in joyous victory if she wins. Philip does not share this passion. As soon as the race begins he disappears from the front of the royal box to sequester himself in the back, where he quietly watches a portable television.

Half-time is tea time, and often the winner of the most important race is invited to the queen's table, a supreme reward. Valets serve watercress and cucumber sandwiches, chocolate cakes, and tea. All around the royal box, in the area called the royal enclosure, several hundred racing fans, all well-born and most of them owners of racing stables, do as the queen does on tables set by their chauffeurs on the immaculate lawn. On the other side of the barrier, commoner racing buffs have their tea in a gigantic cafeteria, or stand in line at one of many portable bars.

When the races are over, the procession of royal carriages re-
verses its earlier route. Back at Windsor, everyone changes for
dinner. Since the queen is blatantly fond of military marches, the
Royal Guards' brass band always plays at one end of the dining
room, even during the most intimate dinners. Sometimes evenings
are devoted to the showing of a film in the throne room. Pages in
red livery set up the screen in front of the noble gold throne, so
that the queen and her guests can gaze on the horseback-riding
exploits of John Wayne in a Western, one of the court's preferred
cinematic subjects.

The queen also has at her disposal several other residences,
among them Sandringham, which is her own personal property
and where she always spends the Christmas holidays. She very
rarely goes to Holyroodhouse in Edinburgh, her official residence
as the queen of Scotland. Also in Scotland, however, is one of her
favorite abodes—Balmoral Castle, constructed on 35,000 acres
(now 80,000) by Prince Albert in 1855, and designed to resemble a
castle in his native Germany. The queen and Prince Philip spend
two months there a year, where every morning they are awakened
by a troupe of bagpipers who march back and forth in front of the
castle. Depending on the season, large fishing or hunting parties
are frequently organized; the queen's preference is stag hunts. Dinner takes place in the great dining hall, whose walls are covered
with the emblems of the Scottish clans; a band of bagpipers plays
constantly in the background. Evenings often end with a session of
traditional Scottish dances. The prince is so adept at the jig that he
is always one of the liveliest and most unrestrained participants,
while the queen, with uncharacteristic gusto, shouts the traditional
joyous cries at the appropriate moments.

Queen Elizabeth's visit to Balmoral provides opportunities for
garden parties for her Scottish subjects (similar to those events at
Buckingham Palace), an occasional banquet for the local nobility,
and investiture ceremonies for new knights. The investiture ceremony and what the English call the Honors' List date back to the
Middle Ages and are among the court's solid traditions of monarchy.

Most Englishmen, in their heart of hearts, hope one day to carry
the title of "sir," and some of them dedicate their lives to works
that will make them eligible to receive this honor. Others are ready
to buy their titles through the guise of charitable or other kinds of

Off for a ride, one of the royal family's favorite pastimes, at Ascot. (British Information Services)

Princess Anne with her son Peter at Gatcombe Park, their country home in Gloucestershire. (British Information Services)

The Queen Mother demonstrates her expertise at billiards at a reception for her eightieth birthday at the London Press Club. (British Information Services)

The queen attends to official duties even at Sandringham Castle, one of her private residences and favorite retreats. (London Pictures Service)

Proud parents with Prince William in the walled garden of Kensington Palace. (London Pictures Service)

contributions. They join the ranks of rich knights who have contributed neither to the renown of the queen's army nor to the glory of the arts and sciences.

This quintessentially British system of hierarchical honors was introduced to the British Isles by a Frenchman, William the Conqueror. In William's day, any owner of a plot of land, preferably large, was considered a knight, and was expected to take up arms to defend his king. In the seventeenth century James I created hereditary baronetcies to enrich the treasury. But from the nineteenth century on, power began to pass from the sovereigns into the hands of Parliament and the government. The king or queen had only to confirm the government's recommendation and award the honor.

According to the complicated system of honorifics, all sirs are not equal. Baronets, also called sir, are superior to knights, but still quite inferior to lords. Prestige and rank depend upon the order with which one is affiliated. There is no comparison whatsoever between the mediocre Order of the British Empire and the royal Order of the Garter. Except for the monarch and certain members of the royal family—direct descendants of Edward III, who founded the order around 1348—there are only twenty-four knights authorized to wear the blue and gold garter and its motto, *Honi soit qui mal y pense* (Evil be to him who evil thinks). But any common functionary serving in some hot and uncomfortable colonial outpost can cling to the hope that he will one day be named to the Order of the British Empire. Between the summit and the valley of English social aspirations are several other knightly orders: the sought-after and most distinguished Order of St. Michael and St. George; the most honorable Order of the Bath, instituted in 1399; and the extremely noble Most Ancient Order of the Thistle, a Scottish order. Certain other orders have disappeared since decolonization, such as the Very Eminent Order of the Indian Empire, and the Imperial Order of the Crown of India.

Just as there is a hierarchy of sirs, there are also all categories of lords. For example, among the 1,172 members of the House of Lords, there are 3 peers of royal blood, 25 dukes, 26 marquises, 126 earls, 104 viscounts, and 862 barons. Of these, 349 life peers subdivide into lords temporal and lords spiritual. The latter classification comprises all members of the Church of England who, on attaining the rank of bishop, automatically become members of this house. At present there are also 24 bishops and 2 archbishops in the membership.

The House of Lords is much too small to accommodate the full complement of its members, but it is hardly a problem, since on average only a few hundred lords attend the sessions. The most diligent are the newest members, in particular former politicians and trade union officials. Descendants of the old aristocracy rarely make an appearance. In the house, dukes of the royal blood and newcomers sit on the same benches and hold identical powers. But it is the only place where they are equal. Aside from their titles, there is little in common between a fourteenth earl or a tenth duke and a lord who owes his title simply to his own merits; the latter would almost never consort with the true British aristocracy.

Until recently, most titles were conferred in recognition of political service. Prime Minister David Lloyd George (1916–1922) was accused of having sold titles, most often in the name of politics, on an unprecedented scale. In the course of his six years in office he handed out a vast quantity of assorted noble titles and up to 25,000 nominations for the Order of the British Empire. A few years ago, when the Labor government came to power, the practice of parceling out honors began to provoke ironic comments from some and indignation from others. The merit of some of the honorees was growing more and more questionable. The queen, it was whispered in London, had even asked Prime Minister Harold Wilson to reconsider the names that appeared on one list. Among them, notably, was a Lord Kagan, who had spent several weeks in a French prison before being extradited to England, where he was sentenced to jail for theft.

Today the government presents all nominations for honors to the queen except for those in the four orders she controls: the Order of the Garter, the Order of the Thistle, the Order of Merit, and the Royal Order of Victoria.

Two lists of recipients are published every year in the London *Times:* one on New Year's Day and the other on the queen's official birthday, arbitrarily set in the month of June. On those two days, tens of thousands of transfixed readers pore over the pages of the honorable *Times* (which doubles its circulation for the occasion) with curiosity, disappointment, or joy.

The queen traditionally holds fourteen investitures a year, which take place either at Buckingham Palace or in one of her other palaces. In spite of the frantic pace of the ceremony—one knight a minute—the atmosphere is extremely relaxed and joyous.

THE QUEEN is considered to be one of the richest women in the world. No one, aside from a few bankers close to the court, really knows the amount of her vast personal fortune, which includes investments and many other holdings. She pays no taxes, as is the case with most other members of the royal family. Her stipend from the government is around 3,700,000 pounds a year.

Prince Philip, who accompanies the queen on almost all her official activities and maintains an intensely busy program of his own, draws some 179,300 pounds a year.

The queen mother receives around 321,500 pounds a year, and, according to certain Labor Members of Parliament, it is she who most merits her draw. After the queen, she is the most popular member of the royal family.

Prince Charles is one of the few members of the royal family who decided to submit to the fiscal law of the people. Before his marriage, he set his own taxes at 50 percent of his income from the duchy of Cornwall, which is his property. Today his income is 733,550 pounds after taxes.

Prince Andrew and Prince Edward each receive an annual stipend of 20,000 pounds, which will be increased if they marry.

Princess Margaret draws about 108,000 pounds from the public treasury, and Princess Anne 111,700 pounds. These are the two endowments most criticized by the people, doubtless because of the unpopularity of the recipients. According to a survey conducted in 1983 by *Woman's Own* magazine, Anne won the favor of only 39 percent of the population and Margaret a mere 36 percent. Anne's husband, Captain Mark Phillips, is in even lower esteem. He particularly alienated the English when he declared in an interview, "We are just a young couple trying to make ends meet"— this while living with his wife in the castle at Gatcombe Park, given to them by the queen and estimated to be worth more than a million pounds!

Charles, the heir to the throne, was the nation's adored child and the pet of the English press. These days, when princes must groom their images and speak circumspectly, since their every move or comment is amplified by the media, Charles has succeeded admirably. The English find nothing in the world as appealing as this young man, with his slightly horsey face and his chest somewhat narrow in relation to his hips. The *Woman's Own* survey showed him to be the fourth most popular member of the royal family after Diana took over third place in the public's affections.

Charles devotes a large part of his day to giving audiences, visiting institutions, and appearing at inaugurations, awards ceremonies, and receptions. Every month he receives hundreds of invitations, from which he chooses those events he will attend. He has always spent a great part of his time traveling. In 1970, for example, when he was only twenty-two, he was sent on official visits to New Zealand, Japan, Australia, and Canada, and in 1977 he made a coast-to-coast tour of the United States, visiting eleven cities in twelve days. On a more recent trip to Australia he was accompanied by Diana and their baby son, Prince William.

Charles keeps himself up to date on British public affairs and occasionally visits 10 Downing Street to sit in on regular cabinet meetings. When he recently decided to familiarize himself with the various aspects of British industry, he visited a number of factories, focusing on those in heavy industry and fishing. At the end of a standard visit of this sort, the prince is often asked to make a short speech. This is a challenge that calls for much grace and wit, since the subject to be covered is extremely narrow and specialized. Whereas a politician is expected to propose and follow up on plans of action, the prince must limit himself to comments or judgments on what he has seen, being careful all the while not to imply that any action should be undertaken in response to his words. Charles's predecessor as prince of Wales, his great-uncle David, once caused a scandal by declaring to a group of workers who he thought were dissatisfied with their lot, "Something will be done." Much more adept, Charles, nevertheless, provoked an indignant outcry on one well-remembered occasion.

IN FEBRUARY 1979, while the English government was confronting a long and debilitating series of strikes, Charles decided to make a statement before the Parliamentary and Scientific Committee on relations between the employers and the unions. To blame, he asserted, were the employers, "who don't understand the importance of the human factor" and "who should be ready to talk frankly and honestly with the employees." There were, understandably, violent protests on the part of the employers. But an antimonarchy protest in Portsmouth was called off at the last minute and the Communist paper, the *Morning Star,* wholeheartedly approved Charles's position in an editorial, so repercussions were not as serious as they might have been.

However sterling his intellectual and personal qualities are, and however outstanding his political and social accomplishments, Charles would still be considered incomplete as an English prince if he did not pass a good part of his time in athletic pursuits. Charles, in this as in other respects, is the total prince. He has played rugby and cricket, and he is a remarkable polo player. His father, Prince Philip, also excelled in this sport of millionaires, princes, and playboys, but was forced to give it up because of arthritis in his wrist. Charles took up the standard and has been a member of several polo teams. He also loves to hunt in Scotland and to fish in Ireland. His father and his grandmother taught him how to handle a fishing rod when he was eight years old.

Charles never led the "normal life" of an ordinary British child, but his early years certainly were a great deal more normal than those of any other English heir-apparent. He was never taught at the palace by private tutors. At Philip's insistence, he was sent to the same schools that his father attended—Cheam and Gordonstoun—where he had to make his own bed, take icy showers, and shine his own shoes, just like all the other students. Charles will be the first English sovereign to possess a university degree—a master of arts—which he was awarded after studying archeology, anthropology, and history for three years at Cambridge.

It was Rab Butler, the man the queen thrice vetoed as prime minister, to whom Charles's education was entrusted. Rab had once been minister of education and, at the time Charles was ready for the university, was the director of Trinity, one of the colleges of Cambridge University.

Rab considered Charles gifted in terms of his studies and "very clever, even more so than his parents. . . . The queen and the duke are not university people. The queen is one of the most intelligent women in England, and brilliant in summing up people. But I don't think she's awfully interested in books . . . whereas Prince Charles has a tremendous affinity for books." (Butler had a way of expressing himself that was not exactly to the royal couple's taste.) When Charles was receiving grades that were lower than expected, Butler asked the queen to allow him to concentrate on his studies instead of continually distracting him by sending him off on official trips—a request that severely irritated the prince's parents. Although Butler had hoped that the prince could live on campus like any other student, Charles was not quite reduced to the life-style of his colleagues. He arrived on campus in a blue sports car, although automobiles were strictly forbidden to other students during their first year. And he had a private bathroom and kitchen, unlike his classmates, who had only single rooms to themselves. But rare are they who, freshly minted from the university, become the prince of Wales.

At his investiture Charles, who had just turned twenty-one, kneeled before his mother, took both her hands in his, and declared, "I Charles, prince of Wales, do become your liege man." The following year Charles began five years of intensive military training, during which he learned to command a battleship, parachute from a plane, scuba dive, and pilot an airplane.

AN AFFABLE YOUNG MAN who laughs easily, Charles still expects to be treated with all the respect due his rank. When he appears, women are supposed to curtsy, and men to bow deeply. And even his most intimate friends call him "sir." These marks of respect did not keep Charles from being "the most sought-after bachelor in the world," as the London press happily referred to him for more than twelve years. If all the press reports were to be believed, he supposedly had at least sixty affairs. His briefest encounter with a young woman with any kind of "past" would set off torrents of commentaries in the British and world press. Displaying a genuine and becoming modesty, Charles's only comment on his feminine conquests was that it was very difficult for a girl to separate his position as prince from his intrinsic personal qualities.

For a long time one of Charles's regular companions was Princess Marie-Astrid of Luxembourg. Some observers believed—some even claimed to know—that the pope and the archbishop of Canterbury had been consulted to resolve the problem of the young princess's religion. A law dating from 1689 stated that "the Protestant realm could not be governed by a papist prince or by a king or queen married to a papist." When a member of Parliament declared before the house that a marriage to Marie-Astrid would "signify the end of the British monarchy," he effectively put an end to any speculation in favor of the blue-eyed princess from Luxembourg.

Charles was very much aware of the public's keen interest in his eventual marriage. In a television interview on his twenty-first birthday, he made it clear that he had already given a great deal of thought to the subject. His future bride, he said, would have to be a princess and someone familiar with the intricacies of royal protocol and customs. To tens of millions of viewers, the young prince seemed wistful and far older than his years when he said he would probably wait until he was at least thirty to marry and then would have to choose his bride very, very carefully. "In my position," he added, "I can hardly entertain the possibility of a divorce."

For the next ten years the prince drifted from one love affair to another. He could be seen dancing with one partner at night, horseback riding with another the following morning. Many of the elder statesmen who had lived through the drama of Edward VIII's short reign—his dalliances, his marriage to the American divorcée Wallis Simpson, his eventual abdication—feared that history might repeat itself. Even the queen was apprehensive. At a dinner with some of Charles's former tutors, she openly voiced her fear that her son might become a sort of royal drifter, flitting from one woman to another like his great-uncle David had before meeting Mrs. Simpson. Even worse was the queen's fear that Charles might take after King Edward VII, who spent most of his adult life pursuing earthly pleasures while awaiting either the abdication or the death of his mother, Queen Victoria.

The long-awaited announcement of Charles's engagement, to nineteen-year-old Lady Diana Spencer, finally put an end to all the speculations.

Diana had always known the royal family. As a child she used to play with the two younger brothers of the future king of England, and she grew up calling the queen "Aunt Lilibet." After the engagement the English could hardly contain themselves in praising her virtues—her grace, her naturalness, her capacity to charm the crowds.

The royal marriage, on July 29, 1981, arrived just in time to divert the country's attention from a difficult economic situation. It also gave England the opportunity to show the weight of the monarchic system. What the royal family accomplished on this day could not have been equaled by the most powerful president of a democratic regime, nor by the most conciliatory president of a parliamentary regime. At the moment of this dazzling celebration —the incarnation of a Cecil B. DeMille extravaganza—the England of the strikers and the unemployed was at one with the England infatuated with its traditions and its venerable, privileged nobility. Even the dreaded Irish Republican Army suspended its activities; for the space of one day, it was the prince's peace. In a moment out of time England rediscovered its former splendor and pride.

Throughout the country, the sun rose on houses that were decked with the colors of the Union Jack. Later in the morning, in front of their televisions and massed along the route to St. Paul's Cathedral, the English gazed with joy and deep emotion at the procession of official cars. The chiefs of state led the motorcade. Behind came the foreign monarchs and dignitaries, followed by the English royal family. The procession crossed London to the accompaniment of the crowd's ringing cheers. The last to leave Clarence House, where she had lived with the queen mother during the official engagement period, was Lady Diana, riding in a carriage with her father. For her the crowd had reserved its most enormous ovation.

Royal marriages have not always been as perfectly choreographed and orchestrated as Charles and Diana's. The wedding of an earlier prince of Wales (Albert, the future Edward VII) in 1863 at Windsor Castle, was full of foibles, faux pas, and surprises. The groom's father had recently died, and Queen Victoria, an inconsolable widow, had wanted the church draped in black. She gave up this idea only when her son threatened to bring his fiancée to the ceremony in a hearse. The European kings in attendance, bickering since their arrival, could not agree on an order of precedence, so the place of honor at the ceremony was given to a Maharajah Dulup Singh. The future Kaiser Wilhelm II, then five years old, was also among the guests. During the ceremony, he began tossing his dagger—part of his Scottish costume—like a ball. Then, moving on to another game, he began biting the knees of his uncles. After the wedding luncheon, as the bride and groom took leave of their guests, the duke of Cambridge, following tradition, threw a shoe in their direction, but his aim was so good that it struck the prince full in the face. Later, the archbishop of Canterbury was shaken up by the departing crowd and, because of the confusion, was obliged to sit in a third-class car on the train home, along with the writer

William Thackeray. All the trains were so congested that the great statesman Disraeli had to make his trip home seated on his wife's lap, while thieves liberated the Portuguese representative of his diamond star.

NOTHING REMOTELY similar occurred during the marriage of Prince Charles and his Lady Di. The bride seemed perfectly serene as she entered St. Paul's Cathedral on her father's arm and began the long walk down the aisle to join her fiancé. After a sixty-two-minute ceremony they returned to Buckingham Palace accompanied by thunderous hurrahs from the spectators lining the route. The newlyweds were honored at a palace luncheon attended by 120 guests, comprising the crowned heads of Europe and family friends; the chiefs of state lunched at a banquet hosted by Mrs. Thatcher. A few days later the young couple embarked on their honeymoon voyage aboard the royal yacht *Britannia*.

The wife of the future forty-fourth sovereign of Great Britain and Northern Ireland has the title, until she becomes queen, of Her Royal Highness, Princess of Wales. Princess Di, as the press affectionately calls her, is five feet seven and a half inches tall, with blond hair, a rosy complexion, and an easy smile; her face and form, both beautiful and distinctive, are exceedingly photogenic. She hates hunting and fishing—the favorite pastimes of the prince—but she has everything else she needs as a sovereign rooted in her family tree, and nothing that she doesn't need other than divorced parents. (One point very much in her favor, at least in the eyes of the royal family, is that she had been a virgin bride, a rare commodity these days. Her uncle, Lord Fermoy, had announced the fact before a flabbergasted group of journalists. "Lady Diana, I can assure you, has never had a lover. There is no such thing as her ever having a past.")

After her marriage, Diana instantly took her place at the summit of the royal jet set, leaving far below the other members of the family, including Prince Charles, who was relegated to a secondary role. The monarchy, under the reign of Elizabeth II, had always maintained a rigid demeanor, and its smiles are well-practiced expressions for public occasions. With daughter-in-law Diana, a high-spirited, spontaneous young woman, it was full-blown life, with all its emotions, pleasures, and disappointments intact, that entered the gates to the Court of St. James's. Condemned to pass her summers at Balmoral instead of discreetly traveling around at will, Diana did nothing to hide the fact that she was profoundly bored, and the whole world took notice.

Her youth, her birth, and her familiarity with the customs of the court had seemed guarantees of her docility. They were not. Undoubtedly it was to induce the press to forget her caprices that Buckingham Palace made a very early announcement of her pregnancy. Certain of the English had for some time hoped that the rule of primogeniture (where the firstborn, whether male or female, inherits the throne) would be established in Britain as it had been in Sweden. But Queen Elizabeth had always favored maintaining tradition. The arrival of baby William put an end to the debate for another generation.

The happy event took place on June 21, 1982, at 11:03 P.M. Prince Charles, who was present at the birth, had prepared himself for his new role as father by reading several books on child care. The next day Diana was already at home in Kensington Palace. The new prince, baptized William Arthur Philip George, is the fourth to carry the name of the dynasty's founder, William the Conqueror. In the land where babies are king, and kings are loved, the royal birth was a victory equal to that of regaining the Falkland Islands —a victory against changing times, atrophying traditions, and sinking national prestige, all of which had been having a depressing effect on the English. There was another happy event to celebrate on September 15, 1984, when Prince Henry was born.

Formerly, in a more austere Great Britain, the Bible and beer were the sole distractors of the people, while the aristocracy lived a life of liberty and even license. But now, at the end of the twentieth century, when liberty belongs to the people and the royal family lives enclosed in its gilded cages, the question in many minds is whether Diana will be able to do as she pleases. At the moment it appears that it is the new princess who sets down the rules, at least at home. She spends lavishly on clothes. The queen, partial to a less costly elegance, has often reproached her about her extravagance. Soon after their marriage, Diana compelled her husband to get rid of Stephen Barry, the valet who for twelve years accompanied Charles everywhere. After his dismissal Barry retaliated by writing *Royal Service,* a revealing book on the private life of his former master. Intimates say Diana tries to keep Charles from seeing his friends while imposing on him her own, all in their twenties, even though he, at thirty-six, has little in common with them. Diana has more or less finessed a role reversal. Early in their engagement, it was believed that the prince, although ready to accept their union, was not truly in love with her, his "shy Di." Then, enchanted by her grace, her capacity to charm the crowds, and her vivaciousness, he succumbed, not only to marriage but to his emotions.

Her vitality and imagination have since had a positive influence on Charles, although he does sometimes find it difficult to accept her enormous and increasing power. Nevertheless, he realizes that in his particular case it is extremely useful to have a wife capable of captivating the crowds. While kings and princes are routinely esteemed or tolerated in the European monarchies, it is the women —the queens and princesses—who seem to radiate the charisma, capturing the adoring attention of their subjects. For example, Silvia of Sweden, once an obscure commoner of German origin, reestablished her country's respect for the monarchy almost single-handedly; and Caroline of Monaco, with her escapades, her constant public appearances, and her carefree life-style, is a formidable publicity agent for the principality.

Diana possesses an exceptional capacity to inflame passions. Her talent, if the prince knows how to exploit it, is that of a flamboyant power behind the throne. This talent has been manifested before in the course of history, for instance, in the late Evita Peron. "O my beloved *descamisados*" (ragamuffins), Evita used to say to crowds of disenfranchised Argentines, raising up her arms shimmering with jewels. Diana demonstrated the same genius for manipulating a crowd when she appeared—coiffed with diamonds and draped with fine pearls—before 3 million unemployed Britons and treated them to light-hearted anecdotes and mischievous smiles. The subject was different, but the context was virtually the same—the feminine powers of seduction put to the service of a husband who holds the title or the power.

For Diana and Charles, the future is at the same time radiant and a bit tarnished. Without a doubt there are few positions more desirable in the world than that of the prince of Wales. Yet he risks spending many long years presiding over banquets and smashing bottles of champagne over the prows of ships. The general consensus is that Charles will not be king for a good twenty years; the queen is in excellent health and comes from a family where the women easily reach their ninth decade. Abdication, although occasionally mentioned in discussions of Charles's future, is completely contrary to English tradition. The majority of the English, the queen, and even Charles himself, are not in favor of Elizabeth II giving up her throne to her son any time in the near future.

Nevertheless, Charles is expected to be an excellent king, and there is little doubt that he will succeed his mother nobly. Like Queen Elizabeth, he is obviously wholly devoted to the glory of his crown and his country. His late great-uncle Lord Louis Mountbatten, who was an excellent judge of what was best for monarchs and monarchies, used to say of having Charles as heir to the throne, "It's a bloody miracle."

One can hardly say as much for the other children of the queen. Princess Anne's relations with her husband are shaky, and the couple are rarely seen togther anymore. The youngest, Edward, sarcastically referred to as the "brain" of the family, passed his secondary school exams with grades generally well below average. As for Andrew, the second son, after valiantly proving himself as a naval officer in the Falklands, he became infatuated with a beautiful young woman who would be difficult to introduce into most families, let alone into the British royal family. Koo Stark, the young lady in question, began her film career by starring in a pornographic film called *Emily,* in which she unveiled her entire anatomy. Unfortunately, under no one's lead but his own, Andrew conducted himself with an unbelievable lack of consideration for his mother. He decided it was a fine idea to invite Koo to spend three days at Balmoral with the queen and presented her simply as an actress. He also invited her to Buckingham Palace and later took her on an abortive but well-publicized trip to the island of Mustique.

IN SPITE OF these escapades, the English monarchy seems destined to endure. Throughout their history, the English dynasties have dealt effectively with revolts, intrigues, foreign attacks, and even their own weaknesses. The current royal family descends in direct line from James I, who succeeded to the throne in 1603. A schemer, a notorious homosexual, and the archetype of the corrupt sovereign, James named his lovers to important posts and looked on the public treasury as his personal bank account. His son, Charles I, paid for his own follies with his head, but in this death Charles's noble nature rose above the horror of the moment. On a frigid January morning in 1649, Charles walked to the scaffold wearing two shirts, so that the people would not believe he was trembling with fear. The eighteenth century brought the four Georges from the House of Hanover, followed by Queen Victoria and her descendants, the House of Windsor.

The structure of modern England and the influence and power of the monarchy were handed down by the queen's namesake, Elizabeth I. When Elizabeth succeeded her sister Mary I in 1558, she inherited a country ravaged by wars and internal strife. Addressing her troops on the eve of battle against the Spanish Armada, she said, "I know I have the body of a weak and feeble woman, but I have the heart and stomach of a king, and of a king of England too!" Under her reign, Sir Francis Drake navigated the world and Shakespeare wrote his plays. The English monarchy has almost always known how to adapt itself, not only to the economic and political conditions of the country, but to the aspirations of the people as well.

When Elizabeth II assumed the crown in 1952, the country's disintegration seemed even more complete than it had during the early reign of the first Elizabeth. England had recently emerged from a world war during which, for the first time in almost a thousand years, the country had been devastated by enemy forces; London and Coventry still bore the scars of heavy bombardment. And it appeared that the empire itself was falling away. India, whose crown Queen Victoria had so proudly worn, would remain part of the Commonwealth, but more or less as an independent country. Even Canada and Australia rejected the British embrace except for elegant ceremonies and other official formalities.

The most serious transformation was taking place, however, at the heart of English society. The very foundations of the country's rigid social structure had crumbled away during the war and afterward during the first few years of peace. The middle classes, divided into subcategories by English sociologists as "lower middle class" and "upper middle class," decided to go after the privileges of the aristocracy. They finally took over economic power in England with a time lag behind Europe that they wanted to rectify as soon as possible.

The strength of the royal family is not that it adapted itself to all the new trends, but that it actually embodies them in its various members. Princess Margaret, so often disparaged, personifies as well as perpetuates the social egalitarianism that marks the London of the day. She represents better than anybody this new society in which a hairdresser such as Vidal Sassoon, or a photographer such as her former husband, Antony Armstrong-Jones, can aspire to be the equal of dukes and peers of the realm. Prince Philip, whose plain-spoken language can be dazzling as well as occasionally shocking, who is a devotee of things mechanical and technical and an avid traveler, is representative of the new middle class which wants to modernize England and make it more competitive in the world markets. But it is still the queen mother, in British hearts, who represents all the charm of beloved old English traditions: white Christmas, plum pudding, and the changing of the guard. As for the queen, with her dowdy hats, her chunky walking shoes, and her cool and distant manner—is she not the embodiment of a deeply rooted England which accepts the new trends but still wants to retain the bonds with the past?

The future of the monarchy would look a great deal different if there were no Prince Charles and if, instead, the unpopular Princess Anne were the heir to the crown. But the prince is indeed there, compassionate to the working classes, keeping current on domestic and world affairs, and jetting from one continent to another in the blink of an eye. To look at him, if one didn't know he was the future king, one might take him for a member of the upwardly mobile middle class, one of the top young executives who manage British industry or supervise the quest for oil in the North Sea. He wears the same gray flannel suit and has the same serious and anonymous face.

It is doubtless indispensable for the royal family to present to the country this neatly minted profile. Over the last few decades, the insular character of Britain has slowly faded away. The United Kingdom is no longer an island. Hovercrafts, as well as trains and planes, today link England and Scotland to the Continent. Its economy is in league, albeit somewhat desultorily, with the Common Market, but the bond is growing. Most Britons these days no longer set their sights, as they did twenty years ago, westward across the great Atlantic, but rather toward Europe, their next-door neighbor. Millions of English tourists spend their vacations on the Continent, which they often criticize and underrate but which, nevertheless, continues to influence their habits and their life style.

It is in the context of all these changes that Queen Elizabeth II and her family have had the strength and ability to prove that the monarchy is not an anachronism. According to all the polls, 95 percent of the population believe that the monarchy is a necessary institution, the only one that allows for social stability and a specifically English way of life. In the coming years, even though the few powers and prerogatives that remain to the monarchy will likely be whittled away, its revenues undoubtedly taxed, and its actions surely criticized, the endurance of the crown, and the sovereigns who wear it, seems assured.

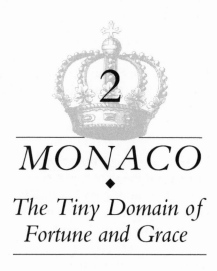

2

MONACO

◆

*The Tiny Domain of
Fortune and Grace*

Looking at a map of the world,
you would need a magnifying glass to pinpoint the minute principality of Monaco, wedged between France, Italy, and the Mediterranean. At this close perspective, you can see Monte Carlo, a city
that bristles with skyscrapers, a city that developed too fast in the
heat of twenty years of frenzied speculation. Today, the exquisite
beaches are in shadows and the fabled charm of this once-great
gambling capital has all but vanished. The smallest country in the
world (just large enough to fit into Central Park without stretching
the seams), Monaco first made its fortune thanks to a legion of
celebrated roulette tables, then went on to become a tax-exempt
paradise for multinational corporations. From financial haven, it
evolved into the popular, family-style tourist attraction it is today,
where the Smiths and the Joneses flock with dreams of breaking
the bank.

His Serene Highness Prince Rainier III of Monaco governs this
principality of 30,000 souls, of which only 3,700 are authentic
"Monégasques." Surprising as it seems he, who has often and
wrongly been compared to the ludicrous sovereigns dear to oper-

ettas, has infinitely more power than her British majesty Elizabeth II with her 900 million subjects. The principality of Monaco exists under a completely autocratic regime. The prince's decree in 1962 read in part:

> By the grace of God, sovereign prince of Monaco, we have resolved to bestow upon the state a new constitution, which, by our sovereign will, from this day on, shall be considered as the fundamental law of the state and cannot be modified except in the terms that we have decreed; we have ordered and we order that:
>
> The principality of Monaco is a sovereign and independent state adhering to the general principles of international law and the specific conventions with France. The principle of government is hereditary and constitutional monarchy.

In practice, however, Monaco is one of the last absolute monarchies of Europe. "Executive power is dependent upon the high authority of the prince, whose person is exercised by the prince and the National Council." It is in the National Council, which consists of eighteen members elected for five years by a direct vote of the people, where debates and votes on legislation take place; but the initiative for new laws, as well as their sanction, lies with the prince. The prince also has the right to pronounce the dissolution of the National Council.

- "The prince represents the principality in its relation with foreign powers." He signs and ratifies treaties after consulting the Crown Council (his personal advisers), whose president and three of its six members he appoints. The three other members are chosen by the National Council, but the prince can reject their nomination.
- "The executive branch of the government is exercised, under the prince's high authority, by a minister of state assisted by a government council. The minister holds the deciding vote over the Government Council." Sovereign ordinances are debated within the Government Council but only the prince's signature gives them executory power. Any decrees signed by the minister of state become official only if they are unopposed by the prince.

Even judiciary power lies with the prince, who, according to the present constitution, has the right to exercise this power in all courts and tribunals. The tribunals render justice in his name. The president of the supreme tribunal as well as its members are named by the prince. Their function and organization are determined by sovereign ordinance.

Conclusion: His Serene Highness Prince Rainier III of Monaco is the only crowned despot in Europe. The National Council made an attempt to take a shred of power for itself twenty-five years ago, but the prince summarily quashed the effort.

The Monégasques were not tempted by even the idea of a revolution, because they knew only too well that should there be dissension in the principality, the administrator of the French Alpes-Maritimes region was empowered to march at the head of his troops into Monaco, with the goal of annexing the principality to France. Thus would come to an end a privilege close to every Monégasque's heart: tax-free citizenship. Herein lies what tempers the strongest republican impulse.

France, meanwhile, was alarmed at the stunning, and growing, number of companies desirous of basing themselves in Monaco in order to avoid taxes; the trend created an obvious disadvantage for France that she felt was grossly unfair.

Urged on by his American consultants, the prince allowed his minuscule country to undergo an enormous economic expansion. With his consent, more than two thousand international companies set up headquarters there, among them Coca-Cola, Bayer Laboratories, Johnson & Johnson, and S. Cumings, the world's foremost arms merchant. In ten years, the volume of business transactions jumped from 150,000 francs to 700,000 a year. For years the French government has dreamed of remodeling Monaco's fiscal regime. But should such an effort ever come to pass, the prince in all probability would refuse to endorse any proposed new laws that would in any way compromise Monaco's fiscal integrity. Isn't he himself linked, if not financially at least morally, with all of the companies that have established themselves on principality territory?

In 1962, President Charles de Gaulle closed the borders between France and Monaco to display his displeasure with the economic situation. The general, piqued by the little prince's ideas of grandeur and independence, wanted the sovereign to remember that Monaco existed only through the goodwill of France. Monaco was thus backed into a "modified compromise" with its neighbor. But the prince heartily defended one point with all the resources at his disposal: "We shall never accept the French fiscal regime. This privilege is directly linked to our independence. Its suppression would signify the disappearance of the principality and would cause serious problems for the Monégasque people, whose interests we are pledged to defend. Knowing that the decisions of the French tribunals are not binding in Monégasque territory [Monaco has its own Supreme Court], I hope that France will not go to the crafty lengths threatened: to cut off our electricity, for example. We have only our loyal goodwill and the sense of our traditions to defend us. The French know this."

A Franco-Monégasque war would be a farce: picture the royal yacht fitted out to encounter the French fleet, while the Monégasque army aimed the Louis XIV bronze cannons, set on the rocky shore, toward France. In order to avoid such a foolish scenario, the accords of 1962 stipulated that everyone then residing in Monaco would forever be exempt from taxes, while anyone who established residence after 1962 would have to pay taxes equivalent to those in France. As for the corporations, they would be taxed on a certain percentage of any profit earned outside of Monaco but at a rate less than it would be in France. Even these few restrictions represented a major economic change for Monaco; before 1962, laws were so lax that a company had only to take a hotel room in Monte Carlo to affirm that its headquarters were in Monaco, and thus avoid taxes.

THE PROBLEMS with France at last resolved, it was then necessary to work out the Onassis-Rainier quarrel, which had been dragging on for more than ten years. Since 1951 Aristotle Socrates Onassis, Greek shipowner and multimillionaire, had been infatuated with Monaco. He hoped to establish his company's maritime headquarters in the old winter Sporting Club, then out of use. But the thought that their posh facility would be leased by a "peasant of the seas" sent a shiver of horror up the spines of several fastidious administrators. This was all Onassis needed to learn: like the tycoon that he was, he bought the whole place. Shortly thereafter, Onassis gained a solid foothold in the SBM, the Société des Bains de Mer, a private organization comprised of half a dozen luxury hotels, two casinos, and various clubs—and Monaco's main source of income. By 1952 he had secured 520,000 shares out of a total of 1,000,000. In spite of this stunning "coup de force," when Onassis presented himself to the National Council with the assurance of someone who is a majority stockholder in their country, not one person expressed the least opposition. Such passivity was at the least astonishing, since a clause in the statutes of the Société des Bains de Mer forbade anyone to hold more than 200 shares—100 in one's own name and the others by proxy—a rule calculated to protect the prince from the competition of a rival power within the SBM. Onassis, a tough and clever businessman, had cunningly steered around the barrier by dividing up his package of shares among fifty Liberian and Panamanian companies. "We are closing our eyes," confided a government official at the time. "Monaco needs money and we hope that Onassis is going to revive the SBM." Everyone, it seems, kept silent, for fear of letting this inestimable fortune escape. Suddenly, the "peasant of the seas" became the savior of a vessel in distress.

The Greek shipowner became an habitué of the palace—he dined with the royal family, took cruises with them, and attended many official affairs; it was indeed a mutual admiration society. Alas, in the space of a few months, the romance turned sour. Neither Onassis nor the prince could transact business deals without the other's consent; the two former friends stymied each other at every turn. Onassis's palace visits grew further and further apart and finally ceased altogether.

In spite of everything, the two men continued to live within the same borders, after a fashion, until 1959, when they agreed to meet in order to define once and for all their respective rights. The time was ripe for action, since Monaco was finding itself increasingly outclassed by the other resorts along the French and Italian coasts. Onassis was reproached for doing nothing to improve Monaco's image. Untrue, retorted the millionaire. Had he not added three stories to the celebrated Hôtel de Paris? This work had indeed been completed but with funds from the Société's reserves, not with the contribution of fresh assets. As for the real estate projects proposed by Onassis, they never materialized.

But the real problem lay in accomplishing anything concrete while two opposite and antagonistic powers were at loggerheads. Aristotle Onassis, believing that the principality's future was tied to upscale international tourism, was resolutely hostile to the more democratic views of the prince and his entourage. "It's necessary to choose between hot dogs and roulette," he declared with contempt. The prince, playing the populist, opted for hot dogs. He feared unpopularity if he gave his country a too luxurious image. He did not want Monte Carlo to continue as the world's gaming capital. (Even today, if someone associates his principality with gambling, Rainier goes into one of his famous rages.) Following the lead of its prince, the government decided that there were two ways to set the economy on its feet: appeal to mass tourism by creating more inexpensive hotel rooms, and greatly improve the services that the SBM doled out so stingily. Onassis, believing otherwise, made his ill will extremely apparent. But the Monégasque authorities held fast and would not give in; the era of the grand dukes was over.

Meanwhile, the directors of the SBM sat and sighed in their offices above the sculpted and gilded woodwork of the gaming rooms; they felt that the government's accusations and demands were unreasonable. What was more, the directors had profound doubts about the viability of the prince's development plan. They were opposed to placing the projected large investments at the mercy of tourism, which in any case seemed to be on the decline. In addition, no one knew whether the company's charter would be renewed when it expired in 1987. So was it prudent to hazard any long-term investments?

The dispute deteriorated into a private quarrel between two men both known for their fiery personalities. The prince believed himself monarch by divine right, while Onassis felt himself to be all-powerful, since, according to him, his success as a businessman was due to divine inspiration. Finally, Onassis agreed to be reimbursed for his 520,000 shares—worth about 85 million old francs ($17 million) in cash from Monaco's treasury. With Onassis paid off and thus out of the picture, the Onassis-Rainier duel was over.

The prince had won his battle, and Monaco lost its glamour. The gaming tables that had made Monaco the most famous and exclusive resort in the world became a mass-market tourist attraction. The elegant international clientele that once flocked to the tables to lose, nobly, a generous inheritance or the fruits of twenty-five years of work, left the scene. They were replaced for a brief time by Arab multimillionaires who hoped to dazzle some of the snobbish elite who were traditionally drawn to the place; but the caftaned princes soon left disappointed, finding nobody worthy of interest. Today, having drawn up the balance sheet, His Highness must ask himself if perhaps his old enemy, the late Onassis, was not right after all: "Roulette is more profitable than hot dogs."

IN THIRTY-FOUR YEARS of reign, Prince Rainier has had ample time to make mistakes as well as score triumphs. After World War II, during which he received both the French and Belgian Croix de Guerre, the twenty-six-year-old Rainier began to involve himself in affairs of state, at the request of his grandfather, Prince Louis II. (Louis's daughter—Rainier's mother and heir-apparent to the throne—had divorced her husband and renounced her right of succession.)

On April 28, 1949, Prince Louis II designated Rainier to manage the principality's affairs. This interregnum was extremely brief; Louis II died less than two weeks later in Monaco. The death was not unexpected, since Louis was seventy-nine years old. What made it somewhat remarkable was that, since Antoine I (1667–1731), no reigning prince had died within Monaco, most having spent the major part of their lives in France. The Monégasques had in fact nicknamed Louis II "the absent prince."

During Louis's funeral, the principality revived an ancient tradition. The prince's body was carried by representatives of Monaco's oldest families, dressed in the black and white costumes of medieval penitents. Mourning lasted six months, during which the flag of the royal family, the House of Grimaldi, flew at half-mast. It was not until November 19 of that year, the name day of St. Rainier, that Rainier III actually became the thirtieth prince of Monaco. In concert, the ancient cannons and the palace chapel bells proclaimed that the new sovereign had just taken his place on the red velvet and gilt throne beneath its richly embroidered canopy, where the princes of Monaco officially sat only once in their life, the day of their accession.

It was upon this same throne that six years later the prince first saw the ravishing vision that would transform his life. Encouraged by audacious journalists, the young and beautiful American actress Grace Kelly, in Cannes for the screening of her latest film, *The Country Girl,* requested an audience with the prince of Monaco. On

May 6, 1955, at 2:30 in the afternoon, the actress, escorted by photographers, entered the court of honor of the Grimaldi palace. For the occasion, she was dressed in a white summer suit with a light silk scarf at her throat; her blond hair was neatly twisted into a chignon. Delayed by another appointment, the prince was an hour late, leaving Grace ample time to play princess in the great ceremonial rooms. Exhausted but dazzled after an hour's guided tour, the future princess, who perhaps had an inkling of her destiny, sat down for a short rest on the throne of Monaco. This crime of high treason made her radiant, since it was the first time in her life that she had sat on a real throne. Lost in her dream, she did not hear the door open. Suddenly she noticed someone standing before her, a man not very tall and casually dressed in a navy blue blazer. Grace, somewhat disconcerted by the silent appearance of the prince, jumped off the throne and sank into a deep curtsy. Beguiled by her charm, the prince perhaps forgot the pain of having to give up his first love, Gisèle Pascal.

Rainier escorted his guest out to the private gardens, then to the cages where lions were kept. Relations between animal and man had always intrigued him; in other circumstances, he might have been a lion tamer. He calmed Grace's fear of the growling beasts by entering the cages and gently caressing the animals. "The day that man can live in peace with the animal kingdom," Rainier explained to his trembling companion, "he will be at peace with himself and will have found paradise on earth." The young actress was visibly impressed by the prince's daring. The captivated "tamer" had in turn captivated the star. They went on to visit the exotic gardens and, in all, spent more than two hours together. Naturally, the day after such an unorthodox audience, newspapers around the world posed the same question: After thirty-three years of bachelorhood, would the prince succumb to the charms of the lady from Hollywood? One man in the prince's entourage, Reverend Father Tucker, certainly hoped so.

In 1950, the pope had dispatched the American priest to Monaco to take over the parish of St. Charles. Very quickly the prince's chaplain and confessor became his intimate friend and confidant. Father Tucker, who looked upon the prince as a son, helped him get over the loss of Gisèle Pascal.

The lovers had met during the winter of 1947 in Paris, where the prince was spending several months. One evening Rainier went to see a play at the Alhambra Theater, and with his first glimpse of the leading lady on stage he was smitten. Without delay he sent a huge bouquet of flowers to her dressing room. After the performance, he invited her to dinner. Gisèle accepted, thus beginning a seven-year romance.

Rainier set his love up in a magnificent villa in St.-Jean-Cap-Ferrat, the Villa Iberia, which was surrounded by a large park filled with flowers and animals. Unfortunately for Rainier, his grandfather, the reigning prince Louis II, had at the age of seventy-five married an actress, Ghislaine Domanget. Conservative factions in the principality complained that the dynasty had an annoying tendency to confuse show business with the aristocracy. Louis II himself agreed with the assertion and coldly declared, "One actress in the family is enough." Understanding his grandson's situation, however, Louis did not demand a breakup of the affair, and the two young lovers, who were exactly the same age, continued to make a perfect and extremely discreet couple. There was no change in their relationship even after the death of Louis II. The gossip of the day was that the Crown Council opposed an alliance because of the extremely humble origins of Gisèle's parents. (Her father, Monsieur Tallone, was in the wholesale fruit business.) Months passed, years passed. Whenever the flags that flew above the palace were lowered, as they were each time the sovereign was absent, the Monégasques would remark, "Well, Rainier is off to visit Gisèle." At the Villa Iberia, happiness reigned: Gisèle prepared dishes of the Midi redolent with herbs and spices, while the prince closed himself up for hours at a time in his workshop, to indulge in his favorite pastime. He could repair almost anything like a professional—he did welding, woodworking, and masonry, and like Louis XVI he was addicted to the art form of metalwork. Alas, the idyll lasted so many years that it became more and more difficult to transform it into marriage. One day, as Rainier knew, it had to come to an end. Or did it? They were still in love. Rainier confided his crisis of conscience to his best friend, Father Tucker. The man of the church told him, "She's charming. I would marry her in a minute, but I can't because I'm a priest. You can't either because you're a sovereign prince."

Why then was Grace Kelly a more acceptable candidate for princess? Her name did not figure any more than Gisèle's in the international social register. But she was American, which struck a patriotic chord in the priest, and she was very rich as well, opening up the possibility of vast new economic channels for the little principality. Her father was an important contractor in Philadelphia, in constant contact with the world of American big business, and Monaco at the time was ripe for economic revival.

In the mid-1950s, and for several years previously, despite the excellent receipts taken in by the casino, the SBM was in trouble. On one single night, December 31, 1954, three million francs were dropped on the green felt tables. The sums were the stuff of dreams, yet they still did not prevent the SBM from sliding dangerously close to bankruptcy, a circumstance which made a possible link with America extremely welcome.

In spite of the disapproving Monégasques, who would have preferred that their prince marry a Frenchwoman, and in spite of the bastions of European society (already somewhat contemptuous of the prince) who had hoped he would align himself with a more illustrious genealogy, everything was settled when Father Tucker gave his stamp of approval to the young American.

Rainier's only remaining problem was how to approach his intended. He and Grace had seen each other only once, and after that there had been no communication. Luckily, providence intervened. In July 1955, Grace's uncle Russell Austin and his wife Carrie arrived from Philadelphia to spend a vacation on the Riviera—St. Tropez, Cannes, Nice, and Monaco. During their stay in Monaco, the Austins discovered to their delight that the elite Sporting Club was holding its first gala of the summer. Unfortunately, all the tables had been reserved long in advance. No problem, decided Uncle Russell; the only thing needed was a little call to the sovereign—after all, Grace had managed to see him and, in addition, had found him quite charming. Direct and efficient American that he was, Uncle Russell telephoned the palace: "Hello, I'm the uncle of Grace Kelly, who . . ." Soon, the Austins had the best table. As soon as he put down the receiver, Rainier called in his *éminence grise,* Father Tucker, and, as a sort of special envoy from His Serene Highness, charged him with establishing contact. After all, there was nothing like the proper approach to slant the family bias in one's favor. Very hospitable and understanding, the Austins invited the sovereign to visit them in Philadelphia, and at the end of that autumn Rainier left for the United States. No proposal of marriage had yet been formulated, but the prince nevertheless carried with him an engagement ring. One never knew. The ring was superb: a double band of gold set with diamonds and rubies, created by Monsieur Balanche, official jeweler to the royal family for thirty years.

On Christmas day the Austins rang the doorbell of the Kellys' home. Accompanying Russell and his wife were Father Tucker and His Serene Highness Prince Rainier of Monaco. Introductions were made, and the somewhat incongruous group, despite a certain apprehension, spent a relaxed evening together. Everybody found the prince extremely nice. "He seemed so simple and unpretentious," Mrs. Kelly said later. "His manners were so democratic we had trouble remembering that we had before us an absolute monarch."

Events were proceeding rapidly and well. Certain skeptics believed, however, that the whole affair was a vast publicity stunt orchestrated by Metro-Goldwyn-Mayer, with whom Grace had just signed a contract. But the gossips soon had to take back their words; early in January, Father Tucker officially asked Mr. Kelly for Grace's hand in marriage in the name of the prince. Shortly thereafter, the engagement was announced.

Neglected for several weeks, Jean-Pierre Aumont, the French actor whom Grace had recently been seeing, received a telephone call from her the night before the official announcement. The young woman he loved and who seemed to love him told him she had accepted Rainier's marriage proposal. It was over as simply as that. All the marvelous moments they had spent together had vanished. Exit Jean-Pierre and his despair, as well as Oleg Cassini, the high-fashion designer, who was devastated upon reading the news in the papers—he also had hoped to marry Grace.

In a few short years, Grace had traveled a long road from the day she was refused admission to Bennington College—known for its excellent courses in dramatic art—because of poor grades. Luckily, the friend of a friend of Mrs. Kelly's, whose daughter had just entered the American Academy of Dramatic Arts, introduced Grace to the director of the school. Thus, Grace was soon accepted into one of the best schools of its kind, whose alumni included Lauren Bacall and Kirk Douglas. To attend, however, it was necessary to move to New York, a den of iniquity as far as the Kellys were concerned. For a very strict Catholic family, the idea was more than an adventure; it was dangerous. To protect Grace from the hazards of the big city, Mrs. Kelly installed her daughter in the

Barbizon Hotel for Women. Grace applied herself with ardor and enthusiasm to her classes in dance, dramatic art, and diction (to the great relief of friends long tortured by her nasal voice). Although she received a generous allowance from her father, for Grace the most exciting part of her new freedom was the opportunity to earn her own living. Her career début was in a series of Coca-Cola advertisements, and she proudly left the photographic session with her payment of seven dollars. Gradually her fees rose to twenty-five dollars, but the photographers saw no future for her—she was too polite, had no bust, no "pep," no éclat.

Completing her course at the academy, Grace began her quest for her first real part as an actress. But everywhere she went she heard the same depressing response: "You have a lot of talent, my dear, but unfortunately you're too tall." Five feet eight inches was indeed a handicap, since, contrary to appearances on the big screen, many leading men were quite short. For Grace, it was a time of despair and tears, which finally abated when she found her first role in a Broadway play. This role opened the doors to television and then to Hollywood and the movies; in 1952 she appeared in *High Noon*.

One day, her agent made an appointment for her at the office of director Gregory Ratoff to audition for a role in a film called *Taxi*. When she pushed open the door Ratoff looked at her thunder-struck. She was wearing an old tweed skirt, a button-down shirt, and flat shoes. Her hair looked as though she hadn't combed it since the night before. "She's perfect," cried the director, who was looking for a girl of the streets. "What I like about her is that she's not pretty. She's perfectly plain." She was so perfect that the producer thought a slightly more attractive girl might actually be better. Fortunately, John Ford and Alfred Hitchcock saw the end of the tryout and realized that this plain Jane could be pretty. Ford found her just right to play the abandoned English wife suddenly smitten with lion-hunter Clark Gable in *Mogambo;* Hitchcock thought her ideal for *Dial M for Murder* and *Rear Window*. What pleased Hitchcock was precisely what she had tried to conquer: her lack of expression.

Grace Kelly signed a seven-year contract with Metro-Goldwyn-Mayer, who decided not to bank on her themselves, but to lend her out to other studios. Fox paid $20,000 for her to appear in *The Bridges of Toko-Ri*. Metro's price rose to $50,000 when Paramount wanted to engage her for *Rear Window*. In return for the privilege of hiring her out, MGM paid Grace $10,000 per picture, content to use her as a commodity while competing studios were cashing in on her sudden fame at the box office to the tune of hundreds of thousands of dollars. When critics jeered at the cowardice of MGM, the studio moguls responded, "Our competitors are making us a star." In reality, the company was not optimistic about the long-term success of this flat-chested, icy actress with the horn-rimmed glasses. But what MGM didn't know was that, since early childhood, whenever young Miss Kelly decided on something, she always got her way. So when she decided to become an actress, nothing could make her change her mind.

When she decided to become a princess, she settled on the idea with the same strength of will. In spite of the number of suitors that any young and beautiful actress attracts, it was the shortest among them (he humorously nicknamed himself Shorty) who, in Grace's eyes, dominated all the others. Prince Rainier obtained a "yes" in less than two months.

Announcement of the engagement instantly mobilized the world press. Radio Monte Carlo interrupted its regular programming to broadcast the terse text of the first telegram: "His Serene Highness Prince Rainier is happy to announce his engagement to Miss Grace Kelly, daughter of Mr. and Mrs. John Kelly of Philadelphia." The following day, portraits of Rainier were displayed in all the shop windows in Monaco. The government sent close to three hundred pounds of flowers to their future princess. Enthusiasm seemed widespread, even though there were those who kept silent at the news. But as one member of the government said, "A happy prince is a happy principality."

Upon learning the big news, Aristotle Onassis immediately sent a gift of a million francs (about $200,000) to the Monaco Red Cross, directed by Princess Antoinette, Rainier's sister. Antoinette, conforming to her official duty, stated that she was happy with her brother's choice.

For the Kellys and the prince, it was now necessary to focus full time on the details of the marriage: to set the date, send out the invitations, decide on the place, and so on. Negotiating from one end of the Atlantic to the other, they finally decided that both the civil and religious ceremonies would take place in Monaco, in spite of Mrs. Kelly's initial wish that the festivities be held in Philadelphia. In Hollywood, meanwhile, Grace was preparing herself: she studied French, organized her trousseau, scheduled fittings, and answered a flood of mail. She wrote countless "thank you" notes for an endless stream of gifts. MGM had to clear out a huge room to store them. Grace was honored by several bridal showers, one of which, a lingerie shower, was given by Hollywood costume designer Helen Rose. Actress Rita Gam brought bras, Celeste Holme a set of silk panties, Ann Blyth a rose lace dressing gown, and Dolores Gray a pale blue slip for Grace to wear under her wedding gown, which was being designed by the hostess.

Back on the Continent, the principality was in a frenzy of preparation, particularly since there were no existing laws regulating nuptial ceremonies in Monaco. In order to find an account of a marriage of a reigning prince on national territory, it was necessary to delve deep into Monégasque history. A special commission was appointed to haul out the dusty archives and come up with an appropriate protocol suitable to the grandeur of the occasion. On his return from Philadelphia, the prince set to work on the festivities, fifteen hours a day. He wanted to be, at one and the same time, director, producer, stage manager, and principal actor in his own marriage. He ordered a facelift for the entire principality. Façades were cleaned, whitewashed, or replastered; street lamps, railings, and even the police barracks were repainted. Sixty workers labored at the palace, repairing, regilding, trimming; the sixty Carrara marble stairs on the grand staircase outside were carefully repolished. Close to a million dollars was allotted for "set decoration" on this elaborate production. Two thousand flagpoles sixty-five feet high were installed along the roadways, and eighty loudspeakers were set up at regular intervals throughout Monte Carlo to permit the entire population to follow the ceremonies. Fifty microphones, sixteen thousand feet of cable, twenty-five telephone stations for the fifteen hundred journalists, thousands of flowers, five hundred shrubs: Cecil B. DeMille could not have done better. Max Factor created a special makeup for the princess to harmonize with her gown. The bra manufacturer sponsoring the radio broadcast of "the greatest romantic event since Romeo and Juliet" promised not to advertise its wares during the program, so that the nuptial mass would not be interrupted by commercials urging women to have a "high, firm bustline." The American influence was already being felt.

All along the Côte d'Azur, movie theaters were packed: on the screen, Grace Kelly. The most successful film by far was *To Catch a Thief,* in which Cary Grant innocently asks the heroine, seated on a beach near Monaco where the film was shot: "So, if I understand correctly, you've come here to buy yourself a husband." The theaters echoed with laughter, in spite of the fury of Rainier, whose autocratic powers could not extend all the way to Nice.

For the historic event everyone—that is, everyone whose social references were known and recognized—received an invitation. Nevertheless, to avoid social affronts, the complete lists were never published. The royal families of England, Holland, Sweden, and Denmark were represented only by their local consul. France sent François Mitterrand, at the time minister of justice.

DEPRIVED of natural resources, the Monégasques, Rainier among them, had long ago realized that after gambling and tourism, the princely family constituted a promising investment. Indeed, the marriage revealed itself to be a marvelous financial and public relations operation for the principality. The commemorative stamps alone, showing a portrait of the two sovereigns, brought in millions of dollars and covered many of the wedding expenses. Windows overlooking the route of the procession were renting for 50,000 to 100,000 francs, then equivalent to around $100 to $200. Tourism was booming. The service staffs of restaurants, hotels, bars, and nightclubs were doubled and occasionally tripled. Three months before the ceremonies commenced there was not a single available hotel room in the principality or within a fifty-mile radius. At a meeting of the town council, one of the members even suggested that the city think about renting rooms in the prison which, located on the rocks in the middle of the St. Martin gardens, had a better view of the principality than any other building. For want of criminal convictions, the model prison was completely empty; criminals didn't know what they were missing. The thirty individual cells, painted pale green, spacious, and complete with a shower, were more than welcoming. The beds were covered with thick white sheets, and the meals, carried in twice daily from a neighboring restaurant, were quite acceptable.

On April 12, 1956, the U.S.S. *Constitution* entered the port of Monaco. On board was the fiancée, accompanied by her entire family—parents, sisters, brothers, uncles, aunts—and more than eighty guests. At dawn, dozens of trunks holding Grace's trousseau had been unloaded at Cannes. A flotilla of small boats had taken to the water, each hoping to be the first to encounter the future sovereign as she sailed from Cannes to Monte Carlo.

In a few days she would be Her Serene Highness, Princess of Monaco, four times a duchess, eight times a countess, and four times a marquise—in brief, one of the most titled women of Europe. She would be called Highness or Madame, but "Madame" with an intonation that left no doubt of the sovereign significance. Her Highness would be addressed in the third-person singular after being honored with a bow or a curtsy. But on her arrival this April 12, Grace was still simply Miss Kelly and as yet had no right to military honors—no cannon salutes, no parade. As bride-to-be, Grace was welcomed in her future country by her fiancé, and as the future Serene Highness she received the homage of the Monégasque population through compliments carefully recited by the palace concierge's son and the palace pastry chef.

At the palace, another ceremony awaited her. Very solemn, the Grand Chamberlain presented to her the palace staff, lined up on the grand staircase according to a rigorous hierarchy. Like a general on inspection, Grace passed before the aides-de-camp, the secretaries, the cooks, the dressmakers, the maître d'hôtel, the chambermaids, on down the line, greeting in all about thirty people. She was then led inside to her apartments, three Empire-style rooms which the prince had had elegantly fitted out to do justice to his beautiful fiancée. She rested for just a half hour before a lady-in-waiting came to ask her to luncheon in the name of the sovereign. Thus began the constraints of the princess's role.

Six days later, at 11:15 A.M., amid massive confusion, the wedding guests were led into the palace throne room. Shortly after, the bridal couple made their entrance. Miss Kelly wore a street-length dress of rose satin and lace with matching satin shoes and hat. The prince wore a morning coat. Both seemed extremely tense, strained, and unsmiling. Two armchairs had been placed for them in the center of the room. Grace, seated on the edge of her chair, stared fixedly in front of her, trying to overcome her shortness of breath and trembling hands. The prince, without raising his eyes, gnawed on his index finger with an air of dismay. Not even a shadow of a smile relieved the tension that enveloped the entire assembly. Several minutes before the beginning of the marriage ceremony, Fernand D'Aillières, chief of protocol, fainted, exhausted by sleepless nights and long days of work.

At a signal from the sovereign, Monsieur Portanier, an eminent member of the government, began the civil ceremony. He forgot nothing, not even the reading from the civil code on marriage, which stated that the husband must aid, protect, and shelter his wife, while she must love him and be faithful to him. Amen. Finally he reached the essential part of the ceremony: "Mademoiselle, do you take for your husband His Serene Highness the Prince Rainier III Grimaldi, Sovereign Prince of Monaco, here present?" In the press room where the journalists were following the ceremony, there was suspense. When the great star murmured yes there was a collective sigh of relief. "Monseigneur, Your Highness," Monsieur Portanier continued, "may I ask most respectfully of Your Serene Highness if he consents to take as wife and legitimate spouse Mademoiselle Grace Patricia Kelly, here present?" In a firm voice the little prince answered yes, even though that morning he had received a discouraging anonymous letter, "Do not marry Grace Kelly. This marriage is not worthy of you."

Bowing before Grace, the magistrate concluded, "In the name of the statutes of the sovereign family and the law, I declare your Serene Highnesses united by the bonds of marriage." For some reason, not a sound, not a whisper, arose from the stony-faced guests. Embarrassed, timid, respectful of etiquette? At first glance, a princely marriage did not seem as joyous or festive an occasion as the simplest bourgeois wedding.

After the newlyweds' appearance on the palace balcony, the people of Monaco were received in the palace gardens, following the Monégasque tradition that at every important occasion the sovereign receive all his people. Louis Veuillot, a French royalist of the last century, wrote, "If I had the ambition to reign, I would be tempted by only two thrones: that of the czar, who reigns over 120 million souls, or that of the prince of Monaco, who knows all his subjects by their first name." Rainier is the only reigning prince who could even gather all his people into his garden. To commemorate the occasion, everyone was allowed to take home a champagne glass. The glasses were decorated with a delicate design in red and white—the Monégasque colors—and engraved in gold with the newlyweds' initials as well as the date of the religious ceremony that would take place the next day. In the evening all the theaters and concerts were free for the citizens of Monaco (but nowhere was there a Grace Kelly movie playing). For the royalty and their guests, there was a gala soirée at the opera. The new princess made her appearance before the international and Monégasque elite wearing a sumptuous diadem, a diamond and ruby necklace, and matching earrings, gifts from the Monaco National Council worth millions of dollars.

At 9:50 the next morning, the cathedral bells began to peal at full volume. An escadrille flew over the principality, while along the parade route sailors from the French, English, Italian, and American fleets stood in formation—twenty-five men representing each country. Alpine troops were stationed at the cathedral steps. But it was the prince's personal Monégasque guard that formed the cordon of honor up to the cathedral's central portal under an immense red and white awning stamped with the Grimaldi coat of arms.

At 10:00 A.M., the princess's procession waited at the top of the grand staircase of the palace for the signal to depart—the boom of twenty-one cannons. The father of the bride, in top hat and tails, took his daughter's arm. Slowly they descended the seventy steps. The princess watched her feet, careful not to step on her cathedral train, trimmed with nineteenth-century Brussels lace. Her bridal gown was made entirely from rosepoint lace, with a pearl stitched in the center of each flower; the sleeves were long and narrow, the skirt lavishly full. Her veil was held by clusters of flowers. She carried a bouquet of lilies of the valley.

At precisely 10:35 A.M., Grace crossed the threshold of the cathedral. She was preceded by two pages in white carrying velvet cushions on which rested the wedding rings, and four little girls crowned with flowers. Eight bridesmaids were dressed in light yellow organdy and satin. Pale with emotion, the bride was greeted under the portal by Monsignor Barthe, Bishop of Monaco. The prince, the last one to leave the palace, stepped out of his car just as Grace reached the altar. He was resplendent in a uniform he had designed himself. Enamored of the sea, he at first had thought of wearing an admiral's uniform. But being supreme head of the Monégasque army (eighty soldiers), he then considered dressing as either a general or an ordinary soldier. Finally, he decided he would wear a unique outfit of a decidedly modern cut, somewhat inspired by the uniform once worn by marshals of Napoleon's empire.

The beautiful film star on the arm of her prince—a fairy tale come true.
(Sygma)

Toning down the traditional adornments he deemed excessive, the prince designed two pairs of epaulettes, one pair magnificently trimmed in gold for evening wear. A constellation of medals covered his chest, and on his head was a jaunty cocked hat with plumes. Chewing nervously on his mustache, Rainier shot a brief glance at Grace and the ceremony began. At the end of the service, the organs blared out a grandiose "Hallelujah Chorus" to celebrate the union as the prince and princess waved to the crowd massed outside the cathedral. Then they stepped into a gleaming white Rolls-Royce and drove slowly to the port through narrow, rocky roads and wide, palm-lined boulevards. The car drew up in front of the Chapel of Sainte-Dévote, where Princess Grace stepped out to lay her bridal bouquet of lilies of the valley in honor of the patron saint of Monaco. It was her first official act as princess.

At one o'clock 750 guests, the men in top hat and tails or dress uniforms, the women in magnificent gowns, arrived at the palace for the wedding luncheon. In the courtyard, under the arches of the Hercules Gallery, lavish buffet tables had been set up, but seating had been provided only for the bridal couple and their families, on the landing of the double grand staircase. At the end of the meal, six liveried valets appeared before the prince and princess with a monumental construction weighing 212 pounds and standing almost six feet tall. (Earlier that morning, the master pastry chef of the Hôtel de Paris, creator of this masterpiece, had been wrestling with an apparently insoluble problem of transport: 212 pounds of frosted cake in six layers separated by sugar colonnades was not an easy proposition. Large drops of perspiration rolled from under poor Chef Battistini's large toque blanche, down his temples, and into the rolls of his neck. If the cake was not there on time it would be a catastrophe: no more job and, above all, a reputation in tatters. Finally, a solution was found—the chef d'oeuvre, complete with an enormous sugar crown at the top, was transported in nine separate pieces and reassembled at the palace.) Hand in hand, the newlyweds cut the first slice of the 100,000-calorie architectural wonder. Shortly thereafter, they disappeared to board the sovereign yacht *Deo Juvante* for a traditional honeymoon. The demanding tasks inherent in any position of power awaited their return.

———

THE LIFE of a reigning monarch is full of small duties. Princess Grace, for example, was president of the Monaco Red Cross, a job she took over from Princess Antoinette. She organized day-care nurseries so that Monégasque women could work outside the home. She traveled the country in a drive for blood donations and gave the annual gala Red Cross Ball, which was the top social and financial event in Monaco's year. She was also president of the Girl Scouts and Boy Scouts, president of the Garden Club (and actively involved in an international flower competition), honorary president of the worldwide Association for the Protection of the Child, and sponsor of the Notre-Dame-de-Fatima nursery. In addition, she created the Princess Grace of Monaco Foundation to aid and encourage artists and artisans from the principality, as well as a Monaco–U.S.A. association to promote cultural exchanges. As part of the latter program, the princess even went on tour in the United States to recite poetry in American universities—a small way of reentering the hitherto forbidden theatrical limelight.

Princess Grace, perfectly adapted to her role, committed only one single faux pas in her career. One day in March 1962, in spite of the prince's interdiction, Princess Grace announced that she would like to return to the screen in an Alfred Hitchcock film. After violent protests from the Monégasque council and a vociferous outcry from the press, Grace had to renounce this desire on pain of tarnishing her image as princess as well as the ancestral coat of arms which had been given the Kelly family.

Officially, Princess Grace did not get involved in politics or business, but this did not stop her from being an informed businesswoman who knew what American big business was all about. Her major contribution to Monaco, however, was that she reestablished a certain prestige in the principality. "My wife is my best public relations agent," the prince once acknowledged; perhaps his best real estate agent, too.

THE PRINCE'S OFFICE, situated in the clock tower that rises above the palace, is crammed with books, folders, files, photos, and a hundred sundry objects, but he finds it no problem to work amid the room's great clutter. Miraculously, he always finds a free space to answer his mail, previously opened by his two secretaries. Letters arrive by the dozen every day, some serious, others harebrained: "Dear Cousin, You don't remember me, but we spent our vacations together at the seashore. . . ." Conclusion: a request for money. If it is not financial aid that is solicited, it is a request for an audience, or sponsorship of some project. The prince rarely answers these letters himself, leaving the task to his secretaries. Later in the morning the chef arrives in Rainier's office to present his proposed menus for the day, which the prince either vetoes or approves. He thus avoids having to eat roast lamb with green beans three days running, followed by three days of grilled salmon and boiled potatoes. When it comes to wine, the prince appreciates the best vintages and has an excellent cellar at the palace.

With all his little administrative chores out of the way, the prince then holds private audiences in the ceremonial office next to his own. If the visitor is coming to the palace for the first time, he or she is first introduced to the chief of protocol, who gives a quick lesson on appropriate conduct. The visitor is then accompanied to the tower and met by either a secretary or a valet who leads the way into a waiting room. Earlier in the century, people were expected to dress formally for an audience with the sovereign: a man in a morning suit, a woman (on the rare occasions when a woman was permitted an audience) as elegantly as possible. Today, only shorts and blue jeans are forbidden. Yet, despite the obvious democratization of its politics and governmental affairs, the Monégasque court remains the most formal of any in the world.

For private or official receptions, precise etiquette is carefully established far in advance. In general, official receptions take place in the state salons; particularly important events take place in the throne room. This grand chamber, whose ceiling is adorned with seventeenth-century frescoes, is hung with crimson damask tapestries from which portraits of Monégasque ancestors are suspended. At the beginning of any reception, the sovereign waits in a small adjacent room, called the Louis XV Salon or the Blue Salon, to receive the respects of each guest. For private receptions, members of the royal family make their appearance only after all the guests have arrived.

Princess Grace managed to do away with the requirement that women wear hats during luncheons or teas at the palace. But for the most part the entire Monégasque court, and above all the palace staff, is firmly entrenched in the rites and customs that regulate daily palace life. "Even I," explained the prince, "if I suddenly decided that at dinner my fork should be placed at the right of my plate, I could not have it that way. The staff who work here, some of whom have been in service forty years, could not bear it. So the fork stays on the left, the wine is served by the maître d', and food is presented from the guest's left." This whole system of complicated rules did not in the least put off the young American princess, who, in spite of a strict Catholic upbringing, had been accustomed to a freer, less confined life style. "The advantage of a strict protocol," she explained, "is that one knows exactly what should be done at all times; each moment is programmed and each attitude is dictated in advance. Far from being a constraint, protocol is a help. Very quickly I realized that I didn't have to torture myself in wondering what attitude I was supposed to take at every moment. Everything was foreseen. Nevertheless, at the beginning of my marriage, the transition between my life in New York and the life at the palace was rather difficult, even more so because I had abandoned a career I liked enormously and in which I was a success, for another one about which I knew absolutely nothing and whose responsibilities were so much more important." The princess took her new role immediately to heart and mastered almost all of its obligations perfectly, except perhaps for the French language. (Twenty-five years after her marriage, she still spoke with a pronounced American accent and had a limited vocabulary. Among themselves, the family all spoke English. The three children, Caroline, Albert, and Stephanie, as well as the prince, are all bilingual.)

ON JANUARY 23, 1957, at 9:27 A.M., the sound of twenty-one cannons announced to the Monégasques that their princess had just given birth to a little princess—Caroline Louise Marguerite Grimaldi. To mark the occasion, the prince gave his wife a necklace of tiny pearls and a pair of diamond earrings. It was a major event for Monaco, as the other royal births would be, particularly Prince Albert's on March 14, 1958.

Caroline was hardly out of the cradle when her photo appeared on the covers of magazines around the world. (These photos, taken by the prince within the intimacy of the family, had cost the press a fortune.) Even though Caroline, after the birth of her younger brother Albert, no longer had the right to carry the same title of "Madame" as her mother, even though she had lost the right to the crown, and even though the guards no longer saluted her when she passed through the palace gates accompanied by her white-uniformed Swiss nurse, the little princess was still great public relations material for the principality. With the cooperation of her parents, Caroline became a truly commercial commodity. The newspapers that featured her doubled their circulations, while the paparazzi never had to worry about unemployment. Caroline was the beacon that drew interest, and eventually visitors, to Monaco.

Caroline and Albert had their early schooling at the palace with a private tutor; two other children Caroline's age attended class with them. Academically, Prince Albert, fourteen months younger than Caroline, could not keep up with the others, and acquired a bashfulness and insecurity from this early experience that he has never quite outgrown. When he reached his teens, he entered Monaco's public school, where he would complete his studies. Every morning he walked to the school, situated on the coast overlooking the Mediterranean. Although he was seemingly unaccompanied, a palace soldier vigilantly followed several yards behind. Caroline was enrolled at the school of the Dames de Saint-Maur, where she remained until early in her high school years, and was then sent to St. Mary's, a Catholic school in Ascot, England. She later took additional courses at a French lycée in London. In 1974 Caroline returned to Paris to prepare for her baccalaureate exams at a small boarding school which her sister Stephanie (born February 1, 1965) would also attend.

Caroline passed her "bac" with honorable mention and, to please her father, enrolled for the preparatory year at the Ecole des Sciences Politiques in Paris. At the end of the last trimester, gossips were saying that she had failed her exams. The official version asserts that she never took them. It seems, nevertheless, that the young princess preferred shopping and the nightlife of fashionable Paris to more scholarly pursuits.

During these years, the family was separated, the men living in Monaco and the women in Paris. In Paris, Her Serene Highness Princess Grace once again took up the worldly and glittering life to which she had been accustomed during her Hollywood days. Occasionally, Prince Rainier and Albert came to join them for the weekend. But more often the princes went to the castle of Marchais, a family estate situated in the Ardennes region of France. Rainier occupied himself at Marchais with numerous renovation projects, fixing the castle up comfortably for the day when he could retire there, as soon as Albert was ready to assume the throne of Monaco.

As for Caroline, two years after her wedding to commoner Philippe Junot, nothing was going right. They were married on June 28, 1978, "for better or worse . . ." but Caroline, at the tender age of twenty-one, had married only "for better," while her parents, opposed to the match from the beginning, knew it would be "for worse." In order to avoid a scandal, such as an elopement, Grace and Rainier had resigned themselves to the inevitable, and the marriage was celebrated in Monaco before six hundred guests. The sovereigns smiled, but their expressions were rigid rather than joyous. Young Caroline had been seduced by an overripe French playboy who made her laugh with his Belgian jokes. Caroline didn't realize that Belgian jokes, very quickly, wear thin. In the official palace biography, Philippe Junot was listed as a financial consultant with a diploma from the New York Institute of Finance. But the Institute protested that it had never awarded a diploma to any Mr. Junot. On the other hand, very select clubs such as Régine's and Castel in Paris could certainly have given him glowing references for unfailing attendance and assiduous application to activities at hand.

Carried away in the whirlwind of galas, balls, dinners, parties, premieres, fashionable restaurants, and jet-set cruises, the couple never had a chance to really get to know each other. The divorce wished for by the sovereigns was pronounced in September 1980.

The shock of the divorce seemed to have a sobering effect on the young princess. Caroline began taking an increasing part in official palace functions alongside her parents. She declared herself fascinated by journalism and asserted that she now wanted to undertake serious pursuits. But the "new Caroline" was short-lived. She soon was constantly by the side of her childhood friend Roberto Rossellini, the son of Ingrid Bergman and Italian film director Robert Rossellini. It was even said that they were living together at the "Clos Saint-Pierre," a tiny pink and green cottage two minutes from the palace that her parents had given Caroline to help her forget her failed marriage. Grace would have preferred a more illustrious partner for Caroline, but she was ready to accept a second marriage as long as it put an end to this "irregular" situation. But Caroline was in no hurry. She did not want to make any more

Right: On her arrival in Monaco aboard the USS *Constitution*, Grace Kelly is greeted by her fiancé. (Maestri/ Sygma)

Below: The prince and princess of Monaco with daughters Caroline (*left*) and Stephanie (*right*) at their winter chalet in Switzerland. (James Andanson/Sygma)

Left to right: Caroline, Albert, and Stephanie wait with their parents to greet celebrity guests at Monaco's Grand Ball for the Red Cross. (Yves Coatsaliou/ Sygma)

Glamorous Princess Caroline attends a star-studded gala in Monte Carlo (James Andanson/Sygma)

mistakes. After a year and a half of relative calm, scandal broke out anew. Princess Caroline of Monaco was infatuated with the Argentinian tennis star Guillermo Vilas. Thanks to a series of indiscreet photographs, taken with a telephoto lens, the whole world was able to see the couple tenderly entwined on an isolated beach in Hawaii.

Stephanie, like her sister Caroline, has the Latin blood of the Grimaldis, a fierce taste for independence, an unfettered spirit, and a strong tendency to let herself be guided by her own pleasure. In spite of her mother's protests, the youngest of the family would go out every night and not return until dawn. Stephanie lived as she pleased. Expelled from the Cours Saint-Dominique—a private school in Paris—for misbehavior, Steff enrolled in the Cours Charles de Foucauld in Neuilly, where she somehow managed, in spite of everything, to pass her baccalaureate exams in 1982.

In contrast to his sisters, Albert developed a sense of duty and dignity early in life. He quietly received his BA degree in political science and economics from Amherst College in Massachusetts without fanfare from the press. He then signed up for a brief stint of military training aboard a French ship, the *Jeanne d'Arc*. Today Albert is working in a New York bank. Whenever he returns home, he presides at minor ceremonial events—such as awarding the cup to the winning Monégasque soccer team—in preparation for his future role as sovereign. Albert has never been involved in any long-term romantic relationships; he has had a few flirtations, but all have been extremely discreet.

ON SEPTEMBER 14, 1982, the roulette tables suddenly stopped spinning, the lights went out, the sky seemed to ominously darken; a profound sadness blanketed the principality. Princess Grace was no more. Disturbing and unpredictable fate. As the wife of the prince of Monaco, Grace had seemingly escaped the pressures, the pains, and the tragedies associated with the most successful film stars, such as Rita Hayworth, Judy Garland, and Marilyn Monroe.

Grace was headed toward a peaceful old age, with wrinkles and overweight her only enemies. She would have died in her bed like the other sovereigns of the twentieth century, like Queen Mary, grandmother of Elizabeth II of England, or like Queen Wilhelmina, grandmother of Beatrix of Holland. She would have died thirty years hence, after seeing her grandchildren grown and her great-grandchildren born. But, violently, she was in a way recaptured by her original destiny. She put her whole heart into living like a princess, and yet she died like a star. Like James Dean in 1955, at the wheel of his Porsche.

It was barely ten o'clock on Monday, September 13, 1982, when the princess, at the wheel of her Rover and accompanied by Stephanie, left the family retreat in Roc Agel to return to the palace in Monaco. It was a winding route full of sharp curves through the hills that Grace, having driven it hundreds of times, knew intimately. Dominique Toci, leisurely driving his truck behind the princess's car, was horrified when he suddenly saw the Rover shoot straight ahead right before the road's last hairpin turn. The car spun out of control off the road and plunged three hundred feet, rolling over several times before landing in Sesto Lequio's garden. Mr. Lequio testified, "I thought an airplane had crashed. The car was lying on its side with flames coming out of it. I ran to find an extinguisher before it exploded." Notified by Sesto Lequio, the Monaco police arrived in ten minutes. To remove Princess Grace from her steel prison, it was necessary to pull her out, unconscious, from the rear left window.

According to Dr. Chatelain, when the princess arrived at the hospital in Monaco that carried her name, she was already in a deep coma. "We began treatment without losing an instant. She had a fractured clavicle, rib, and right leg." An emergency call was immediately made to Dr. Jean Duplay, a chief neurologist in Nice. Yet it was not until eight hours later that the princess was taken to the nearby clinic of Dr. Michemouron to undergo tests with a CAT scanner, the only one in Monte Carlo. The examination confirmed the doctors' fears: the princess had suffered a major cerebral hemorrhage.

During the night the princess took a turn for the worse; the doctors put her on life-support equipment to keep her heart and lungs functioning. By noon, it was evident that there was no more hope. Finally, at ten o'clock that evening, Prince Rainier, Albert, and Caroline, heartbroken, decided to have the machines turned off.

An autopsy revealed that two hemorrhages had occurred. The first one, just prior to the accident, was an attack that would not have been serious had it happened while she was at home. The rupture would have been more of a mild warning signal, causing a sudden dizziness or loss of consciousness. Alas, at the wheel of a car on a dangerous road, it was fatal. From the results of the autopsy and Stephanie's description of the accident, Dr. Duplay concluded that Grace had lost control of her car because of the dizziness or fainting from the first hemorrhage, and that the second hemorrhage, much more serious, had been brought on by the shock of the accident.

Lying in state at the Palatine Chapel, Princess Grace received the final respects of hundreds of tearful Monégasques who filed past her open coffin. The funeral took place on September 18, in the chapel where, twenty-six years earlier, the young American actress answered yes to the question, "Do you take for your husband His Serene Highness . . ." Hunched in his red velvet chair, Rainier looked as if he had aged ten years in five days. With his black-gloved hand, he wiped away the tears he could no longer hold back. Caroline watched him with sadness, while Albert stared straight ahead. A profound emotion gripped the entire assembly.

Rainier divided the duties Grace had performed so well between his two eldest children. Since the accident, Caroline in particular has been a constant help to her father. It is even said that it was she who organized the funeral, drew up the list of guests, and chose the music. Perhaps misfortune had succeeded where all else had failed to tame the untamable Caroline.

Today Caroline has a husband by her side to help with her numerous responsibilities as first lady of the principality. She met Stephano Casiraghi in 1982 at Jimmy's, a famous nightclub in Monte Carlo. In October 1983 they were secretly engaged. And suddenly, in December, the news of their wedding was splashed on the front pages of newspapers around the world. Caroline's three-year reign as the world's most sought-after divorcée had come to an end.

Stephano is three years younger than his wife. He works in his father's business empire (oil, real estate, shoe and textile exports to the United States); he also owns some shares in a nightclub in Milan. He is very handsome, very rich, and very well known as a Milanese playboy. Or perhaps former playboy, since his friends say, without hesitation, that this time he is really in love.

The wedding ceremony was carried out with dispatch and kept suspiciously low-keyed. Rumors were circulating that the princess was pregnant, which might explain why the Grimaldi family did not wait for the Vatican to grant their request—or not—that Caroline's first marriage be annulled. The Vatican was not pleased by the hasty wedding. As far as the Catholic Church is concerned, Caroline is guilty of adultery.

On June 11, 1984, Caroline gave birth to a 6-pound, 6-ounce son, Andrea Albert.

So . . . in the limelight another of Monaco's love stories, but in the shadow the uncertain financial future of the principality (although the new bridegroom is reputed to be a billionaire).

In her time, Grace Kelly had brought to Monaco a formidable business know-how inherited from her father. For twenty-six years she had succeeded in attracting the world's grand and wealthy to her doorstep to attend charity balls and other social events that took place in one or another establishment of the SBM. Hotel and casino directors today seem somewhat lost and bewildered without their guiding spirit. Will Rainier, devastated by the pain of his loss, be able to hold on to the Americans, the tourists, and the businessmen that Grace knew how to lure to Monaco?

In the view of his closest associates, Rainier is a shattered man who hopes to be replaced by his son as soon as possible. Is Albert ready? Will he be able to conquer his shyness in order to face up to his responsibilities? The general consensus in Monaco is that Albert should marry soon, since the population would take less kindly to being governed by a bachelor, and a young one at that. Europe still has sufficient royal dynasties to offer Albert his choice of appropriate fiancées.

But there is no urgency. Neither the death of Grace nor the tumultuous lives of her daughters have seriously shaken the Monégasque principality. Monaco has survived other scandals and other reversals of fortune in its history, and can abide a few more; a revolution that would upset the throne is not foreseen for tomorrow. In any case, this throne, regilded again and again, is more like a sturdy office chair. As His Serene Highness Prince Rainier III Grimaldi-Polignac himself has stated, "I consider myself more like the chief executive officer of a corporation"—a hereditary corporation just waiting for its father's son.

3

DENMARK

◆

Just the Queen Next Door

O n a late spring morning in the early 1950s, a blond, curly-headed young girl with a book bag slung across her shoulders was skipping her way to school accompanied by her mother and two small sisters. In a piping voice the young girl rehearsed the history lesson that she was going to present in class later that day. With the blithe spirit of a thirteen-year-old, Princess Margrethe, the eldest daughter of Denmark's King Frederik IX and Queen Ingrid, hardly seemed to realize that, as of the night before, she had become heir to the Danish throne.

When King Frederik and Queen Ingrid succeeded to the throne in 1947 on the death of King Christian X, they already had three daughters, and the arrival of a fourth child seemed unlikely. Under Denmark's Salic law, a nineteenth-century legal code, females were excluded from the line of succession. The heir to the Danish throne, therefore, seemed to be Prince Knud, the king's younger brother. But at this moment, inspired by British example, there was a powerful national movement fulminating in favor of abolishing the Salic law—which had in fact never been applied, since all kings in the previous one hundred years had produced sons.

The initiative for a constitutional measure abolishing the law derived from no particular political party. It was a reform, studied for several years by a specially appointed government commission that crossed party lines. Although the measure would mean a radical change in the constitutional monarchy, there was certainly little danger of transforming this thousand-year-old kingdom into a republic. Even the Socialists, when they first came to power in 1926, had voluntarily struck out the first line of their program, which called for the abolition of the monarchy.

On Sunday, May 28, 1953, the Danish people spoke through a national referendum, which posed this question of such immense importance to the future of the monarchy: Would a female member of the royal family be permitted to succeed to the throne? The "ayes" just barely carried a majority; the schoolgirl of that spring morning would become the first Danish queen since her namesake, Queen Margrethe, ruled in the late 1300s.

Although certain hapless husbands mused bitterly over their mugs of beer about the inevitable advance of feminism, the future queen was already extremely popular in Denmark, much more so than her uncle Knud, who kept such a low profile that he was almost invisible. Margrethe's arrival into the world, on April 16, 1940, one week after the onset of the German occupation in World War II, had a stirring and long-lasting effect on the Danish population. Menaced by an aerial bombardment that would have burned and bloodied the capital, the Danish army had been forced to capitulate. The humiliation of this defeat weighed heavily on every heart. The birth of Margrethe was like a benediction from God—a portent of a hopeful future.

During this dark period in its history, Denmark grew closer to its sovereigns. As soon as the princess saw the light of day, the Danebrög—the Danish flag—was raised high in every village, in spite of the foreign occupation. A crowd of Danes, partly out of allegiance to the royal family, and partly in defiance of the Germans, gathered in front of Amalienborg Palace in Copenhagen to sign the traditional registers of congratulation. For the first time since Nazi boots had stomped through the streets, the people, through their silent demonstration of affection and support for the monarchy, manifested their faith in a brighter tomorrow.

At the age of five, Margrethe began learning to read and write in a kindergarten set up in the heart of the royal palace. The classroom was on the third floor, just across from the office of her grand-father, King Christian X. Six little girls of her age were "requisi-tioned" to study with her, under the guidance of Miss Marie Elizabeth Barfod. Everything was set up so that Margrethe's edu-cation would lack for nothing: there were blackboards, desks, ink-wells, a piano for dancing and singing, crayons, giant sheets of white paper for drawing, even a gym. Margrethe's program con-formed precisely to the mandatory requirements of the Danish school system and included all kinds of field trips: zoos, museums, farms, exhibitions, and of course athletic excursions such as skiing and hiking—essential to any royal education.

In 1949, when the "Amalienborg School" closed its doors, Mar-grethe was enrolled at the N. Zahle School, one of the last remain-ing private schools in Denmark. Queen Ingrid believed it was very important for her daughters to meet children from all walks of life, in order to be able to freely choose their friends. To her great joy, Margrethe could walk to school with her younger sister Benedikte like any other little Danish schoolgirl. (Later on, they were joined by Princess Anne-Marie, the youngest, who would one day marry King Constantin of Greece.) They were accompanied on foot by their mother or their governess. Often on cold, dark winter morn-ings, passers-by could see their queen hurrying to the school hold-ing her daughters by the hand. Following at a discreet distance was a chauffeur-driven car, which would take Queen Ingrid back to the palace. (Never during any of these outings were they bothered by a crowd of gawkers or the press. Respect for the individual, royalty or commoner, is one of the principal tenets of Scandinavian life. Everyone, professional photographers included, seems to realize that a private life, especially a child's, must be protected from the glare of a potentially harmful limelight.)

At school, the princesses were treated just like the other students —no special privileges, no special teachers, and no titles. They even brought their own lunch—cheese or pâté sandwiches made in the royal kitchens.

At about 2:15 P.M., their classes over, the girls returned home. A few hours later, the king, the queen, and the children would gather in the family quarters of the palace for tea. The king, who loved this ritual, once remarked: "There are two things I would not miss for the world—the sessions of the Private Council and tea with my daughters." Tea time was not, however, always totally relaxing, since the king found his daughter Margrethe "noisy, inquisitive, and unbearable," but, he added magnanimously, "always my darling."

Family life at the palace was warm and spontaneous, without pomp and without protocol. Most of the showy, stiff ceremonies had long since passed out of existence. The great receptions to celebrate royal birthdays had been done away with; what remained were small family gatherings with a cake baked by the children. The traditional New Year's celebration, along with the royal hunts, had been considerably scaled down. Gone was the closed society of princes and princesses, barons and baronesses; in Denmark it was the era of the businessman, the artist, the industrialist, and the politician.

The king, the queen, and the children loved to travel, as much within Denmark as abroad. From April to October, when the rigors of winter had abated, there was a flurry of trips between the royal residences. The family went from Amalienborg Palace in Copenhagen, one of the lovliest rococo castles in Europe, to Fredensborg Castle, about twenty-five miles from the capital. Vacations were spent at Graasten Castle in Slesvig, near the German border; here, in the park, the three princesses had built a little wooden hut where they often invited friends to play. A chalet in Trend, isolated in the middle of a forest of huge pines, served as the royal retreat. It had been given to the king as a gift from his people, on his marriage to Princess Ingrid of Sweden in May 1935, when he was still crown prince. Here in Trend, one of the most deserted areas of Denmark, the royal couple and their daughters celebrated Christmas. Usually one or two servants accompanied them. But occasionally, for one reason or another, the couple found themselves alone. A visitor might have come upon the king then, an apron around his waist, vacuuming the floor or dusting the furniture while the queen was busy in the kitchen.

With the good summer weather came cruises aboard the royal yacht, the *Danebrög*. Margrethe, who knew the boat from the bilge to the bridge, was a born sailor like her father. In the autumn, King Frederik and Queen Ingrid traveled to Rome, and for several years Princess Margrethe accompanied them. She took advantage of these trips to indulge her passion of archeology, often with her grandfather King Adolf VI of Sweden along as her very competent guide. If history had not tapped her to be queen, Margrethe would

Playing a game at a children's party, the "prince," grandson of the Swedish Ambassador, kneels to Princess Margrethe. (Danish Ministry of Foreign Affairs)

Margrethe and a school friend wearing the traditional red and white student's cap. (Danish Ministry of Foreign Affairs)

January 15, 1972: "King Frederik is dead, long live Queen Margrethe," proclaims the prime minister. (Danish Ministry of Foreign Affairs)

certainly have become an archeologist. She took part in several digs organized in Denmark, Italy, and Greece, and in 1962 was part of an important Scandinavian expedition to the Sudan.

After six years of study at the N. Zahle School, Margrethe spent a year at a little-known boarding school in England, North Foreland Lodge, where she perfected her already fluent English, learned at the knee of an English governess. On her return to Denmark, the teen-age princess began intensive studies at the palace "school" to prepare for her role as the future head of state. This school, which came into being only periodically, was inaugurated in the late nineteenth century when the future King Christian X had to prepare for his exams. When Christian terminated his studies, the school closed down, to be resurrected years later for his son, Crown Prince Frederik. It was once again in business for the future Queen Margrethe II. The school, the smallest in Denmark, was made up of one royal classroom for one royal student, and a faculty highly qualified in all the disciplines. At the end of a year and a half, still alone in her classroom and surrounded by books and notebooks, the young, spirited princess was on the brink of depression. Subsequently, a friend, Birgitta, daughter of the grand chamberlain, Gregor Iuel, was called in to be her classmate. "All alone," explained Margrethe later, "I don't believe I could ever have finished." But together she and Birgitta passed the final exam with honors.

For relaxation Margrethe loved to swim, fence, play tennis, go horseback riding, and ski. To keep in shape, she often ran with her lady-in-waiting, Countess Kitty Wara Armfeldt. Head of a group of certified female pilots, Kitty had often participated in cross-country competitions with her colleagues. Three miles across a difficult, hilly terrain didn't faze this big, sturdy girl in the least.

April 16, 1958, marked Princess Margrethe's eighteenth birthday; she had reached the age of majority. For the first time, Margrethe could sit at Parliament next to her father as heir to the throne. She could also attend sessions of the State Council, presided over by the king. By nine o'clock on that April morning, a curious crowd of onlookers had gathered in front of Amalienborg Palace to watch the royal procession pass on its way to Christianborg Castle, the seat of Parliament. At ten o'clock, the princess, dressed in a red coat and small matching hat, left the palace with the king in a black Rolls-Royce (the return trip would be in a golden carriage, reserved for special state occasions). Throughout the trip across the city, Margrethe smiled and waved to the crowds. Meanwhile, as the princess and the king made their way to Parliament, there were nonstop comings-and-goings at the palace gate as birthday gifts arrived continuously—bouquets of flowers, boxes of chocolates, a car, the deed to a 111-acre farm known as "North Garden" in central Denmark, from a group of Danish farmers.

To signify the importance of this day, King Frederik presented Margrethe with the highest honorary award in Denmark. She became Chevalier of the Order of the Elephant, an exclusive royal order created by King Christian V in 1693. Since her eighteenth birthday, for major ceremonies, Margrethe has always worn the decoration she received that day, a little elephant suspended from a silk ribbon. Symbolizing intelligence, nobility, and chastity, the elephant is set with a cross of diamonds on its side and forehead, carries a little tower of red enameled gold bricks on its back, and is led by a Moor. Margrethe was also allocated an annual stipend of 75,000 Danish crowns by Parliament, a sum which would increase to 100,000 crowns when she turned twenty-one. With this birthday, Margrethe had reached a major milestone. "A chapter of your life has just come to an end," King Frederik told her. "You have said good-bye to childhood. From here on in, little by little, you will enter the adult world." For Margrethe, these simple paternal words underlined the importance and seriousness of the role she would have to fill.

WHILE she was pursuing her studies in philosophy and law at the University of Copenhagen, Her Royal Highness, Crown Princess Margrethe of Denmark opened exhibitions, visited nursery schools, and sat at Parliament. Then, for one year, she took a leave of absence from her official obligations to devote herself entirely to her avocation of archeology. She enrolled at Girton College, Cambridge University, taking up residence in a closet-sized student's room and immersing herself in courses in ancient history and archeological studies. When she returned to Denmark, it was to a new university—this one at Aarhus—where she took postgraduate courses in constitutional law, international relations, business, political science, and economy, all necessary for a future head of state. The princess, who in most ways was still a typical young woman, also took cooking courses like most of her friends. But unlike her friends, she attended meetings of the State Council twice a week, and became regent of the country when the king traveled abroad.

In 1963, after a short stint at the Sorbonne to improve her French, the princess took her first official trip, to Asia. It was for the most part an educational journey, where meetings with various heads of state were interspersed with visits to historic and cultural sites. The trip—a heavy dose of people, places, and protocol—was important to Margrethe, because it helped her acquire the savvy and culture necessary to her perfectionist image of a role she took very much to heart. She was a young, intelligent, incisive woman who knew exactly how to make the most of the solid, extensive training her parents had provided for her.

Although Margrethe was fulfilling her academic and international responsibilities admirably, her people were still waiting for her to fulfill the old Danish adage: "All food will one day be eaten, and every girl will find a husband." Not an easy task for a princess, and a crown princess at that, who stood slightly over six feet tall. But in 1965 she finally found a man who measured up, in the person of Henri-Marie-Jean-André de Laborde de Monpezat, a tall, thirty-two-year-old third secretary at the French embassy in London.

They met in England, where Margrethe was attending classes at the London School of Economics. They first saw each other at a dinner given by mutual friends. As Margrethe said later of that meeting: "There was no follow-up; by follow-up I mean in the 'dating' sense. We saw each other again only by accident the next spring at a friend's wedding in Scotland. After the marriage, once again by accident, we ended up taking the same plane back to London. After that, though, we saw each other quite often, on purpose! When I went back to Denmark, we wrote to each other and met secretly, and then, *voilà*, we were engaged." Once engaged, Henri de Monpezat no longer had to enter Amalienborg Palace through the service entrance, the collar of his raincoat turned up to his ears and a soft felt hat pulled down almost over his eyes. He walked, instead, up the grand staircase of honor.

The engagement was announced on October 4, 1966, at the opening of Parliament, since protocol dictated that the news be announced by the prime minister to the convened members. When the king and queen and Princess Margrethe and her fiancé arrived, they were greeted by the president of Parliament, Julius Bomholt, who led them to the royal box. The prime minister, Jens Otton Krag, delivered a welcoming speech, but the consent of the house would not be given until after the departure of the engaged couple.

> According to information we have gathered, no legal objection can be raised against the wish of Princess Margrethe to unite with Monsieur Henri de Monpezat. The latter has made known his intention to request Danish nationality. He has also given us to understand that he will embrace the Lutheran evangelical religion. With great conscientiousness, the crown princess has prepared herself for her future task. She has often represented our country abroad in satisfactory fashion. My impression is that Henri de Monpezat will know how to nobly assist the princess in her duties. . . . I am sure that all the Danish people are ready, along with me, to wish them a happy and harmonious marriage, one in which they will mutually support each other in the mission they will have to accomplish.

The king signed the document giving his consent. In effect, according to the law of succession, no person having the right to one day assume the crown could, without losing his right, contract a marriage without the king's consent given at the State Council.

Nothing seemed to stand in the way of the marriage, and yet the decision was far from welcome among the Danish people. Why, they wondered, did the future queen of a millennium-old kingdom choose for her mate a foreigner of modest origins—an obscure secretary of an embassy and a Catholic to boot, whose cool, studied demeanor was so at odds with the naturalness and simplicity of the Danes? Why? Love, probably.

THE MONPEZATS were a family of country gentlemen from Béarn, in the Lower Pyrénées, who lived on and from the land. The nobility of the family (they call themselves "counts") remains a questionable assertion. Certainly there are the official letters, various licenses dating from 1655, the family registration in the Parliament of Pau, records of 130 years of nobility tax payments, and the possession of noble lands for well beyond the requisite hundred years—but all this is not quite enough to convince specialists in such matters that the Laborde de Monpezats belong among the nobility.

Henri, Margrethe's fiancé, was born near Bordeaux on June 11, 1934, the second of eight children, six of whom are still alive. A few months after his birth, Henri left in his mother's arms for Indochina, where his paternal grandfather (also named Henri) had installed his family at the turn of the century when Indochina was France's beckoning new frontier. An extremely colorful character, Grandfather Henri worked briefly for the colonial government, but he was hardly cut out for the life of a civil servant; he decided to tackle the hostile and deserted brushland of Annam—the central region of Vietnam. A pioneer and planter during a major *époque* of French colonial history, Monpezat became a "personality" in Indochina. His greatest renown came from the founding of a newspaper, *The Indochinese Will,* from whose platform he led a merciless battle against the "carpetbagging" representatives of the leftist Popular Front, against demagoguery, and against political weakness. Above all else, Henri was a warrior who battled for his ideas.

In 1904, Henri married a girl of Swedish origin, an alliance that brought the Monpezats only one step away from finding common ancestors with Queen Ingrid, Margrethe's mother. The couple had two sons, Jacques and André, the future father-in-law of Margrethe.

When war broke out in 1939, André de Monpezat, now married and the father of four children, took his family back to France. He had already served in the French Foreign Legion, and now he enlisted in the Royal Air Command. He later fought with the Resistance and was eventually awarded the Croix de Guerre with a bronze star.

In 1947, André returned to Indochina with his wife and children to manage his vast agricultural holdings in Tonkin. He soon realized the necessity of setting up guards and a self-defense militia; this private force, of which André remained chief, would considerably aid French troops until 1954. Born with the same courage as his father, he often fought in skirmishes against the Vietminh. He was among the last of the French to leave Haiphong and Hanoi in 1957 and was forced to abandon everything—the industrial installations, the farms, the buildings he had put up. (After having cultivated thousands of acres in Tonkin, André today tends just fifty French acres of vines and small crops.)

André's young son Henri, who spent the first five years of his life in Asia, spoke Vietnamese more fluently than French. When his family returned to France in 1939, he studied at home with a private tutor and a piano teacher until the age of thirteen, when he was sent to a Jesuit school in Bordeaux. From 1948 to 1950 he attended a lycée in Cahors, in southern France, then returned to Indochina for two years, where he finished his secondary studies at a lycée in Hanoi. At eighteen he discovered Paris and moved into a smart little apartment on the Boulevard Saint-Michel. He enrolled in law school and at the same time decided to prepare for a degree in literature. An attractive, popular student with blue eyes and chestnut brown hair, he loved to join his friends in the nightlife of the Latin Quarter. Later, naturally fascinated by the Far East and gifted in language and design, he decided to switch majors, enrolling in the Oriental language department of the Sorbonne, where he earned his diploma in Chinese and Vietnamese. In 1957 he was awarded a university grant that enabled him to spend a year in Hong Kong, a base from which he visited Vietnam, Laos, Cambodia, Thailand, and India.

Henri's Oriental idyll was over in November 1959, when he was called up for military service. He was sent to a training camp in Besançon in preparation for his new position as a supply sergeant stationed with French troops in Algeria.

Back in civilian life in November 1962, Henri joined the Far Eastern department of the Ministry of Foreign Affairs in Paris, where from nine until six he served as a functionary. His elegance was almost overbearing, his relations with others always somewhat distant. His evenings were spent with friends, indulging in the sophisticated Parisian pursuits he craved—exclusive clubs, expensive restaurants, the right parties. In January 1964, he was transferred to the French embassy in London as third secretary. Before long he established himself as a high-living man about town. He set up housekeeping at Bryanston Square, behind Hyde Park, in a comfortable ground-floor apartment. Mary, the concierge, acted as his housekeeper. It was she who carried in Henri's breakfast every morning before he went speeding to the embassy in his dark green sports car. Everything *chez Henri*—from the closet in the living room to the bathroom and the kitchen—denoted an orderly, meticulous, well-organized bachelor. His impeccably cut English suits ran the gamut from medium gray to charcoal gray, and most of them had tiny, subtle pinstripes; his shirts were silk or hand-woven cotton, his sweaters cashmere; brightly printed ties, scarves, and pocket handkerchiefs in multicolored Indian silks filled his dresser drawers. In the bathroom bottles of toilet water were lined up next to bath oils and perfumed soap, and in the mahogany-furnished living room everything was always at the ready—whiskey, sherry, cognac, glasses, cocktail snacks—to receive anyone at any hour. He loved to surround himself with friends.

HENRI was perfectly adapted to the life of the gilded youth of London. Almost every night he could be seen at the Maison de France, a favorite restaurant of Philip of Edinburgh, Douglas Fairbanks, Jr., and rich Indians. For intimate dinners, though, he preferred the Chinese restaurants of Soho. During the wee hours, he could usually be found, at least every other night, at Annabel's, one of the most sophisticated and expensive private gaming clubs in the world, frequented by still-moneyed lords (a dying breed), starlets, models, and particularly Arab millionaires. (Henri's passion for gambling often kept him at the tables until well past dawn.) At the end of the week, like any self-respecting Englishman, he left the capital to visit friends with great country houses. It was at one of these gatherings that he met the beautiful Princess Margrethe of Denmark.

Before marrying the princess, Henri de Monpezat wanted to wed her religion—Lutheranism. This conversion was not, however, a prerequisite of his marriage. According to the terms of the Danish Constitution, a Catholic may become prince consort, but with certain restrictions: for example, he can never, should the occasion arise, become regent of the kingdom; also, the children of the royal family have to be raised in the Lutheran religion.

Nevertheless, the future Prince Henrik made his decision to convert, and he notified a representative of the pope that he would be giving up Catholicism. Henry de Monpezat's entry into the Lutheran church was a simple procedure, with no particular authorization or ceremony. An adult who is already a member of another Christian community need simply express the wish to become Lutheran to be automatically inscribed in a register of the faithful in an accredited parish. In fact, in the eyes of the Scandinavian evangelical clergy, the choice is simply a personal affair between an individual and God. There are no such things as stringent examinations of theory, tests of faith, or ritualistic swearings-off of old beliefs. Everyone, Danish or not, resident or not, has the right to enter the Danish church. Officially, it is the church of state, but spiritually it is open to all souls.

If Henri's first marriage was with the Danish religion, his second was with the Danish nation. To marry a Danish princess, it was essential to be of Danish nationality. In France, Henri arranged for a decree to be published in the *Journal Officiel Français,* which stated that Henri de Monpezat was "authorized to be naturalized abroad." The decree was signed by Prime Minister Georges Pompidou and Minister of Foreign Affairs Jean-Marcel Jeanneney. And so it was that Henri de Laborde de Monpezat became, by the will of King Frederik IX, Prince Henrik of Denmark. From this point on, all the conditions having been fulfilled, the real marriage could take place.

On the morning of June 10, 1967, a little before ten o'clock, the guests were already assembled in Fredensborg Castle. In several minutes the official presentation of gifts would begin—an array that ranged from a classic table service to 220 pounds of French meringues and that included a rug, a piano, two Irish brood mares, and two and a half acres of prime Corsican land. After a reception held at eleven o'clock, everyone left to attend the civil ceremony at city hall. Dressed in a knee-length, green silk-print dress and coiffed by a small gold tiara, the radiant princess waved to the crowd as she had been doing for so many years; beside her, his smile a bit taut, was Prince Henrik, who seemed as stiff and formal as one of his invariable three-piece suits. After the ceremony, a luncheon was held for family and friends, not at the royal palace, but at the Lenguilinie Pavillonen, a restaurant overlooking the port. For a finale, Margrethe and Henrik boarded a motor launch and circled the port, to the booming of cannons and the cheering of sailors.

The religious ceremony took place the next day at 4:30 in the afternoon at a little baroque church that had been used in the sixteenth century as a blacksmith's shop to forge anchors for King Frederik II. The two families, as well as special guests, sat inside the old church, with its bleach-whitened walls and splendidly sculpted woodwork. Because of space limitations, all the other guests were sheltered under a canopy outside. Prince Henrik's arrival created a stir among the onlookers because he appeared, not on the arm of his mother in the Danish custom, but in the company of his brother Etienne. Certainly no rule stipulated that the future groom *had* to enter the church on his mother's arm; nevertheless, among the traditional Danes, such a breach caused astonishment. The explanation, it seems, was that Henrik's parents, who were fervent Catholics, wished to participate in the ceremony as discreetly as possible. When his parents did arrive, André de Monpezat, like his son Henrik, wore the flashy Order of the Elephant across his chest and was also decorated with the Order of the Danebrög, reserved for members of the royal family. At the end of the religious service, the Lutherans were in for another surprise—the exchange of rings. Although such a custom did not exist within her religion, Margrethe wanted to make this sentimental gesture to the Catholic origin of her husband.

Seven kings and queens, twenty-three royal or imperial highnesses, and two presidents of the republic attended this lavish wedding. (For once, unassuming Scandinavian simplicity was nowhere in evidence.) On this special day, Monsieur André found himself on equal footing with King Frederik IX; his wife Reneé and Queen Ingrid were seated side by side at the church (and at the banquet later); his younger son Etienne was seated across from the king of Sweden; and his daughter Madame Bardin sat in the same row as Princess Benedikte. All of this was more than satisfying for the French country squire, who also happened to be an unconditional monarchist. "Even for 100,000 francs," his neighbors used to say of him, "you couldn't get Monsieur de Monpezat to shout 'Long live the Republic,' " and this was never truer than on his son's wedding day.

FIVE YEARS LATER, on New Year's Eve, when King Frederik IX appeared on television to broadcast his annual greetings to his people, he appeared extremely tired. Three days later, on Monday, January 4, 1972, a radio bulletin announced that the king had been taken by ambulance to the communal hospital in Copenhagen. He had influenza and even the beginnings of pneumonia, but what most alarmed the doctors was the weakness of his heart. Princess Margrethe was named regent of the kingdom. On January 13, Frederik IX took a turn for the worse; on January 14 he went into a coma from which he never emerged; at 7:30 that evening the end came. His Majesty died, at the age of seventy-three, in a public hospital, like the most humble of his subjects. At eight o'clock the death of King Frederik IX of Denmark was proclaimed, followed by the announcement that Margrethe was queen of Denmark.

The following morning, according to custom, the prime minister shouted from his balcony, "King Frederik is dead. Long live Queen Margrethe!" Everything remained closed that day—theaters, movies, sports arenas, restaurants. Radio and television stations interrupted their regular programming to broadcast the classical music that the king, who had once conducted the Copenhagen Orchestra, loved.

The body of the king lay in state for five days in the chapel of Christianborg Castle. From January 19 to 23 the Danes filed by their king, one of the most popular monarchs Denmark had ever known. The funeral took place on January 24 in the Cathedral of Roskilde—eighteen miles from the capital—where all Danish monarchs are buried. A letter from the king, opened after his death, set down the entire funeral service as he wished it to be: Forty-eight men from the Danish navy would draw the funeral wagon from Christianborg Castle to the central railroad station in Copenhagen, where it would be put on a special train; as soon as the train arrived at its destination, the same men would once again draw the wagon to Roskilde, marching to a cadence of sixty-four half steps a minute, the traditional pace for Danish funeral ceremonies; there would be two months of national mourning.

"My father having joined his ancestors, I become your new sovereign," Margrethe began in her short open letter to the Danish people, delivered to the government. With this letter, the regent crown princess effectively became queen without any, or hardly any, further formalities (since 1840 official coronations had been abolished). All that was required, in addition to the letter, was the formal declaration of Parliament, where Margrethe appeared, dressed and veiled in black. She announced that she would now be called Her Majesty Queen Margrethe II, doing away with the long litany of Danish sovereign titles—Queen of the Wends and the Goths, Duchess of Slesvig, Holstein, Storman, and so on. She took as her motto, "Help of God, love of my people, strength of Denmark."

Following tradition, Jens Otto Krag, the prime minister, offered his resignation to the queen; she, also traditionally, refused. Mr. Krag, a Social Democrat, willingly affirmed that "the Danish monarchy is not an obstacle to the development of democracy or social progress." But it might seem as if it were, especially if one referred to Article 13 of the Danish Constitution, which states: "The sovereign is not responsible!" A startling statement at first glance, these words simply mean that, according to the principles of the Danish constitutional monarchy, all acts of the chief of state—the sovereign—have to be countersigned by a government minister, the only one accountable or "responsible" before Parliament.

AS CHIEF of a constitutional monarchy—or, if you will, as queen of a crowned democracy—Margrethe II has no actual political power. Although she is the "administrative head" of the affairs of state, the essential part of her role is symbolic and inspirational. She presides over the State Council and can, as a member of this council, attend sessions of Parliament; she also gives sanction to laws passed there. Most governmental decrees are published in her name and signed by her, but only as a matter of form. The decisions themselves do not come from the queen; it is she who follows the lead of her ministers. Margrethe can take no initiative. Her strength resides in tradition and in her position as figurehead; she represents, as nothing else can, the continuity and unity of the nation. As former Prime Minister Hans Christian Hansen once said, "The importance of a king in a modern constitutional monarchy rests not in the influence that he exerts over politics but in the confidence he generates as well as in his function as a symbol of the country's unity." Placed by the laws of blood at the tip of the hierarchical pyramid, the queen or king must at no time become involved in the partisan quarrels of parties and candidates. The Danes like to quip that they have given their monarch absolute power on the one condition that he never use it. There is, however, one exception to the rule. In the case of a political crisis, when representatives of various parties in Parliament cannot channel enough power to elect one clear winner, the queen can call in a new prime minister.

The life of Queen Margrethe has been compared to the life of any working woman in an executive position. At eight in the morning she has breakfast with her husband and two sons, sixteen-year-old Crown Prince Frederik—next in line to the throne—and fifteen-year-old Prince Joachim. After reading several Danish and foreign newspapers, she meets with the grand marshal of court or the master of ceremonies to go over the day's events: inaugurations, visits to institutions, ship christenings, and so on. Her activities also include attending military maneuvers, taking part in hunts, organizing parties, and receiving artists. At 10:30, she goes over her agenda with her secretary. Wednesday is the queen's "official day" at court. She receives the prime minister and the minister of foreign affairs, who keep her up to date on events in their domains. Next she receives the commander of the army, followed by the commander of the navy. Twice a month the queen holds a public audience at Christianborg Castle, as her father did before her and his father before him, a tradition Margrethe values greatly because it brings her closer to the people.

For Margrethe, her royal career is a "job that never ends. It involves me twenty-four hours a day, three hundred and sixty-five days a year, and will last my entire life. But it is, after all, our life; we have been raised for that." Her position, for that matter, seems to agree with her. It should be noted that she possesses all the qualities necessary to exercise the job well: a great will to do it, steady nerves, the art of pleasant repartee, and a sense of authority that never lets her forget she is queen. She is often compared to Queen Victoria of England, or to Juliana, Queen Mother of the Netherlands.

As long as the Danish sovereign assiduously fulfills her assigned duties she will continue to occupy an important place in Danish life —but not the sort of place she would have occupied one or two generations earlier. There is very little Danish pomp and flourish left these days. The throne itself has been relegated to a museum, as have the crown jewels, which sparkle within a glass cage; the ermine robes packed in mothballs are shut away in a dark closet; the carriages are rarely taken out. Only the royal guard remains as a vestige of what the monarchy once was.

In denuding their monarchy and diluting its power, the Danes are completely opposite in spirit from the English, who would not know how to get by without a minimum of royal flash and glitter: "They would be ready to deprive themselves of their boiled mutton with their famous mint sauce, or their beer, even of their tea with a cloud of milk," wrote a British journalist, "to save the

Queen Margrethe and Prince Henrik visit Greenland on the occasion of the country's transition to home rule in 1979. (Danish Ministry of Foreign Affairs)

Crown Prince Frederik (*left*), next in line to the throne, and Prince Joachim (*right*) with their parents and the family pet. (Danish Ministry of Foreign Affairs) essential—the sovereign panache, the crown jewels, and the Royal Guards of Buckingham Palace, so dear to Kipling, to Churchill and even to the Rolling Stones." And a member of Parliament from the Labor party, known for his acerbic wit, once declared: "I certainly wouldn't want a monarch like Denmark's that would just go around on a bicycle in the street. There must be some magic, some splendor, and I for one am ready to pay what it takes to have it."

The Danes, however, need have no fear of tax increases to support their monarchy, since the queen shows a pronounced taste for economy. Her annual stipend has risen to 16.8 million Danish crowns (only about $2 million!). The maintenance of the royal residences—Amalienborg, Fredensborg, and Graasten—as well as salaries for the majority of royal personnel is the responsibility of the government. The queen has only twenty people in her charge. Her husband, the prince consort, has no allotment of his own, so he too relies on his wife's purse for funds. Ingrid, the queen mother, and Princess Benedikte benefit from yearly allotments of 4 million crowns each. Although the queen's extensive years of study in different fields may seem excessive for eventually becoming an "irresponsible" sovereign, at least her courses in economics serve her well in administering her holdings to advantage.

While there are no questions and no surprises regarding the precisely described duties and role of the queen—the sovereign's responsibilities have been codified for so many years—there are, on the other hand, absolutely no constitutional rules concerning the status of a queen's husband, since there has been no precedent in modern Danish history. So, from the beginning, Prince Henrik was on his own.

In marrying Margrethe, Henri de Laborde de Monpezat joined the little international troupe of prince consorts. How would this modest French diplomat assume the role that George VI of England had described to Philip of Edinburgh as being much more difficult than that of king? Although Henri had not hesitated for a moment to change his church, his country, his language, and his culture, the Danish people were not so quick to respond to these gestures of good faith. In fact, the Danes were just waiting for this overly refined foreigner to make his first mistake. They sorely missed the jovial, simple, spontaneous style of their good King Frederik, a former sailor whose arms, shoulders, and torso were covered with tattoos. Prince Henrik was rather cold and reserved, an aesthete who always dressed to the nines, with a sense of humor more compatible with a flute of champagne than a mug of beer, and a taste for luxury that annoyed the Danes.

While Margrethe was occupied with official duties, Henrik undertook the redecoration of the royal apartments at Amalienborg Castle. (The royal residence is actually composed of four small, identical castles situated thirty-two yards from the Copenhagen docks. Queen Ingrid lives in one of these little castles; Prince Knud, Margrethe's uncle, lives in another. The third dwelling is home to Margrethe, the prince consort, and their children. The fourth castle is reserved for official receptions and is far and away the most richly decorated.) To redo the Amalienborg quarters, Henrik enlisted the aid of his long-time friend Jean-Louis de Maigret. All the furniture is antique, mostly Louis XV. It is a style the Danes do not understand at all; they would have preferred that Henrik had chosen modern Scandinavian furniture, just as they would have preferred him to drive a Volvo rather than a Ferrari. "He has made the palace into a palace fit for a millionaire," wrote a Danish journalist. "No less than 130 million crowns has he spent for furniture. He gives grandiose receptions and sumptuous dinners with menus printed in French, even though the two palace cooks are Danish. He insists on having fresh flowers every day in all the rooms, even in the salons that are opened up only once a month. And for whom, all these extravagant indulgences? For his friends alone. Not a day goes by without the Rolls leaving the palace to pick up one of his buddies from Paris at the airport."

Another of Henrik's early quirks was his penchant for uniforms, an idiosyncrasy often derided by "his" people. Everyone remembers the time he showed up at a ball in the post–World War I uniform of an infantry officer. And no one will forget the funeral of the king of Sweden, where Prince Henrik appeared in the formal dress uniform of an admiral of the fleet—he who had never navigated anything more complex than a small pleasure boat on a social-set outing. As for his official title of Colonel of the Danish Air Force—which corresponded to his position as prince consort—people were well aware that Henrik had ended his military service as no more than a humble sergeant. The bad-mouthers had found in him the personification of the hero in the popular Danish book *The Dictionary of Vanity*. People even went so far as to insinuate that the prince consort fancied himself as queen. It was plain that

the open, easygoing Danes were not taking easily to their dandi-
fied, snobbish, and French prince consort.

He did nothing to help his cause when, shortly after his marriage, he infuriated Danish parents by stating during an interview
that a good spanking never did a child any harm. Or when he made
public his position favoring Denmark's entry into the Common
Market before it was put to the people's vote, thus causing a scandal among opponents of the issue. The opposition even distributed
leaflets in the street stating that instead of a leader "capable of
making the voice of Denmark heard in the concert of nations, the
late king has left behind only a weak woman and a frivolous
Frenchman who thinks only of enjoying himself."

Since his early days in Denmark, marked by excesses and faux
pas due to inexperience, Prince Henrik has learned his lessons well.
He has found his proper place in the order of things: second. He
has thus become a full-fledged member of that small coterie of
distinguished, well-mannered men who know how to fade into the
background three steps behind their wives, as protocol requires,
carefully maintaining their stations, hands generally crossed behind
their backs, wearing their obligatory smiles, and obediently carrying out their fuzzily defined duties. Today, at least Henrik knows
enough to say: "I think as the queen does." He realizes now that
everything is not always rosy at the beginning. "I finally feel one
hundred percent Danish," he confides. "There was, the first two
years, a difficult period of adaptation on both sides, mine and the
people's. But I'm no longer the Frenchman who just got off the
boat." These days the prince speaks Danish fluently, which would
be considered quite an accomplishment even for, say, an expert in
Oriental languages. Of course, his accent is far from perfect, but
few would reproach him for that. He conscientiously fulfills the
duties incumbent upon the spouse of a king: He is commissioner
of the Danish Red Cross; he is president of the Danish section of
the World Wildlife Fund; he oversees organizations involved with
landmark and neighborhood preservation; and he sponsors the promotion of Danish industrial design abroad.

Henrik's afternoons are usually divided between inaugurations
and recreational sports activities. He grew fond of sports rather late
in life, a fact clearly reflected in his ability, or lack of it. (What he
plays best, in fact, is not tennis, golf, or polo, but cards. It would
be dangerous to risk a fortune against him in bridge or poker.

Margrethe enjoys being queen and Prince Henrik has finally adapted to his proper place—second. (Danish Ministry of Foreign Affairs)

"He's got the devil's own luck," his friends say.) At five o'clock in the afternoon, when Danish professional life draws to a halt, Henrik commences his long, leisurely family evening. He plays Monopoly with his sons or teaches them to play cards. Often, in the winter, he takes them to the movies, since there is no projection room in the palace, and the queen does not enjoy films. The hours after dinner are peaceful. Everyone is busy around the fireplace, Henrik reading (when he is not on a trip to another corner of the world), Margrethe embroidering, and the boys playing.

In recent years Margrethe has been criticized for smoking too much, for being too fond of the good life, and for talking a bit too loudly during official dinners and ceremonies. Moreover she has begun to exhibit—some might say flaunt—a burning passion for bridge, a means perhaps of drawing closer to her husband, who has a distressing tendency to ignore her. If he is not traveling in some far-off land, Henrik shuts himself up in his sculpture studio, which he installed in the attic of the castle. But all this seems inconsequential and beside the point when considering the present and future of the Danish kingdom. Through their commitment and responsibility to their work, Queen Margrethe and the prince consort give meaning to the royal functions they fulfill, and in doing so are, in all probability, perpetuating the monarchy. In periodic popularity polls of public figures in Denmark, they are usually found at the top of the list. And if one day the Danish monarchy were to disappear, the queen would most likely be elected president of the new republic, but her powers probably would not be much enhanced because of it.

4

SWEDEN

◆

The Citizen-King Takes a Commoner Queen: An Unexpected Royal Renaissance

There was a time, not so long ago, when the Swedish monarchy lavishly displayed all the signs of royalty. At sumptuous banquets given by King Gustav Adolf VI, grandfather of the present king, regal razzle-dazzle and monarchical protocol were reminiscent of Louis XIV's Versailles. Before dinner, guests would await the sovereigns in the White Sea Salon, a great ceremonial hall decorated with rare Savonnerie tapestries and rich lilac satins that shimmered in the light of a blazing fireplace. Liveried footmen, frozen at attention, flanked the doors, which were flung open to admit the master of ceremonies, dressed in a glittering uniform. Advancing several steps into the room, he would stop short and, his face a mask of marble, tap three times on the floor with his silver-knobbed staff to announce the entrance of the royal hosts.

After greeting their guests, the king and queen would lead the party into the Charles XI Gallery, where under twinkling chandeliers the yards-long dining table, covered with a white damask cloth embossed with the Swedish coat of arms, stood ready and waiting. The king's page, decked out in patent leather boots and green velvet livery trimmed with silver braid, stood in attendance behind his majesty's chair. He would take each plate from the servants and serve the king himself. The queen's courier would attend her in the same fashion.

A leather case containing two vermeil egg cups sat on a special place mat before the sovereigns, a tradition that dated back to the Middle Ages. (Since eggs could not be poisoned, it was wise—in those days of palace intrigue and skulduggery—to always have a few on hand.) The sovereigns also had their own salt and pepper shakers.

More frequent, smaller parties were less stately, but still quite formal; black tie and long gowns were obligatory. Dinner would be served at seven o'clock sharp, after which some of the guests would chat over liqueurs or play canasta, one of the old king's favorite pastimes. While playing, the gentle sovereign liked to munch on hard caramel candies, his one small vice. At 10:30 sharp, as tradition dictated, the guests would depart.

If the Versailleslike pomp has today practically disappeared from Sweden's court, there has been a marked change in the sovereigns' daily life as well. King Carl Gustav XVI and Queen Silvia arise at 6:30 and cook their own breakfast in the kitchenette of their six-room apartment, lost among the 608 rooms of the eighteenth-century palace. The king, in a dressing gown, prepares ham and eggs, keeps an eye on the toast, and makes coffee. The queen sets the table, and when her husband is not on a diet (which he frequently is, since he gains weight easily), she makes hot cereal.

After breakfast, the sovereigns repair to their respective offices within the castle. The king spends a good part of his day answering mail and holding audiences—as many as ten in the morning and two or three in the afternoon—with ambassadors, businessmen, or government officials who come to brief him on political matters.

Although the king is fully cognizant of the symbolic aspect of his role, he is no less persuaded of its utility. "The people know," he explains, "that they can write to the king for help—for example, if they need to obtain a driver's license or hope to reduce a prison sentence. One day I received a letter from a father who asked my advice on how to persuade his little boy that he had to have his tooth pulled." (It is hard to know whether this is an example of the king's naïveté or his subtle humor.) "I want to be myself," he adds. "It's fundamental to being a good king." He keeps abreast of what

An official portrait of the monarchs, with Silvia looking every inch the queen in her fabulous sapphires. (Swedish Information Service)

Children of Stockholm congratulate their king on his thirty-seventh birthday. (Swedish Information Service)

is happening in everyday Sweden by talking to people from all walks of life. A few years ago, after a conversation with some young people about drug-related problems, he came to the conclusion that "it is much more worthwhile to play sports." He feels that his grandfather's early advice has been particularly helpful: "Never permit flatterers, courtesans, or sycophants to come between you and the Swedish people. You are one among them, you live among them. You must share their joys and their pain. That is monarchy. You represent Sweden, you must 'live' Sweden."

HIS MAJESTY Carl Gustav XVI is today no more than one of his country's business representatives; yet he does not even have the right to sign a contract. He no longer has the right to vote; nor does he have any advisory power. The Constitution of 1810, upon which the present Constitution is based, stipulated that "Sweden must be governed by a king." But already in the early nineteenth century royal powers were limited to appointing the prime minister according to parliamentary rules; to presiding over the Council of Ministers once a week; and to reading the Address from the Throne at the annual opening of the Riksdag—Parliament—a showy, traditional ceremony.

Today, even these sovereign tasks have been struck from the Constitution. The Swedish prime minister is now named by the president of Parliament. And perhaps the crowning blow, the Address from the Throne, formerly presented by the king, is now read by the person who traditionally has always written it—the prime minister. Carl Gustav has even lost the symbolic title of chief of the armed services and has ceased to participate in any meetings of the government. Most of his duties now fall to the president of the Assembly. The last time the young king presided over the Council of Ministers—which convenes every Friday at the palace —was on December 31, 1974. The amended Constitution, which did away with the last remaining powers of the crown, took effect the next day. So it was that on January 1, 1975, Carl Gustav stored away his scepter and his crown, which he had received on the death of his grandfather a little more than a year earlier. He would have no further use for them, just as he would no longer have occasion to mount the silver throne, a symbol of the Swedish monarchy dating from the seventeenth-century reign of Queen Christina. The only things left for the king to do are to participate in ribbon-cutting ceremonies, to unveil new statues, to distribute the Nobel prizes each year, and to christen ships.

Such diminishing measures were not implemented during the reign of Gustav Adolf VI, who was extremely popular. Unfortunately, Carl Gustav, unlike his grandfather, was hardly esteemed by the Swedes. "We don't want him as king. He should look for another job," the students at Stockholm University railed. He was perceived as a spoiled prince who preferred to live at night, and for whom the nickname "His Highness Casanova" seemed hardly out of place. (To keep him from the throne a bit longer, the constitutional age at which Carl Gustav could assume his new role was raised from twenty-one to twenty-five.)

King Gustav Adolf VI, courtly and kindhearted, was beloved by all. An enlightened, cultured man, he was fond of music and the arts. He possessed a library of eight thousand diverse volumes and a large collection of exquisite Scandinavian ceramics. He was passionately interested in archeology and spent all his free time, or almost all, participating in digs in Italy and Greece. A connoisseur of Chinese antiquities, he was consulted by specialists from all over the world. His own collection of Chinese antiques—2,500 pieces in all, dating from primitive times—was one of the most extensive and beautiful in the world. These consuming intellectual pursuits did not, however, prevent the king from being an excellent tennis player and golfer, as well as an enthusiastic gardener. He designed the palace flower beds and experimented with creating unusual hybrids. On weekends at his castle in Sofiero, he cultivated orchids and camellias.

The king married twice; his first wife was Margaret of Connaught, princess of Great Britain and Ireland, by whom he had five children. After her death in 1920, he married Louise Mountbatten, sister of Louis Mountbatten, Viceroy of India, and aunt of the future Prince Philip of England.

On August 18, 1973, the king was rushed to Hälsingborg Hospital suffering from internal hemorrhaging. Three days later he was operated on for a bleeding ulcer and placed in intensive care. (In spite of his ninety years, Gustav Adolf had been in basically good health, which he attributed to a hearty appetite, no cigarettes, and a nonalcoholic, rice-based drink.) A slight improvement was closely followed by a relapse, and the weakened king sank into a coma. The telephone lines to Sofiero Castle were jammed with calls from well-wishers, while hundreds of telegrams and bouquets of flowers flooded the castle. Several people, on hearing that the king's kidneys had failed, offered one of their own for a transplant attempt. "It's absolutely out of the question," declared his personal physician. "There's no way he would be able to sustain the operation." On September 15, at 8:35 P.M., the beloved old king died after a twenty-three-year reign.

Following a brief religious service in the presence of the new king, Carl Gustav XVI, and his four sisters, the body of King Gustav Adolf VI lay in state in the chapel of the royal palace; for three days the grief-stricken people filed past their king. He was buried on the grounds of Haga Castle, near Stockholm. Services in memory of Gustav Adolf were held in every church in Sweden; in tiny backwaters of the country as well as in the major cities immense crowds turned out for all of them.

At the solemn enthronement ceremony of the new king, the dynasty's seventh heir, Carl Gustav XVI, wearing the full-dress uniform of an admiral, astonishingly resembled a portrait of his ancestor, Karl Johan XIV, formerly Marshal Bernadotte of the French empire. Karl Johan had traveled an extremely unusual route to the Swedish throne. Born in the town of Pau, in southwestern France, the son of a modest notary, Charles Jean-Baptiste Bernadotte was to become the founder of the Bernadotte dynasty and father of the contemporary sovereign families of Sweden and Norway.

IN 1807, King Gustav IV of Sweden decided, against the will of his people, to declare war on France. He believed that God had chosen him to annihilate Napoleon, and that by doing so he would ensure the everlasting friendship of the Russian czar. (One of the Swedes' greatest fears was that Russia would conquer neighboring Finland and the king hoped to remain in the czar's favor.) Unfortunately, the czar had already allied himself with Napoleon and suddenly, to his consternation, King Gustav found himself fighting Russia as well.

Marshal Bernadotte, stationed in the Baltic with Napoleon's army, got into a conversation with a captured squadron of Swedish officers about Sweden's dilemma—a subject that seemed to fascinate him. Bernadotte remarked that it was unlikely that the czar would give in on the Finnish question and that Sweden, Norway, and Denmark were in imminent danger of invasion by French troops. He recommended that Sweden save itself with an armed neutrality. "And if you absolutely must have a confederation of states, align yourself with Norway, and let Finland go." With this advice, Bernadotte sent the Swedes home, and a friendship was born. (Some, particularly the French, would later consider Bernadotte's attitude a betrayal of France.) On their return, the Swedish officers went directly to the government ministers to explain the situation and enlist their aid in compelling the king to withdraw from the war. The king turned a deaf ear.

In 1809, after losing Finland to Russia, the Swedes deposed Gustav IV, who was now certifiably mad, and proclaimed his uncle, Karl XIII, king. This new sovereign, old and sick, was not much of an improvement. Having no children to succeed him, Karl XIII adopted a young relative, Prince Christian August von Holstein-Sonderburg-Augustenburg, and named him successor to the throne. One year later the young prince died in an accident. The Swedish Diet (an assembly of princes and landowners) met to choose a new heir. The king of Denmark, brother-in-law of the recently deceased candidate, and his younger brother, the duke of Augustenburg, both proposed themselves as candidates, to no avail. (The deposed King Gustav IV, living in exile in Switzerland, did have a son. But since everyone knew the king was crazy, little credibility was attached to his son.) And so Sweden dispatched envoys to its new friend, Marshal Bernadotte, to sound him out on the situation. Several weeks later, the Swedes were suddenly met with the news that "His Highness Jean-Baptiste Bernadotte, prince of Pontecorvo, marshal of France, with the consent of his majesty the emperor of the French, has accepted the crown of Sweden." Louis XVIII, from the depths of exile, declared, "All of the crowned heads are more than a little bewildered at the decision of the Swedish states. An ordinary individual, of humble birth, a French general, and thus one of my subjects, is chosen to be crowned by the free will of the people." Charles Jean-Baptiste Bernadotte was to spend several years as crown prince before being crowned Karl Johan XIV of Sweden on the death of his "adopted father," Karl XIII.

On September 19, 1973, Karl Johan's XIV's great-great-great-

great-grandson Carl Gustav XVI, officially mounted the silver throne and was paid homage by ministers, Parliament, high military and civil dignitaries, and the various constituent bodies. After taking the oath of office, the new king addressed the nation. His voice was firm: "I will strive to the best of my abilities to fulfill the responsibilities left to the monarch in this day and age. My grandfather, a man admired and well loved, became a symbol for the modern monarchy. I am firmly committed to following his example." The young king, twenty-seven years old, also appealed for "understanding among all Swedes for the good of the country."

Carl Gustav got through the first five days of his reign without making a wrong move, to the surprise of some of his skeptical subjects. On September 20, he presided for the first time over the Council of Ministers, assisted by his uncle Bertil, third son of the dead king. (If Gustav Adolf VI had died before his grandson reached the age of majority, Prince Bertil would have become regent.) Standing before the council, the youngest sovereign in Europe uttered the ritual formula: "Since my beloved grandfather Gustav Adolf VI is dead, I assume his succession as king of the country." Does the office of king automatically endow the ability to meet its demands? Doubtless it does, because the young man who woke up that day in Stockholm Palace scarcely resembled the one who had been living under the same roof just three months earlier.

Fate had not been particularly kind to Carl Gustav Folke Hubertus. He was born on April 30, 1946. Nine months later his father, Gustav Adolf, forty years old and next in line to inherit the throne, died in a plane crash on a flight home from Holland, where he had been a guest of Prince Bernhard. The plane had made a brief stopover in Copenhagen, then suddenly burst into flames as it took off for Sweden. There were no survivors, and to this day, no one has ever learned what happened.

That same evening the Swedish royal family—called the "Haga family," since they spent most of their time at Haga Castle—were gathered around a big fireplace in the living room. Four little princesses, wearing their prettiest dresses, were elbowing each other and giggling, badgering their mother again and again with the question: "What is Papa going to bring us?" Princess Sibylle, teasing, would answer, "You'll see. . . ." The children's excitement peaked. Finally a car approached the house, its headlights reflected on the snow. When the doorbell rang, Sibylle ran to welcome her husband, followed closely by the little girls crying, "It's Papa, it's Papa." But instead of the long-awaited prince, Sibylle found Queen Louise, her face distorted with grief. "Send the children to bed quickly . . . the plane crashed."

The news was a terrible blow to Princess Sibylle; she had lost everything—love, hope, and ambition. The air disaster robbed her of the father of her children, and of her chance to one day wear the crown. Daughter of one of the innumerable German princes who, before World War I, reigned over small provincial courts, Princess Sibylle de Saxe-Coburg, although a great-granddaughter on her father's side of Queen Victoria, did not seem destined for a life of prominence. She had spent a lonely, rather isolated childhood in the modest city of Coburg. But the day came when, at the wedding of the duke of Kent and Princess Marina of Greece, Sibylle met the man who would one day become her husband and change her life. Among the crowd, the tall, shy young man, grandson of King Gustav Adolf of Sweden, noticed the pretty young German girl. They were married in 1932 at Coburg; she was twenty-four, he was twenty-six. Princess Sibylle bloomed in the atmosphere of the Swedish court, unprepossessing though it was. Installed in Haga Castle, near Stockholm, the young couple knew fifteen years of real happiness. Four daughters—Margaretha, Désirée, Birgitta, and Christina—were born between 1933 and 1943, and in 1946 the long-awaited son arrived. Then the tragedy struck.

The Swedes wept for their prince, but they did not weep for the fate of their princess, widowed at forty with five children, because they did not love her. Sibylle was a German, and the war was still only yesterday. (To compound matters, her father had thrown in his lot with the Nazis during the war.) Naturally reserved with a haughty appearance, she was extremely conscious of her position as "queen manqué" and as mother to the future king. A terrible snob, she was the first to condemn her husband's brothers for marrying commoners. Some said Sibylle's attitude resulted from a solitary and provincial education and suggested that when her protective shell was pierced the princess—nicknamed "Mother Superior" by her detractors—was a charming, warm-hearted woman. Be that as it may, her severity and her principles were unshakable, particularly where her nearest and dearest were concerned.

Her children, her daughters in particular, were deeply affected by the constraints their mother's authority and hierarchical sense brought to bear upon them. She broke up the marriage plans— scandalous in her eyes—of her eldest daughter, Margaretha, and a nightclub pianist, Robin Douglas-Home, nephew of Sir Alec Douglas-Home, at various times minister of foreign affairs and prime minister of England. It might have been a good marriage, if the young man had only chosen another profession; "nocturnal pianist" was little valued at court. Princess Sibylle was on the verge of saying no as well to the marriage of her second daughter, Dési- rée, to Gregor Lewenhaupt when the young man died in a skiing accident. It took a lot of courage and more than a few drops of noble blood to dare ask for the hand of one of her daughters. Even so, not all the girls made "important" marriages. Margaretha mar- ried John Ambler, a British businessman, in 1964. Désirée married a Swedish baron, Nicolas Silfverschold, in 1965. Birgitta, in 1961, married Prince Johan George de Hohenzollern, the only "high" marriage of all her siblings. The youngest, Christina, married Tord Magnusson, a businessman and agent for Pommery champagne, in 1974. Princess Sibylle did not live to see the marriage of her last daughter, nor that of her son, Carl Gustav. She died of cancer in 1972.

LITTLE PRINCE CARL was the palace darling. Whose turn was it to comb his beautiful blond curls? Who would dress him up in his cutest outfit? Even the old king was charmed by his grandson's blue eyes and cherubic smile. When the prince was three, the king officially declared him the youngest soldier in the kingdom, and the little prince enjoyed dressing up in the blue uniform of the Royal Mounted Guard and the cross of the Noble Order of the Seraphim. To Carl Gustav's delight, he often accompanied his grandfather to official events. The duke of Jemtland, for such was the small soldier's official title, also loved to organize complex tactical maneuvers with his mechanical toys. The vast rooms of Haga Castle were often transformed into "restricted territory," where electric trains and miniature jeeps whizzed around in a great commotion. In quieter moments, he enjoyed constructing scale models of battleships on his small workbench.

When he turned five years old, most of the royal family were in favor of sending him to nursery school. For a child swathed in a cocoon, fussed over by his sisters, and coddled by the staff, the experience of mingling with children his own age from all ranks of society would certainly have helped him overcome the problems of integration he suffered later in life. But Princess Sibylle was inflexible—a future king must never mix with the people. And so a private teacher was hired. His classmates—for he needed at least a few—were chosen with extreme care. As far as Princess Sibylle was concerned, etiquette and tradition were the basic principles of education. The students were ordered never to address Carl Gustav by his first name but as "Prince." When his classmates were reprimanded for occasionally forgetting this directive, Carl Gustav blushed with embarrassment at being the cause of the scolding. In spite of the rules and the reprimands, the young prince was very popular, due in large part to his unpretentiousness, his kindness, and his gentle, handsome face. Very sensitive and yet outgoing by nature, he suffered from being constantly set apart by his surroundings and position. Today he retains rather bad memories of those early years.

When Carl Gustav turned seven, Sibylle finally permitted him to leave the palace every morning at 8:30 to attend Broms, a private school in Stockholm. There his classmates called him neither "Prince" nor "Highness," but by the nickname "Chabo." Chabo was far from being the most well-behaved child in his class. He was mischievous, indeed undisciplined, but happily his angelic smile made up for all his little sins. He participated in all the school activities, and one day he was sent with the rest of his classmates to a certain area of the city to direct traffic. The news spread like wildfire. The press came to photograph the event; motorists stopped in the middle of the road to stare. The resulting traffic jam was so immense that the police had to be called to rescue the trapped prince; humiliated and ashamed, it was only with a great deal of self-control that he was able to hold back his tears. This incident compounded two problems he had worked to overcome throughout his early school years: pronounced dyslexia, which left him with a lifelong dislike of books, and a shyness that was almost pathological.

At thirteen, Carl Gustav was sent to a boarding school in the town of Sigtuna, finally leaving the easy palace life for regimented communal living. Like his classmates, he went to bed every night at 8:45. Ten Swedish crowns (about two dollars) was his monthly pocket money. No special courses were instituted for the crown prince; he followed the regular curriculum. In Sweden, schoolchildren are first given a good basic education deliberately oriented to the useful, practical side of life. The instructors seem to have a certain disdain for culture and philosophical ideas; rather, they attach great importance to the vocational arts. Each high school has woodworking and metalworking courses, and a large part of the curriculum is devoted to sports. Nothing could have corresponded more closely to the interests and tastes of the young crown prince.

Carl Gustav could never be accused of having been a brilliant student. At the rather advanced age of twenty, he finally passed the Student Examen signifying the end of his secondary studies. (The finale of the Student Examen is a showy, tradition-bound ceremony, with the boys in black tie, the girls in white dresses.) The graduates that year, including Carl Gustav, paraded through the streets singing. When the Swedish people learned the good news of their prince's success, announced by an official court communiqué, there was a general explosion of joy, almost of triumph. Forgotten was his age; hope was reborn; the monarchy would endure.

In the fever of victory, nobody dreamed of asking what his grades were or where he ranked among his fellow students. It sufficed that if the grandson of a king as cultured and literate as Gustav Adolf VI had passed his exam, he could only be the most brilliant student in the world. Alas, even future kings are betrayed. A copy of his grade book mysteriously turned up on the desk of the director of one of Stockholm's most important newspapers—a disaster. The heir to the throne had received fair to poor grades in every subject except geography. He had made it through school, but just barely. The grades caused a scandal: there was talk of establishing a republic.

Lèse-majesté—a crime committed against a sovereign—did not exist in Sweden; the monarchy belonged to the people and they were free to vent their indignation. "Such an incompetent young man would certainly be out of place on the throne of Sweden," his detractors complained. "We can hardly see a prince so mediocre in literature handing out the Nobel Prize. Better the republic immediately."

Had the revolution in Sweden finally arrived? For several years the dynasty had been squeezed drier and drier by the Socialist party. The prince's shortcomings—especially his poor scholastic record—would serve well as a pretext to do away with the throne completely. Many Swedes were wondering if the monarchy had not become a superfluous institution. In bluntly posing the question to Parliament, the Socialists were successful in obtaining the nomination of a commission charged to study the possibility of constitutionally replacing the kingdom with a republic. Only the strong personality and enormous popularity of King Gustav Adolf VI could have put the brakes on this movement.

ARE THERE MANY DEFENDERS of the throne today? Recent polls show that more than 70 percent of the population is in favor of retaining the monarchy—a far cry from the low results of polls taken in previous years. What could possibly have caused this turnabout, especially now when all monarchies appear somewhat antiquated?

For one thing, the new king is no longer the Casanova of yesterday; for another, he gave Sweden a queen who knew just how to revive the monarchy. The crown prince who frittered away his bachelorhood escorting pretty girls to nightclubs has become a serious, conscientious king. His royal "role" has brought about a complete metamorphosis. He who confided, not long ago, "I think I am rather a night person . . . one who needs at least a whole morning to pick up one's natural rhythm," now begins his days early, faithful to his grandfather's motto: "Duty above all." He studiously keeps himself informed on what is happening in the world, and most particularly, in every domain of Swedish society, frequently visiting various public works, organizations, and institutions.

At the beginning of his reign, Carl Gustav was fortunate enough to have the help and guidance of his uncle Bertil, who watched over him like a surrogate father. During the early years of his grandfather's reign (Gustav V), Bertil had been fourth in line of succession to the throne—after his father and two older brothers—and assumed that he would simply make the navy his career. But he moved one step closer to the throne when his brother Sigvard, despite royal opposition, married a commoner and lost his right to the crown. (The Swedish laws of succession are actually rather strangely conceived. Crown princes are not permitted to marry outside royalty. If they violate the rule, they and their children are automatically excluded from succession, losing their privileges and their titles. On the other hand, once they are kings, they can marry whomever they wish. When Bertil, at the age of twenty-three, fell in love with a commoner, his father forbade him to marry her, and the heartbroken Bertil bowed before the royal will.)

In 1950, when Gustav VI ascended to the throne at the age of sixty-seven, Prince Bertil remained as the only son to assist him with the affairs of state. Karl Johan, the youngest, had followed the example of Sigvard and relinquished his right to the throne by marrying a commoner. And the eldest son, Gustav Adolf, had been killed several years before. According to the laws of succession, Gustav Adolf's son Carl Gustav, rather than Bertil, became the next heir to the crown, thus setting up a situation whereby the succession to the throne would skip an entire generation. Prince Bertil, in the meantime, functioned as regent of the kingdom. And once again, at his father's insistence, he was compelled to renounce marriage to a commoner, Lillian Craig, a dancer whom he had met in London during World War II. But this time Bertil capitulated only on certain conditions, because he would not give Lillian up. "I will fulfill my functions as regent of the kingdom as it is stipulated in the Constitution," he told his father, "but do not ask too much of me. . . . Each time the affairs of state permit, I will rejoin Lillian abroad. I will share myself between the state and the woman I love until my nephew Carl Gustav reaches his majority. Then I will take up my liberty . . . and I will marry Lillian."

Prince Bertil had to wait more than a quarter of a century until the young King Carl Gustav found his queen and they produced an heir. Then, and only then, was Prince Bertil able to liberate himself from the tyranny of the state and make his life with the woman who had so faithfully waited for him.

Several years before the death of his grandfather, Carl Gustav had already discovered his own heart's desire. But unlike his uncles, who lost their titles and their heritage by prematurely marrying commoners, he knew how to be patient. On assuming the crown in 1973, after the death of Gustav Adolf VI, Carl Gustav entered a period of mourning, following royal convention, and did not immediately reveal his intention to marry. For almost three years more his love for Silvia Sommerlath was kept a secret from the public.

THEY MET DURING the Olympics in Munich. On March 16, 1972, the president of the German Olympic Committee had scheduled a large reception. Silvia, who at the time was an official hostess for the committee, was arranging placecards on a dining table when she noticed one card bearing the title "His Royal Highness Prince Carl Gustav of Sweden." The young prince arrived at the reception very late that evening and, to make matters worse, had lost his invitation. At the entrance, where the explaining, pleading, and cajoling of aggressive would-be guests was incessant, the head usher finally lost his patience: "Royal Highness or not, without an invitation you don't get in." The president of the committee was called. Accompanied by Miss Sommerlath, he said to Carl Gustav, "Your Highness, the best of our hostesses will serve as your guide." The royal connoisseur surveyed with pleasure the pretty face, the dazzling smile, and the long chestnut hair lightly pulled back to reveal a lovely neck and perfect shoulders. Five feet ten inches tall, with a shapely figure and an elegant, stately presence, she made a ravishing hostess for a playboy prince. (Although delighted with her new assignment, at the time of this meeting Silvia was in love with a thirty-six-year-old financial consultant, who was divorced and the father of a ten-year-old girl. Silvia was hoping to marry him, but he was reluctant to tie himself up for a second time.)

The Olympic games over, Silvia and Carl Gustav did not appear intent on seeing each other again. But chance—or fate—had other plans. "During the winter of 1973, I fulfilled my contract with the German Olympic Committee," Silvia relates, "and I began working for the Innsbruck Winter Games Committee in Austria, where I met a Swedish couple. One evening they arranged a party for me and a few friends. You can imagine my surprise when I saw King Carl Gustav there." The two skied together and dined quietly at their friends' home, avoiding obtrusive photographers. In the spring Silvia made several trips to Stockholm. On arrival in the Swedish capital, she was always met by a chauffeured car that sped her straight to the royal palace.

By 1975 the king was master of his own destiny, and the meetings multiplied. Journalists, sensing that this was a serious romance, pursued them relentlessly. To escape harassment, Carl Gustav hired a double, and Silvia wore a wig and dark glasses. She had by this time become a palace regular. Everyone was familiar with her pert, lively face—the king's colleagues, the palace staff, the secretaries—and greeted her with deference because they were certain that she would one day be their queen. The royal family aided and abetted the romance; convention went by the boards. Uncle Bertil and Aunt Lillian lent the couple their lovely house on the Riviera; Princess Birgitta, the king's sister, turned over Stenhammer, her chalet in Switzerland.

On March 22, 1976, the official announcement of the engagement of King Carl Gustav XVI to Miss Silvia Sommerlath was greeted with resounding apathy by the population. This was a bourgeois affair, without fanfare or fancy trappings. Silvia arrived at Stockholm Palace in a car unadorned with flags or ribbons, and without even a motorcycle escort. No cheering crowd waited anxiously to catch a glimpse of the future queen. The few spectators chatted casually among themselves, as though they were discussing the latest television game show. Silvia was greeted by Princess Margaretha's husband, John Ambler, who was no more a prince than Silvia was a princess. She entered the royal courtyard waving cheerfully to the sparse gathering of onlookers. The scene was worlds away from the feverish activity that surrounds Buckingham Palace on such special occasions.

But if the public remained indifferent, European nobility did not, giving free reign to sarcastic comments, while reporters probed the bride-to-be's family tree.

Silvia, who at thirty-two looked ten years younger, had the kind of radiant beauty born of good health, athletics, and an appetite for life. She was a natural for her new position: intelligent, poised, forthright, and fluent in several languages. In spite of the awesome gift destiny had placed in her lap, she kept a cool head always. She was a precise young woman who would manage her kingdom like a household. A princess of the bourgeoisie, Silvia was born into the highly professional world of European business and had worked all her adult life. When a journalist asked what she thought about becoming queen, she responded, innocently: "I don't have the impression that I am abandoning my professional life in becoming queen. I have simply changed one job for another. In fact, the job is the same; only the setting differs."

Silvia was born on December, 23, 1943, during the Allied bomb attacks on Heidelberg, Germany. Her mother and brothers had left Berlin shortly before to escape the air raids there. Her father, unable to leave his job, remained behind, but made round-trip visits as often as possible. Toward the end of the war the company he worked for was bombed and all of Berlin lay in ruins. Unemployed and with almost no resources, Mr. Sommerlath left to join his family in Heidelberg. By working at odd jobs, he somehow managed to keep food on the table. When the war ended, he realized that in order to resume his career he would have to leave Germany, where everything was in chaos.

The first time Walter Sommerlath left Germany was in 1920, when he was only twenty years old. He had decided to seek his fortune in Brazil, against the will of his father, who wanted him to go into the family tobacco business in Heidelberg. "I will never give you a penny," his father told him, "but if you want to come back, I'll send you the ticket." Nevertheless, Walter left for South America, where he became a sales representative for a German metallurgy company. At the end of the 1920s he met Alice de Toledo, a nineteen-year-old Brazilian from an old aristocratic family; a few years later they were married. In 1938, on the eve of World War II, the Sommerlath family, which now included two little boys, returned to Germany, where for the first time Walter had the opportunity to become an industrialist in his own right.

Left with nothing at the end of the war, Walter Sommerlath decided to return with his family to Brazil, where he had been offered a job as branch manager for a Swedish firm. But he had to wait two years before the Allied authorities would furnish the papers he needed to leave the country.

Brazil, in contrast to Germany, was extraordinary: abundant food and clothing, jobs, a decent place to live. Home for the Sommerlaths was a large pink and white villa, surrounded by palm trees and flowers. Although a serene, pleasant way of life was certainly possible, the elder Sommerlaths were not beguiled. The children were raised in an austere Northern European milieu. And yet, for four-year-old Silvia, it was the beginning of a happy childhood. When she was seven, she was sent to an extremely disciplinary private school. After school, Silvia was given private lessons at home in sewing and languages. She seldom played with her friends, and certainly never with boys. It was forbidden, and her father expected complete obedience, but this rule seemed to have no effect on her sunny disposition.

In 1957, the family returned to Heidelberg because Silvia's mother could no longer tolerate Brazil's humid climate. Silvia by now spoke fluent Portuguese, Spanish, and English, but had serious difficulty with German. She was enrolled in a very strict private school for the daughters of high society. The building was surrounded by walls thirteen-feet high, so there was no question of scaling them to freedom. Silvia remained there for eight months, until the family moved one more time, to Dusseldorf, where she attended Luisenschule, a high school for daughters of the conservative bourgeoisie. The students shunned makeup and dressed like aged spinsters. Silvia had problems adapting, first because she still spoke German badly, and second because her upbringing had been even more rigid than that of her classmates. (Her parents would not allow her to go anywhere unless she was chaperoned by one of her brothers.) She always felt like an outcast. After she passed her final exams, Silvia enrolled in the famous interpreter's school founded by Professor Paul Schmit, who had translated all the rantings of Adolf Hitler into the world's major languages. Completing four years of study, Silvia found a job in the Argentinian embassy for $300 a month. She later worked for a Spanish firm as an interpreter at international conventions. In 1972, she was chosen from among fifteen hundred candidates as chief hostess for the Olympics in Munich. And it was there that fate brought her together with the handsome prince, whom all the aristocratic European dowagers plotted to snare for their dinner parties and seat next to their eligible granddaughters.

Silvia married Carl Gustav on June 19, 1976. It was the first royal marriage celebrated in Sweden since 1797, when Gustav IV married Frederika von Baden. In the eighteenth century the ceremony was marked by lavish and exuberant display. By 1976, times had changed drastically: Hadn't the young king chosen as his motto "For Sweden in its time"? Had he already foreseen his marriage? "I will make a marriage of love. It's fundamental for being a good king," he declared while he was still crown prince.

In all the other kingdoms of the world, when a king marries a commoner for love, it's a tragedy. Parliaments rebel, archbishops threaten, public opinion splits, the king ends up abdicating, and the condemned couple leave the palace at nightfall to wander the rest of their days among the arid lands of exile. In Sweden, where the throne is just an office chair, the royal union was no more dramatic than a little family celebration.

For the wedding, the king wore his formal admiral-of-the-fleet uniform bedecked with medals. The future queen wore a high-waisted, rather simple white satin gown by Marc Bohan of Christian Dior, its long train held by two pages. Atop her lace veil was a tiara, made of cameos surrounded by pearls and set in red gold, that had been handed down from the marriage of Oscar I, son of the first Bernadotte (Karl Johan XIV), to the granddaughter of the Empress Josephine.

Storkyrkan Church was decorated with a new breed of roses—named, of course, Queen Silvia—that had been developed by Gustav Adolf VI's personal gardener. The bride and groom were seated in special red velvet chairs before the altar. At 1:15 P.M., Olof Sundby, the archbishop of Stockholm, asked the king, "Before God who knows all, do you, Carl Gustav, take Silvia to be your wife?" "*Ju* [yes]," he responded. A few moments later, Silvia, who already spoke a little Swedish, also murmured *"Ju,"* and became the twenty-fifth queen of Sweden. The archbishop was assisted by the court chaplain, and Silvia's uncle, Father Ernst Sommerlath, who read the psalms in German. He brought smiles to the faces of the assembled guests with his words, "It is the duty of the spouses to love each other and together to take care of the house." The rings were presented to the archbishop on a blue velvet cushion by the oldest bridesmaid, Carmita Sommerlath, Silvia's niece. After the exchange of rings it is customary for the groom to kiss the bride. Carl Gustav omitted it. Forgetful, shy?

In spite of the reprobation of the European royals and the nobility, almost everyone attended the wedding: Baudouin and Fabiola of Belgium, Margrethe and Henrik of Denmark, Constantin and Anne-Marie of Greece, Beatrix of Holland with Prince Claus, Simeon of Bulgaria, and Lord Mountbatten, quite remarkable in his impeccable suit as full of decorations as a Christmas tree. Only the pompous court of England snubbed the wedding. Her Majesty the Queen of England sent only the duke and duchess of Gloucester to represent her—eighth in the line of succession. Annoyed, the Swedes didn't fail to remark that the duchess in question had been no more than a secretary before her marriage. The behavior of the British queen was not without rancor, since Carl Gustav had never been taken by the charms of her daughter Anne, now married to a certain Mark Phillips.

Members of government were also present. Several Socialist ministers grumbled: "We didn't even have a real king, and suddenly we have a real royal couple before us." In diminishing the attributes of the "little king," the republicans had hoped to be able to rid themselves, slowly but surely, of the monarchy. But the royal marriage threw everything back into question, to the consternation of many government officials. The behavior of Prime Minister Olaf Palme was particularly telling. The Socialist leader arrived at the ceremony in a light blue business suit, in flagrant contrast to the tailcoats, full-dress uniforms, and gowns of the other twelve hundred guests. And his mocking smile seemed to say, "They can have their fun playing out this little comedy; the real boss is me."

On leaving the church, the king paused to put on his admiral's hat and buckle on a sword handed to him by his valet.

A four-in-hand coach, with two footmen in position at the rear, waited to carry the newlyweds through the streets of Stockholm. Surrounding the carriage were four mounted escorts: the Master of the Horse, the Commander of the King's Royal Cavalry, and two of Sweden's most famous jockeys. This colorful assemblage was led by the king's mounted guard, smartly dressed in light blue uniforms and white-plumed silver helmets. It was a masterpiece of production, due to the behind-the-scenes direction of Queen Silvia, former chief hostess evolved for the occasion into chief of protocol.

Swedes came from the four corners of the country to line the three-and-a-half-mile route; they were there to applaud the royal couple as well as to participate in the fairytale renewal of the monarchy. The triumphant path was staked out by twenty orchestras, from symphony to pop, as well as a drum corps, a rock group, and the Salvation Army band. There was something for everyone.

Back at the palace, Queen Silvia was greeted by a welcoming address from the palace governor: "Welcome, Madame, to this house, which will henceforth be Your Majesty's." Then he bowed formally to kiss her hand. In the middle of the courtyard the king, with Silvia at his side, mounted the small platform set up at his request. Addressing the Swedes, he said: "I present to you my spouse, my queen. She will reign with me; love her. Here before the Swedish people . . . here is the woman I have chosen for my wife."

More than 5 million people watched the event on television. Women viewers identified with the new queen, while men saw in her their wives, mothers, and sisters. She was not complicated, she

Carl Gustav and Silvia posing in front of a sixteenth-century tapestry—a wedding gift from the people of Delft, Holland. (Swedish Information Service)

was not fancy, she was not difficult; she liked her simple pleasures. She was a good housekeeper; she knew how to cook and sew; she dressed simply; she never went to the hairdresser, and the hairdresser certainly never came to her. All in all, she was just an average Swedish woman. She had simply exchanged her two-rooms-plus-kitchen flat and monthly income of $500 for a 608-rooms-plus-kitchen castle and a share of the king's annual stipend —slightly more than 8 million Swedish crowns, or approximately $2 million.

King Carl Gustav's personal fortune runs to several millions more. He inherited close to $800,000 from his grandfather, almost $200,000 from his father, and $40,000 from his mother; he inherited another $500,000 when he married. Moreover, he owns real estate, stock (approximately 95,000 shares in several large Swedish firms), jewels, and antiques. But these holdings do not support an extravagant way of life. Shortly after his marriage, the king declared: "We are going to cut down on daily expenses, living in a more contemporary way with a much smaller staff. My wife and I do not want to live removed from the people in an isolated, luxurious world. We want to live as though we were no more than high civil servants of the state." Certain antimonarchist journalists were skeptical. Nevertheless, according to a resident at the castle, nothing is thrown out these days. The new economy measures even extend to the candles, which are not replaced until they have burned down to a few inches. Silvia does not have a personal maid, and she has done away with curtsying at court: "I do not want old women much more important than I am curtsying to me." Queen Silvia intends to fulfill her role as though it were any other job, no different from that of a sausage maker or a receptionist.

THE QUEEN OF SWEDEN works for her kingdom from nine until five. After catching up on the world news and reading and answering mail, she spends the rest of the day receiving delegations of athletes, students, and artists; visiting hospitals, foster homes, and the handicapped; and engaging in a variety of other activities that enable her to better understand Swedish society. She frequently represents Sweden on official visits abroad. She instinctively knows exactly the right thing to do whatever the occasion. During a visit to a Swedish paper factory, for example, Queen

Silvia helped the workers stack packages stamped with the royal coat of arms, a move that couldn't help but endear her to the people —and win good notices in the press. More important, she has succeeded in transmitting her composure to the king, who had always been extremely shy and incapable of making a spontaneous gesture in public. On a visit to a glass factory recently, he surprised and delighted everyone by blowing a delicate glass vase (which he later presented to his wife), something that would have been unimaginable for him while he was still crown prince.

The queen often drops into her husband's office to discuss various matters and sometimes finds him meeting with important government officials such as the Grand Marshal of the Kingdom, or even the head of the government. Like the king, the queen must never become involved in political matters. But occasionally, when the sovereigns and politicians are having a private get-together, they do exchange their points of view. The queen has a certain authority, which stems in part from her remarkable diplomacy. She exudes confidence, yet remains always feminine, reserved, and discreet. From all the evidence, she is quite pleased with her job, a fact that never ceases to amaze a king who, given the choice, would much prefer the life of a gentleman farmer.

Silvia's commitment to being a model queen does not interfere with her role as a mother. When Princess Victoria Ingrid Alice Désirée was born on July 14, 1977, it was of little consequence that she was the daughter of Her Royal Highness; in the hospital she was simply number 770714-0021 in the official register of all newborn Swedish babies. Citizen Silvia has the right to an annual maternity allowance of 2,800 Swedish crowns (about $400) until her daughter is sixteen. The same applies for Carl Philip Edmond Bertil, born on May 13, 1979. He was called the "surprise baby," since the queen's doctor had estimated his arrival for June 15. But at five o'clock in the morning on May 13, the king, traveling in Germany, received a phone call from the housekeeper announcing that the queen was about to deliver at the palace, and not at the hospital as planned. The little prince was born at seven o'clock, an hour before the king's return. At 2:30 that afternoon, the navy fired off forty-two cannons, and all of Stockholm knew a prince had been born. The latest addition to the royal family is Madeleine, born at Drottingholm Castle on June 10, 1982. The children are cared for by two Swedish women: sixty-year-old Martha, the nurse-in-chief,

The king and queen, Prince Carl, and Princess Victoria learn about candle-making at the Culture House at Skanse, Stockholm. (Swedish Information Service)

At the summer palace in Drottningholm. Princess Madeleine is perched on the shoulders of future Queen Victoria while brother Carl Philip looks shyly at the camera. (Swedish Information Service)

and a young au-pair girl. The king's former nurse, Ingrid Bgörn-berg, who had looked after him until she was well past the age of seventy, is still there to supervise; she is called, with a great deal of respect, the Old Lady. The queen's office is close by the children's rooms, and she makes an effort to see her children as much as possible during the day. In the evening, she always helps with their baths and tucks them into bed.

Lunch at the castle is served family-style in the modernly furnished private quarters, decorated with antique rugs, paintings and *objets* borrowed from other rooms in the palace. Every Tuesday the sovereigns have the high palace staff in for lunch—fifteen people whose titles still have a very monarchical ring: the First Marshal of Court, the Grand Marshal of the Kingdom, the First Lady-in-Waiting, and so on. Apart from the traditional lunches, family life goes on very much as it does anywhere else. If the weather is good, the royal couple take a short walk in the afternoon with the children and Charlie, their black Labrador retriever.

Favorite royal pastimes are more athletic than cultural. Five minutes from the palace by car is a private stable where the royal family frequently rides. Silver Dream, their pureblood Arabian, always welcomes them with a whinny. There are as well two Lipizzaner stallions, a gift to Princess Victoria, who is still too small to ride them. Easter vacations are spent at Storlien, the royal chalet, where the king and queen, both excellent skiers, have taught the children to ski. The king, queen, and children go by themselves, with no domestic help, and they manage everything—cooking, cleaning, transportation—on their own. During the summer the royal family stays at Soliden Castle, where they have a private beach and an enormous yacht, the *Storo*. And weekends are spent at Stenhammar Castle, fifty-six miles from Stockholm.

Carl Gustav is a wonderful cook and loves to create special dishes for his family and friends. (Even as a child he showed an unusual interest in cooking. By special dispensation he was allowed to bake cakes and practice cooking in the palace kitchens under the watchful eye of the master chef, Paul Arbin.) Whenever the king lunches or dines in a restaurant, he takes along a little notebook in which to jot down the description or recipe for something he especially liked, and if he doesn't have time to make the dish himself, he asks Silvia to discuss it with their chef. Cooking is a passion that the young king shares with his uncle Bertil, and shared with his grandfather, King Gustav Adolf VI. Unfortunately, the old king was never able to indulge in his, since the protocol of his day would never allow a sovereign to soil his hands.

Silvia has made a great effort to rejuvenate the palace, not only its furniture but its services as well. Efficiency has replaced the pomp of antiquated protocol. The palace staff is smaller now and more versatile. The queen herself participates in much of the be-hind-the-scenes planning, particularly when it concerns prepara-tions for an official trip. One staff member reports that she is really a marvel of organization, that she foresees everything down to the last detail. Her experience as a former hostess serves her well.

This inclination to "dust off" the monarchy had led Silvia, in favor of equality of the sexes like the great majority of Swedes, to urge the king to approve the new law of succession, making their daughter Victoria crown princess; in her enthusiasm she totally forgot that the royal word no longer carried any authority. In 1975, Parliament had called for the study of the question of female succes-sion to the throne. The government later appointed an expert to prepare a report on the subject, which was presented early in 1977, before the birth of the princess. The bill subsequently introduced by the government to allow female succession was not adopted until November 1979, after it won a majority vote in Parliament. Until that moment, Carl Philip—crown prince for a little more than six months—was the rightful successor to the Swedish throne in accordance with the Constitution, which stipulated that only male descendants in direct line to the throne could inherit the crown. Now, however, succession is by order of primogeniture or firstborn—thus total equality between male and female descen-dants. The new law of succession was a veritable upheaval, truly a historic first for Sweden. In his heart of hearts, Carl Gustav XVI regretted this turn of events. It is said that on hearing of Parlia-ment's vote he declared in a gently nostalgic voice, "I believe that the majority of Swedes would prefer to have a king."

The next Bernadotte to mount the throne will be Princess Vic-toria Ingrid Alice Désirée. But by the time she reaches the age of constitutional majority, in the year 2002, the preference for a king or a queen may no longer be relevant. Who can say, at the dawn of the twenty-first century, whether the monarchy will still be a flour-ishing reality or merely a fond memory?

5

NORWAY
◆
The Middle-Class Monarchy

An elected monarch! It's too horrible!" wrote the grand duchess of Mecklenburg-Strelitz to her niece, the princess of Galle, sister-in-law of the new king of Norway. Prince Charles, the youngest son of King Frederik VIII of Denmark, was most assuredly king, but a rare king indeed, voted in by the Storting, the Norwegian Parliament, on November 18, 1905, five months and eleven days after the country's proclamation of independence from Sweden. He was the first king of Norway's own choosing in more than five hundred years. The Norwegian crown, which dates from the year 872, had spent five centuries on the heads of various Danish sovereigns and still another hundred years—most of the last century—on those of the Bernadotte dynasty of Sweden. (Norway was part of Denmark from the end of the fourteenth century until 1815, when it was united with Sweden.)

By the end of the nineteenth century, the proud and nationalistic Norwegians had grown weary of their enforced union with Sweden; the Swedish yoke chafed and was no more comfortable than the Danish one that had preceded it. The marriage between the

United Kingdoms of Sweden and Norway had lasted ninety years, but Norway had become an unhappy spouse as awareness of her own particularities and interests grew. Finally, in 1890, the Norwegians decided to emancipate themselves and began to lobby for their own consulates; but it was not until fifteen years later, in the face of intractable Swedish refusal, that the Storting resolved to go ahead and set up Norway's diplomatic bureaus. Oscar II of Sweden refused to sanction the decision. Exasperated, the Storting decreed that there would no longer be a Swedish king on Norwegian territory. Would this mean war? Actually, neither side wanted it. Sven Hedin, the great Swedish explorer, is said to have declared with contempt, "There is not one man in Sweden who considers the current union worth a single drop of Swedish blood." The Norwegians stood firm and on June 7, 1905, after nearly a century-long battle of words, the Norwegian Parliament proclaimed the dissolution of the union. The separation between the two countries was consecrated by the Treaty of Carlstad. After over five hundred years of foreign domination, Norway was once again independent.

What would its new status be? In a crowned Europe—only France, Switzerland, and San Marino, in central Italy, were without monarchies—would a new republic be born? Norway decided that it would remain a kingdom, which it had been traditionally since the late ninth century. Economic considerations also played a major role in the choice favoring monarchy; the Storting believed that a republic would be much more expensive.

There remained only the choice of a monarch. Erasing from memory the centuries of Danish servitude, the Norwegians chose Prince Charles, the youngest son of King Frederik VIII of Denmark. The Danish royal family was descended from the oldest dynasty in Europe and was related by blood to all its reigning members. (In the nineteenth century, Denmark's King Christian IX was nicknamed the "father-in-law of Europe," while Queen Victoria of England was dubbed "the grandmother of Europe.") Another point in the prince's favor was that he had an heir young enough to easily adapt to his new country. In 1896, Charles had married Princess Maud, daughter of Prince Edward VII of England; their son, Prince Alexander of Denmark, was born in 1903.

Before accepting Norway's proposition, Prince Charles wanted assurance that the majority of the Norwegian people were in favor of the move. A referendum was thus submitted to a popular vote on November 12 and 13, 1905. Seventy-nine percent of the voting population favored the monarchy. (At that time only men over twenty-five years old had the right to vote; women obtained the right in 1914.) This referendum was double-edged: if the Norwegians had voted against the monarchy, the present government would have had to resign; the overwhelming yes actually corresponded more to a desire to keep the government in place than to a natural propensity toward monarchy.

On November, 21, Prince Charles disembarked at Christiana, Norway's capital (later given the Viking name of Oslo), his son in his arms, his wife by his side. To establish himself as a continuation of the line of ancient Norwegian sovereigns descended from the Vikings, the first king of the new dynasty chose the name Haakon VII; his son, now heir to the throne, was renamed Olav.

After numerous discussions, the all-powerful Storting concluded that a coronation ceremony was necessary in spite of its fear that, in letting out all the royal stops, a corps of sycophants and royal "groupies" would develop, ready to nurture a veritable monarchical power. In reality there was little to fear; Norway had long since lost its aristocracy, and the crowned and titled personages of Europe preferred the brilliant salons of Vienna and London. Nevertheless, all the crowned heads of Europe would attend the coronation, except the Swedes, who couldn't bear to see "little" Norway become a country in its own right.

On June 22, 1906, at the age of thirty-three, King Haakon VII was crowned with great ceremony in Trondheim Cathedral, the oldest cathedral in the kingdom. To symbolize the unity of the country, one of the government ministers placed the crowns on the heads of the new king and queen. In his right hand his majesty held the scepter, and in his left the golden globe—symbols of royal power. But the new king harbored no illusions about his responsibilities; he understood from the first that he was not to govern but simply to reign. Shortly after his coronation, he wrote to his father, "I listened to several addresses. The essence of them all was that I have the right to say nothing."

NORWAY HAD barely attained its independence when World War I exploded. Yet Norway suffered little, since it proclaimed its neutrality early on; some Norwegian shipowners even amassed fortunes fulfilling the needs of both England and Germany. When World War II broke out, Norway once again proclaimed its neutrality, but this time it was not to last. This time the stakes were too high to respect Norway's decision. The Allies thought of occupying Norway, particularly the city of Narvik, a center for shipping Swedish iron ore to Germany. Hitler, on his part, wanted to turn Norway into a sort of huge, magnificent aircraft carrier as well as use its deep and numerous fjords as submarine shelters. Although the majority of the Norwegians favored the Allies, opposition did exist from an extremely fanatical and powerful National-Socialist party—with close to ten thousand members—led by Vidkum Quisling. (After the German invasion, Quisling became the head of the government and remained in power until the liberation in 1945. He was subsequently tried for treason and executed.)

On April 7, 1940, German troops landed in Norway. Parliament held an emergency meeting to decide whether to fight or surrender. King Haakon and Crown Prince Olav, both in their general's uniforms, declared that they would do battle at the front. In the presence of his minister of foreign affairs the king announced to the German delegation that had come to negotiate, "We refuse to surrender."

Supported for a time by the Allies, Norway was soon abandoned and was finally forced to capitulate on June 10. Pursued by German bombers, the king and his son, who had fled north, were in constant danger. (Queen Maud had died two years earlier; Olav's wife, Princess Martha, and her children were already sheltered in Sweden.) On April 15, 1940, father and son barely escaped a bombing attack by diving into a snow bank.

During the last meeting of the Council of Ministers, which was held in the residence of the bishop of Tromso, the prime minister spoke: "His Royal Highness, the crown prince, raised a question on the occasion of our last meeting: Should he or should he not remain in Norway in the event that the king and government are compelled to leave the country? His Royal Highness informed us of his desire to stay. The government, in accord with the president of Parliament, and after a scrupulous study of the question, has decided that it would be preferable for the crown prince to leave the country so as not to risk falling into the hands of the Germans."

Disguised as ordinary travelers, Haakon and Olav took a train to the west coast of Norway, where they were picked up by a British cruiser, the *Devonshire,* and taken to England.

The king refused to acknowledge the Quisling government and continued his vociferous resistance from England, where the former government had also taken refuge; Crown Prince Olav headed the exiled Norwegian Military Council. Numerous messages made their way from the royal family to the Norwegian people, encouraging them to continue their battle against the invader.

Later in the war, King Haakon VII and the royal family traveled to the United States at the invitation of President Roosevelt and took up residence in exile at Pooks Hill, near Washington, D.C. Olav shuttled back and forth between London and Washington to continue his resistance activities.

On May 13, 1945, shortly after the German defeat, Prince Olav and the ousted civil authorities returned to Norway. Three weeks later the king and his family made their triumphant return. Prince Olav welcomed his father exuberantly: "King and Master! As you once again—and for the first time after five years of absence—put your foot on Norwegian ground, we all wish you, from the bottom of our hearts, welcome: we, the armed forces, your soldiers and your people."

King Haakon VII died in 1957, at the age of eighty-five. Two years before he had broken his thigh bone in the bathroom of his summer residence at Bygdoy, where he had lived happily with Queen Maud and where he continued to spend several months a year after her death in 1938. As a result of his accident, the king was confined to a wheelchair, with only occasional outings on a pair of crutches. He never recovered his health—or rather, he never wanted to recover. He often said: "One is either perfectly alive or completely dead." He decided to die. Fifty-two years of reign had drawn to a close, although in fact it was Olav who had been exercising all the monarchical responsibilities for more than a year.

Crown Prince Olav was alone when he assumed the office of sovereign, since Crown Princess Martha had died in 1954 from hepatitis. The official announcement of the old king's death was presented by His Majesty King Olav to the Council of Ministers, gathered at the royal palace at 4:00 P.M. on September 21, 1957: "It is my duty to inform the Council of Ministers that my dear father, His Majesty King Haakon VII, died today at 4:30 in the morning. In accordance with the Constitution, I become a member of the government as well as king of Norway, and I now take the oath in writing according to paragraph nine of the Constitution. From here on, I will bear the name of Olav V, and will keep the same motto as that chosen by my father: 'All for Norway.' "

On October 2, 1957, eleven days after King Haakon's death, the flags of Oslo fluttered at half-mast; in shop windows portraits of the old sovereign were draped in black crepe. The funeral procession left from the royal palace at 11:30 that morning. Sailors presented arms as the coffin, covered with a Norwegian flag, was placed on a horse-drawn hearse. The day before, cannons had boomed a final salute; this day church bells rang at noon, announcing the end of religious services. King Olav, in an admiral's full-dress uniform, and his son Crown Prince Harald, dressed in a cadet's khakis, accompanied their father and grandfather on his final journey to the railroad station, where a special train waited to carry his body to Trondheim for interment. A popular king in spite of the fact that he did not speak a word of his adoptive country's language (happily most Norwegians understand Danish), Haakon VII was universally mourned.

In contrast to his father, King Olav would have no coronation, since such ceremonies had been abolished by constitutional amendment in 1908. Olav wanted to mark the changing of the reign, nevertheless, by a religious ceremony; in this way he was consecrated, but not crowned, by a benediction in Trondheim Cathedral on Sunday, June 22, 1958—fifty-two years to the day after the coronation of his father. The royal symbols were placed at the king's side: the gold baroque crown, set with a beautiful tourmaline, that dated from the reign of Karl Johan XIV, king of Sweden and Norway in the early nineteenth century; the globe, a ball of gold with the equator and the meridian marked by rows of golden rosettes; the scepter, a twenty-five-inch baton of gilded bronze; and the Sword of State, whose hilt and sheath were of gilded bronze encrusted with mother-of-pearl.

KING OLAV has been a dutiful and conscientious sovereign for more than twenty-six years. Every Friday he presides over one of the meetings of the Council of Ministers. Seated at the head of a long table, he is usually content to remain silent and respond with a nod; lately, because of his advanced years, he has tended to doze

His devotion to the crown for more than twenty-five years has won the king the enduring love and respect of his people. (Norwegian Information Service)

off. But the meetings are, nevertheless, extremely formal. The ministers still request the king's permission to explain their programs and listen with the greatest respect to his comments. They realize that the king speaks from long experience, that he has, in fact, been reigning since some of them were still in diapers. In addition to attending these weekly meetings, the king opens and closes the first and last sessions of Parliament. And when there is a change of government, his majesty asks the departing prime minister who should be called to the royal palace, the first step in naming his successor. As a rule, the chief of state—the king—must follow the advice of the departing chief of government; but when the advice is not sufficient to resolve a crisis, such as when the various parties of Parliament cannot agree on who will be the next prime minister, the king then has the right to intervene as an objective judge. However, the role of the king during a government transition has never actually been formally discussed or specified. This lack of precision can be regarded either as a mark of confidence in the king or an instance of governmental negligence.

In an emergency—a war, for example—the king, symbolic chief of the armed services, has the authority to appoint new generals or defense chiefs, if he deems it necessary. But without question, his most significant—and time-consuming—role is that of figurehead. He goes from inaugurations to exhibitions, from receptions to premieres. Every two weeks he dines with the archbishop, then with the chief general of the armed forces, and finally with the admiral of the navy. Once a week the minister of foreign affairs and the prime minister take their turns at the king's table. And every year the king hosts three lavish dinners at the royal palace—one for Parliament, one for the government ministers, and one for the court of justice. On New Year's Eve, the king delivers his traditional address to his countrymen over television and radio.

Unlike his son Harald, King Olav is open and easygoing and takes great pleasure in meeting new people. The only thing he is inflexible about is punctuality. He takes it as a point of honor to always be on time, and if one of his "audiences" does not respect this elementary law, he withdraws into an angry silence ten times more daunting than a violent outburst.

The king frequently travels abroad to represent his country. Most often these trips are designed to publicize Norway's economic needs. Serving as a sort of business representative without portfolio, he does not have the right to sign the most insignificant contract or come to a tacit agreement even when a formal commitment is in the offing. The king's signature alone is of no legal value; documents are not valid unless countersigned by a member of the government. And although the king's signature is necessary to activate numerous statutes or provisions, it remains only a formality. Yet the king's presence is valued and sought after; he is a living symbol of the country's unity, and as such a stabilizing element.

Though Crown Prince Harald is replacing his father on various official occasions, Olav remains very active in spite of his age, and it is he alone who decides on the parceling out of the sovereign duties. Remarkably well preserved, he drives his own car, with his chauffeur sitting in the back, as if their roles were reversed. Since terrorism has taken on an international dimension, the royal car is now always followed by a police escort. But concern for his safety does not deter the old king from walking alone around the streets in his battered raincoat, which is not much younger than its owner. The king has a horror of change, and it extends from his old raincoat, his faded felt hat, and his ski poles, to the law of succession, which in Norway still does not recognize women as rightful heirs to the throne. In spite of, or perhaps because of, his eccentricities, he remains extremely popular. The king often attends the theater, and although he has a royal box he prefers to sit in the orchestra with a companion. He also enjoys concerts, and dining with his children or with friends in town.

THE VAGARIES OF POLITICS, a general trend toward more democratic customs, and perhaps above all the lack of royal conviction among its sovereigns have resulted in a bourgeois monarchy as boring as any Socialist regime. It was essential, of course, to establish a balance between the egalitarian Norwegian character and a royal chief of state. King Olav has succeeded so well that the royal family is scarcely distinct from an average upper-middle-class Norwegian family. The king himself has noted with bemused resignation that his family has become completely bourgeois, and completely Norwegian, since all his children chose their mates from the Norwegian middle class.

The royal family is actually distinctive in only one area: their problematical and soap opera-ish love lives. As a young girl, Princess Ragnhild, the eldest of Olav's children, had eyes for no one but Erling Lorendzen, son of an Oslo shipowner. But as far as old King Haakon VII was concerned, it was out of the question for his granddaughter to marry a commoner. In 1953, after six years of resistance, he finally gave in to his son's pleas on her behalf. Olav's argument for the marriage carried substantial weight—Lorendzen, a commando officer during the war, had been one of the heroes of the Norwegian resistance who had returned the throne to one of Europe's most venerable monarchs.

The wedding took place on May 15, in the little Chapel of Asker. Immediately after the ceremony, Her Royal Highness Princess Ragnhild, henceforth Mrs. Lorendzen, left with her husband for Rio, where he would manage his father's shipping offices. By her marriage, the princess lost her title of royal highness; her children would not have the right to any title whatsoever. This was the first breach of royal tradition. King Haakon, getting older, relented—once.

With the marriage of her sister in 1953, twenty-one-year-old Princess Astrid was heartbroken. Of course she was happy for Ragnhild, but at the same time she lost all hope of marrying the man she had loved for five years. She was sixteen when she first met twenty-six-year-old Johan Martin Ferner at a New Year's Eve party, and it was love at first sight. But Johan was also a commoner, the son of the proprietor of a men's clothing store in Oslo, and the king said no to any thought of marriage. The continuation of the new Norwegian dynasty, of which he was the founder, could not be jeopardized by disrespect for tradition.

The following year, Astrid's mother died, and the young princess entered a new phase of her life. She became the first lady of the kingdom, assuming all the duties her mother had fulfilled after Queen Maud's death. Astrid's longed-for marriage was now, more than ever, utterly an impossibility. Johan Martin Ferner understood this and decided to take himself out of the picture. To escape despair, he married the ravishing Bitte Hesselberg Meyer, a model and daughter of an Oslo businessman. Two years later the marriage ended in divorce, and Johan and the princess began seeing each other again.

When, on King Haakon's death, Crown Prince Olav mounted the throne, his son Harald became the crown prince, while his daughter Princess Astrid continued as the kingdom's first lady. But the first lady was languishing. For ten years she had fought for the only man she had ever loved. Finally her persistence and faithfulness prevailed. If Olav was liberal enough to allow his daughter to marry not a blue-blooded foreigner but a red-blooded Norwegian, and a salesman at Harrods to boot, it was perhaps because he did not have the means or choice to do otherwise. Princess Astrid, although extremely devoted to her duty, was above all a woman, and a woman of strong character. Having threatened her father with the scandal of running away with Ferner, Astrid embarked on a sort of royal strike, refusing to fulfill certain obligations of the first lady. Olav V gave in; he was a loving father and his daughter had fulfilled her role up to that point with conscientiousness and devotion. The king even decided that Princess Astrid could retain her title. After her marriage she would be called "Princess Astrid, Mrs. Ferner," and continue to carry out all her official duties. But she would have to give up the endowment of 50,000 Norwegian crowns (about $7,000) a year that she received as first lady.

While the liberals rejoiced, the conservatives made their disapproval quite evident. One evening paper bore the headline: "The Royal House of Norway Endures the Greatest Tempest in Its History." Another daily trumpeted: "Is the Norwegian Church Going to Bless the Marriage of Astrid, Who Didn't Know How to Be Faithful to Her Duty?" The real problem was that in Norway the church was divided between the liberals, who accepted divorce, and the purists, who couldn't bear to hear the word spoken. Monsignor Johannes Snemo, who was the bishop of Oslo and primate of the kingdom, refused the king—the symbolic head of the Norwegian church—point blank; he would not unite the couple because Astrid's fiancé was divorced, and Parliament would refuse to sign the traditional congratulatory message. A newspaper publisher wrote in his editorial: "It would have been desirable that Princess Astrid had had the wisdom and the self-control of Britain's Princess Margaret to choose the path of duty, as distressful as that might have been." This was the rerun of the fuss over the Margaret Rose–Peter Townsend romance, but with a happy ending. Astrid's marriage took place on January 2, 1961, in the same church where Ragnhild was married. The benediction was given by Bishop Arne Sjenlbu, of Trondheim, a former member of the Norwegian resistance known for his liberal views.

To many people, this second commoner marriage further weakened the future for the monarchical form of government. But as long as the current king lived, the monarchy was safe. Olav's formidable popularity, his devotion to the crown, and his people's admiration and respect for his wartime efforts remained the unshakable strengths of the regime. And yet, committed as he was to his position, and proud as he was of his people's affection, even he was not able to avoid the trap of sentimental love. The death of his wife, Princess Martha, had left an empty place in the royal nest. In the drawing rooms of Oslo there were whispers that the king had a mistress. (The Norwegian press, although privy to the gossip, had sufficient respect for individual liberties to let pass in silence that which after all would be quite natural. In Germany, England, and France, where the press is quick to speculate on a future marriage or a sentimental drama, old Olav's love life simply did not make for a juicy page-one story.)

LIKE HIS CHILDREN, Olav V did not seem to know how to find love among duchesses or princesses. It was among the commoners that he discovered, in 1958, the extremely beautiful Astrid Blestvik. Fabric designer, high-fashion model, and heiress to one of the most important textile mills in Oslo, Astrid was a radiant, fortyish woman of the world. Abroad, big headlines splashed the dailies: "The Beautiful Astrid Will Marry the King." She herself— with tears in her eyes—made statements to the press (but never in her own country) lamenting her fate: "Alas, we will never be able to marry." At the Norwegian court, there was absolutely no question of marriage. Mrs. Blestvik, a divorced mother who had had several run-ins with the tax authorities, could never replace Princess Martha. Never did Astrid darken the palace portals. The couple met in her sumptuous villa, at friends' homes for dinner, on the ski slopes, or on board the royal yacht. A court spokesman, harassed by foreign paparazzi, stated that should Crown Prince Harald marry a princess to assure the continuation of the Norwegian dynasty, and succeed his father on the throne, then King Olav *might* eventually marry Astrid. But neither Olav nor Harald even dreamed of this dénouement. The former, although extremely liberal, was hardly contemplating marriage, and the heart of the second was already taken. Although no one was perturbed by the king's affair, the noise surrounding it became overwhelming. Exit Mrs. Blestvik.

Prince Harald and Princess Sonja, the future monarchs of Norway. Sonja is well aware of the significant role she will play as queen. (Royal Norwegian Embassy)

Prince Harald, faithful to family tradition, became involved in the same sort of sentimental drama as his father and sisters: he fell in love with Miss Sonja Haroldsen, a salesgirl in her father's clothing shop. And, miracle of miracles, Sonja was neither married nor divorced. They had met at an officers' ball, and, as in the storybooks, it was love at first sight. The king was less than enthusiastic about the pairing. Mr. and Mrs. Haroldsen had the wisdom to send their daughter to France to expand her vision and change her mind. In the depths of Corrèze, working as an au-pair girl, young Sonja would perhaps forget her Prince Charming.

After she left, Prince Harald immersed himself in his official obligations, making numerous trips abroad . . . but never to France. The press reported him engaged successively to the two Greek princesses, Sophie and Irene; to Princess Tatiana Radziwill of Poland; and then to Princess Benedikte of Denmark. But the prince in fact, had eyes for none, and there could be only one explanation—Sonja. She and Harald had never stopped writing to each other, and when she returned to Norway they met secretly as often as possible. Their frustrating fate was discussed in the Norwegian press and within the royal family; both were sympathetic but disapproving.

For ten years, King Olav tried to dissuade his son from marrying Sonja. But Harald refused to give in, even though according to the Constitution he risked losing the throne and the crown for himself and his descendants if he acted against the king's wishes. Harald, dubbed the "sad prince" by the press, held fast: "It's Sonja, or I renounce all my rights." This was a serious threat to the dynasty, since he was the only male heir. "After so many years, my son is not about to change his mind," the king reflected. And so, after consulting the government, Parliament, and the heads of the different parties, the king announced the engagement.

Actually, there was nothing in the Norwegian Constitution that specified that a crown prince had to marry a person of royal blood. The monarchy was indeed becoming middle class, but the trend suited an egalitarian Norway. In a general opinion poll on the impending marriage of their prince, 58 percent of the people questioned approved, 34 percent were opposed, and 8 percent had no opinion. Among those between fifteen and thirty, approval weighed in at 81 percent, while among those over sixty, approval was only 30 percent. The opposition party—the Social Democrats —argued that if the prince married a commoner, Norway no longer had any reason to maintain a hereditary monarchy. But the discussion was closed.

The king himself escorted the bride to the altar on August 29, 1968. Sonja's father had died in 1959, and even though her brother Haakon could have filled in, the king wanted to prove that Sonja was completely welcome in the royal house. In his sermon, the Bishop of Oslo diplomatically emphasized "that a new and very strong bond" had just been formed between the royal family and the Norwegian people.

If Princess Sonja did not have blue blood, she did possess many other qualities essential to her new position as first lady of the kingdom. She was intelligent, cultivated, artistic, and elegant, and her dazzling smile was an important social asset. She had learned how to sew in Paris and had attended a finishing school in Lausanne that taught girls from good families how to run a household. She was fluent in French, as well as in English, which she had studied at Cambridge University. "I was brought up," she once said, "to be a good housewife"; but her upbringing would also help her to be a good crown princess and future queen. King Olav made every effort to have her accompany him to official ceremonies, and it was he who took on the responsibility of teaching Sonja her new profession. She proved to be a very gifted student.

Harald's education had been geared to his future role as king; after high school he was a cadet at the cavalry training academy for six months prior to attending military school. Then it was off to Oxford where, like his father thirty years earlier, the prince studied political science and economics. Harald was never more than a mediocre student, but the Norwegians did not value their hereditary monarch any less because of it—unlike their Swedish cousins who admonished Carl Gustav when his grades became public knowledge. In Norway, even more so than in other Scandinavian countries, the population remains totally discreet when it comes to the royal family's private life.

SINCE MAY 1970, when Harald became regent, he has played an increasingly important role in the monarchy. According to Article 41 of the Constitution, the prince is "temporarily invested with the royal power."

Princess Sonja is well aware of the significant part she will play

The prince and princess with their children, Martha Louise and Haakon Magnus, the future heir apparent, at their villa in a suburb of Oslo. (Royal Norwegian Embassy)

King Olav is an expert sailor. At age twenty-five, he was a member of the yachting crew that won a gold medal at the summer Olympics in Amsterdam. (Norwegian Information Service)

Their love of skiing has endeared the royal family to all of Norway, where the sport is almost sacred. (Royal Norwegian Embassy)

once her husband is king. Her goodwill activities are numerous and include visits to day-care centers and hospitals as well as volunteer work with handicapped children. She is president of the children's aid division of the Norwegian Red Cross. Spare moments are few and far between, since official personal appearances also heavily dot her calendar. "To be the wife of the crown prince and the future queen of Norway to me means that I must always be a role model and must realize that my smallest gestures will be observed and judged," she has stated. Up to this point, Sonja has succeeded perfectly: seated behind her big desk, surrounded by telephones, files, books, and copious mail, she imparts an image of an independent and strong-willed businesswoman. "Life has changed a great deal for first ladies of the country," she says. "Queens and princesses take a much more active part than they used to in representing the monarchy." She presides over large official get-togethers with warmth and exceptional savoir-faire. She know all the provinces of her country intimately and, during her visits, likes to dress in regional costumes. She combines easy accessibility with the bearing of a queen.

Harald, a tall, solid man with a calm demeanor, is much more shy and reserved than his wife, although his shyness does not seem to inhibit his sharp sense of humor. Whenever anyone brings up the possibility of a republic, he responds: "I am at your disposal." Nevertheless, he believes in the future of the monarchy. "As long as it functions as it does today," he states, "I believe that the monarchy has a mission to fulfill."

Norwegian royalty lives in the simplest possible way. King Olav resides alone in the palace, which is casually guarded by young soldiers in curious plumed kepis. Harald and Sonja make their home in a large villa in Skaugum—on the outskirts of Oslo—where the grounds are a children's paradise. Princess Martha Louise and Prince Haakon Magnus, ages twelve and ten respectively, enjoy the park, the playing fields, the farm animals, and the swimming pool whenever they are not in school. Sonja, like King Olav, is athletic, a quality highly valued by the Norwegians. She is an excellent skier, better than her husband, who (although he won't admit it, since skiing is almost sacred in Norway) much prefers trout fishing. But Sonja and Harald share a passion for sailing; Prince Harald even participated in the regattas at the Tokyo Olympics.

The government allots the entire royal family 22.4 million Norwegian crowns (about $3 million), from which King Olav draws 5 million crowns for personal expenses and the maintenance of the castle and other residences. Prince Harald receives 4.4 million crowns; the remaining 13 million are used for food, staff salaries, and insurance. Like all employed Norwegians, the sovereign and his family are obliged to participate in the social security system.

Norway is both a monarchy and a parliamentary regime; the duality is a calm and comfortable one. (As if to symbolize this, the largest thoroughfare in Oslo connects the royal palace to Parliament, each sitting on a hill.) The country is very egalitarian: relations are cordial between factory workers and executives, union officials and government members. Even the Socialists have no wish for a revolution.

Five years of world war reinforced the monarchy's power as a national symbol, and it was a heritage that King Olav, hero of the Norwegian resistance, knew how to preserve. But someday soon the war will be just one more memory among many others filed in the dust of historical archives, and Olav V will be replaced by Prince Harald. The newest generation has already forgotten, if indeed it ever knew, the role the royal family played from 1940 to 1945. Although the Socialists on the left have attempted on several occasions to raise a debate on the principle of monarchy as a form of government, it is still apparent that no conflict exists between the sovereigns, the government, and the people. For now, Olav V is the guarantee of the monarchy; he celebrated his silver jubilee in October 1982, and with him the monarchy lives. It remains to be seen whether the same will hold true with the future King Harald.

6

SPAIN

◆

The Monarch Restores Democracy

W hile Europe has had a tendency to dismantle its monarchies—Constantine of Greece lost his throne in 1973, Michael of Rumania lost his in 1947, and many others toppled beforehand—in 1975 Spain gained a brand-new monarchy and a brand-new king: Juan Carlos I. Thirty-seven when he mounted the throne, he was over six feet three inches tall, athletic, and handsome. He had a smiling wife and three attractive children; it all seemed like a fairytale. But in reality it was far from it. Juan Carlos took on a difficult heritage. His grandfather, King Alfonso XIII, used to say bitterly, "No one ever asked me if I wanted to be king." The prince never had the chance to ask himself the question. From his earliest years, he had undergone intensive training in order to emerge as the champion of the Spanish monarchy. His trainer was the most famous man in the kingdom—General Francisco Franco y Bahamonde. No detail of this forced apprenticeship was left to chance.

The dynasties of Aragon, Castile, Hapsburg, and the Spanish Bourbons had succeeded one another on the Spanish throne. But Juan Carlos was the first "Bourbon-Franco." With pride, el caudillo (the leader), as Franco called himself, could say of him: "This future king is my creation." Today, the shadow of the old general still darkens Spain, but it is fading.

IN 1975, a drama was unfolding at the Pardo, Franco's residence and headquarters. The library doors were wide open and six men passed through, bearing a stretcher. The shape of a body could be discerned under the embroidered mantle of the Virgin of Pilar, brought in specially by the Archbishop of Saragossa in the hope that it would produce a miracle. No sound—no sigh, no moan—issued from the stretcher. Only blood gurgling from the mouth of the skeletal body being transported signaled imminent death. It was the end, the end of a life that it had seemed would never be over. There, surrounded by his loyal followers, lay Francisco Franco y Bahamonde, generalissimo of the armies, master, after God, of all the Spains. Everyone looked with fright at their caudillo. Slowly the mournful cortège descended the ambassadors' stairway to the ambulance waiting below. Inadvertently, one of the escorts bringing up the rear brushed his foot over the dark pool that was beginning to spread over the precious carpet on the steps. "Don't walk on the blood of Franco," roared an escort next to him.

For twenty days nothing in Franco's worn-out body had worked, and physical breakdown followed physical breakdown. The human machine, subject for many years to the pressures of Parkinson's disease, finally gave in everywhere at once.

Absolute master of his country since 1936, the eighty-three-year-old Franco was now no more than an eighty-pound skeleton, a ruined and almost lifeless body laid out on a table, helpless in the hands of medical science. In a nook to the left of the operating room, hastily set up in the infirmary of a police barracks two hundred yards from the Pardo, important men of the country were gathered: Arias Navarro, president of the government; Alejandro Rodriguez de Valcarcel, head of the Parliament; Garcia Hernandez, minister of the interior; Lieutenant General Colona Gallegos, commander of the infantry; and Alvarez Arenas, captain-commandant of Madrid. The prince of Spain, Juan Carlos de Borbón, the interim chief of state for the last several days, had just arrived accompanied by his wife, Sofia, when Dr. Hidalgo Huertas broke into the room crying, "We can't operate, the blood pressure is too low!" Was this the end?

Franco remained the absolute master of Spain right up until his death. The restoration of the monarchy provided for by the Fundamental Laws of Succession, formulated in 1947, had been put off to some imprecise future date. Yet on July 23, 1969, in a quavering, high-pitched voice rendered almost unintelligible by emotion, Franco, garbed in the dress uniform of captain-general, had announced before 519 cheering deputies the historic phrase, "I have decided to propose to the nation as my successor the Prince don Juan Carlos de Borbón y Borbón." He read his speech seated on the enormous velvet-upholstered throne in the Palace de Oriente, the Palace of Kings. Behind him, among the gilded panels, the tapestries, and the stucco of the throne room, which resembled a stage set more than a Parliament, portraits of Isabelle the Catholic and Ferdinand silently presided over the event: the monarchy was conferred on the Spanish people by a little general who took himself for sovereign.

As Franco lay dying, Juan Carlos refused to accept the interim leadership, encouraged by his father, who advised him to turn down any offer of power that would not be permanent. In the face of the country's agonizing situation, the *camarillas,* or entourage, demanded that the prince set in gear the process of succession. To general stupefaction, he flatly refused. The big, reserved, and timid young man, who all his life had only followed the advice of others, said no for the first time. The *camarillas* would have been less astonished at this show of will had they recalled that the prince was a very attentive and retentive student. In July 1974, when Franco first became ill, Juan Carlos was urged from all quarters to announce his presence as interim head of state. This he did. No sooner were the words out of his mouth when Franco opened one eye, then both, ending the brief "interim" and relegating the prince once again to the shadows. Humiliated, Juan Carlos had to withdraw amid sarcastic comments from all over Spain and abroad. The prince understood that this was not the kind of mistake to make twice. When one announces to the people that one is taking power, one keeps it. So, when Franco lingered near death for a second time, Juan Carlos was firmly resolved to do nothing. Caution obliged.

He requested several doctors to keep him precisely informed of the invalid's state of health, regardless of the Franco family's wishes. And when these specialists could tell him that the end was absolutely certain, then and only then would he agree to take over the interim government. President Arias Navarro confirmed the verdict of the doctors: "I can guarantee you that he will never again recover. He's been opened up from here to there," he explained. "Now it's no more than a question of days. I call upon your patriotism."

Referring to Article 2 of the Organic Law—voted in by the Cortes, the Spanish Parliament, and approved by the people—which provided precisely for the situation where a sick Franco could no longer exercise his duties, the Council of the Kingdom and most of the high state officials concurred on the necessity of Juan Carlos's taking charge. On October 30, 1975, at 9:00 P.M., the president of the Cortes announced that Juan Carlos was the interim chief of state. The following morning, while waiting to reign over 35 million Spaniards, Juan Carlos presided over the Council of Ministers. "Let us work with serenity," said the prince. "Once again the sense of duty impels me to take over the direction of the state." The ministers hesitated a long while before pronouncing the caudillo unfit. What if the generalissimo were to open his eyes one more time and call in Madrid's captain-general to say, "This is a coup d'état. Put all these people in prison"?

But at this point there was no longer any question of consulting Franco. After undergoing many blood transfusions to counteract the hemorrhaging that had persisted for three days, Franco sank into unconsciousness. Juan Carlos knew that a chief of state was now essential, and he finally accepted the proffered solution of the interim.

Of course, in spite of everything, Franco was still not dead. He was only "temporarily" unfit to govern. Profiting from the delicate situation in which Spain found itself, Hassan II of Morocco decided to "peacefully" invade the Spanish Sahara without waiting for the date of self-determination agreed upon long before. Juan Carlos remained calm; if up until this point he had been a cardboard prince, he now took on the full dimensions of a king. He went in person to El-Aiun, the capital, to demonstrate his support for the army. The Spaniards were impressed by the action and courage of their prince.

During the night of November 3, in the Pardo barracks, Franco underwent his first operation, but the hemorrhaging persisted. Four days later, on the advice of his doctors, he was transported to La Paz, Madrid's most modern hospital, for a second operation.

Very few people were allowed to enter room 132. Among those who were was the prince.

It was quite obvious that the extraordinary means employed to keep Franco alive for thirty-five days were impelled not by medical ethics but rather by political factors, permitting various players to gain time. No one at the Pardo pretended that the caudillo's choice of Juan Carlos to succeed him would be universally supported. But among the Franco family, sentiments were different. The marriage of one of Franco's granddaughters, Carmencita, to one of Juan Carlos's cousins, Alfonso de Borbón Dampierre, had revived the "dynastic" appetites of some members of the Franco family. Especially those of the woman who was for forty-one years the first lady of the kingdom—Carmen Palo y Martinez Valdez, the daughter of a millionaire and a former beauty queen.

As far as the specialists were concerned, Franco was being treated by hypothermia, but others felt the general had been put into hibernation. Either way, there was no reason to believe this situation could not last for weeks, for months, or even longer. Finally, on November 19, the thirty-seventh day of the crisis, the general's life ineluctably slipped away. At exactly 3:40 A.M. on Thursday, November 20, 1975, Franco died. Diagnosis of death: Parkinson's disease, thrombo-phlebitis, heart disease, bleeding ulcers, bronchial pneumonia, kidney failure, peritonitis, toxic shock, heart failure. A diagnosis that would make even a doctor shudder. At 4:58, before there was even time to make the official announcement, "Franco is dead" was on the wire services around the world. It was the end of the last "monarchy" of Europe, an absolute "monarchy" that had lasted longer than Roosevelt, Churchill, De Gaulle, and Pompidou together had governed.

5:15 A.M.: the embalmers arrived. "The general is so well embalmed," said one, "that he'll remain intact for thousands of years, like the Egyptian mummies."

8:00 A.M.: Arias Navarro arrived at the Ministry of Information's radio studio to read the caudillo's last message to his people: "Spaniards, the moment has arrived for me to lay down my life before the Almighty, and to appear before His judgment without appeal. I ask God to receive me unto Him. . . . I ask pardon from all, and with all my heart I pardon those who call themselves my enemies. . . . For the love I have brought to your country, I ask you to continue on in unity and in peace around the future king of Spain, don Juan Carlos de Borbón, with the same affection and the same loyalty which you have shown me. . . . I would like, in my last moments, to unite the names of God and Spain, and to clasp you all close to me to shout together, one last time, in the shadow of my death: Arriba España. Viva España.''

10:30 A.M.: a short meeting of government ministers established that calm reigned throughout the country; it would be useless and unnecessary to put into play the various devices planned in case of trouble or disorder.

11:00 A.M.: the coffin containing Franco's body arrived at the Pardo.

11:30 A.M.: in the caudillo's antechamber the official death certificate was signed by the president of the government, the head of Parliament, the heads of the civil and military organizations, and the minister of justice.

12:15 P.M.: the official notification of death was given to Prince Juan Carlos, who had been alerted early in the morning and had immediately appeared at the Pardo.

The most important measure was to declare Prince Juan Carlos chief of the armies, even before he was proclaimed king. The decree was enacted that same morning in Parliament and then ratified by a council of ministers. The official point of view was that this action accounted for the ease of the transition. The army was, for the moment, remaining calm, but the caudillo's death nevertheless left an enormous void. He had been a role model who had earned his stripes on the battlefield, and sacrificed his life for his country.

As astonishing as it might appear, at the instant when the electronic brain waves of Franco went flat on the scan, Juan Carlos, interim chief of state, no longer had a position. He had once again become prince of Spain, a prince without a kingdom and without a crown. The actual power was held by the Regency Council, whose members were the president of the Cortes, Rodriguez de Valcarcel; the archbishop of Saragossa, Monsignor Cantero Caudrado; and Air Force General Larrazabal. On Saturday November 22, 1975, before a plenary session of the government, Juan Carlos took the oath of fidelity to the Fundamental Laws of the Franco regime and to the principles of the Movimiento (a unique party formed by the groups and political associations allowed by Franco). This oath was merely a formality, in a way a repetition of the oath that Juan Carlos had already pledged before the Cortes in 1969. By this simple statement, pronounced on the evening preceding the caudillo's funeral, the dauphin became king.

Juan Carlos was not a king by divine right as his ancestors were; nor was he a king voted in by the people. He was more a high government official who had just been named to a new post. King he would be, but without consecration and without coronation, put into office simply through the will of a general who had been prince of the kingdom he had re-created, a kingdom of which the Cortes and the Council of the Kingdom were trustees. The night before the oath-taking, the civil register—the official log of births, marriages, and deaths—of the royal family had been reestablished. The day following the ceremony don Juan, father of the new king and true heir to the crown in the monarchical sense of the term, published a statement in which he expressed his disapproval, although for six years he had had ample time to become accustomed to the fact that his son would be king. The struggle instigated by Franco between father and son ended at the moment when Juan Carlos, as Juan Carlos I, King of Spain, descended the steps of the Cortes to the acclaim of the crowds. Yet don Juan waited to totally renounce his dynastic rights until he saw his son completely clear of the Francoist regime, several years down the road.

On November 23, Juan Carlos presided over the funeral of the caudillo, a ceremony which Franco himself, two years before, had organized down to the smallest detail. The idea had beguiled him. To his family, who had begged him not to do anything about it, the caudillo had laughingly answered, "I am not afraid. I have never been afraid." But when he watched the players in this future drama parade before him in a sort of dress rehearsal, garbed in an assortment of formal white uniforms, violet cassocks, Moorish white turbans, capes, mantillas, and shiny cocked hats, all to his exact specifications, tears began to spill down his cheeks.

After three days of national mourning, the political suspense was at its peak in Madrid. In the course of that first post-Franco week, Juan Carlos presided as king over his first meeting with the Council of Ministers. From the beginning, the ministers noted "an abysmal difference," as one of them put it, between Franco and Juan Carlos. The most obvious difference between them was that one had been eighty-three years old and worn out by power and the other was a young man of thirty-seven eager to hold the reins.

In the Zarzuela Palace, the prince's residence, conversation was

marked with the same respect as at the Pardo, but at the same time
was more spontaneous and more cordial. The little palace, in which
visitors tripped over children's bicycles in the vestibule, had none
of the coldness or formality of the Pardo. Before the meeting, the
dining room table had been hastily re-covered to give it a more
official appearance. One detail immediately attracted the notice of
the ministers: ashtrays instead of the crystal candy dishes that Franco's valets never had to refill, since no one ever touched them.
Franco couldn't bear to have anyone smoke in his presence. But
the biggest difference as far as the ministers were concerned was
that they now had to abandon their long-time practice of passing
little notes. "Franco had a weak voice," one of them explained.
"He spoke without making the least effort. It was necessary to be
absolutely silent and attentive; otherwise, in spite of the microphones, only those closest to him could hear what he was saying.
So we took up the custom of scribbling little notes and passing
them when we wanted to communicate with each other." The
"schoolboys" would quickly begin circulating their personal comments and observations, often having nothing to do with the question at hand, while Franco, like a tormented professor, pretended
to see nothing amiss in his unruly classroom. At the first meeting
under his authority, Juan Carlos intercepted the little notes being
passed under his nose and read them aloud, to the great embarrassment of the ministers. Ever since the notes have vanished.

The reign of Juan Carlos would be a reign of a king unlike any
other. All of Franco's Machiavellianism had made a sort of hostage
of the young prince, a supreme guarantor of his regime after his
death. Juan Carlos would not have an easy task. His consecration
as king did not return the Spanish throne to his family. He was
instead the first in a new line, a king born of Francoism, to which
he owed fidelity. Moreover, his powers were not really those of a
king as much as Franco's were. The caudillo legislated without
consulting the Cortes; he possessed "all the powers of the state,"
"all governmental functions," as well as "the supreme power of
establishing general judicial standards." Juan Carlos was far from
having these powers. Cut off from his family, whose name and
historic weight he still bore, and hostage of a system whose demands he had accepted, the fact remained that Juan Carlos was
more or less a "trial king." For in the Francoist ranks, not all
opinion was favorable to him. The ultra-rightists of the regime,

"the guerrillas of the Christ-King," Franco's first supporters, never had any monarchical inclination. They would have preferred to see one of their own succeeding their caudillo. Still others were awaiting yet another changeover.

JUAN CARLOS, it is said, had planned his accession ceremony in collaboration with his father for several years. The ceremony was actually an investiture and an enthronement rather than a coronation. (Today in Europe only the pope and the king or queen of England are crowned.) The extremely simple ceremony took place on November 25 in the Cortes Palace, where Juan Carlos arrived in the royal carriage. For the occasion, the prince was dressed in a uniform corresponding to the army's highest rank. He wore the obligatory Order of the Golden Fleece and the Order of Charles III, as well as several others he deemed useful. Present at the ceremony were the symbols of his new rank: the crown and the scepter, usually exhibited at the Palace de Oriente. The crown, dating from the time of Charles III, who reigned in the late eighteenth century, was purely symbolic; it would never be placed on the sovereign's head. (In fact, it is rather plain and without any great value; gold-plated silver unadorned with precious stones, topped by the globe and the cross of the Catholic kings. The scepter is much more decorative. Measuring twenty-seven inches, it is a cylindrical baton of gold set with emeralds and rubies and topped by a sphere of rock crystal.) These symbols of royalty were set on a table to the king's right. On another table were the Bible and the crucifix. At the solemn moment of the oath, the sovereign placed his right hand on the Bible, which was held by the president of the Cortes. At this instant the monarchy sealed a pact with the Spanish people. The king recited the oath standing up; only heirs to the throne kneeled.

The following day the solemn Te Deum mass was celebrated in the cathedral. Rows of spectators lined the streets. The royal Rolls-Royce pulled up in front of the church portico at 10:30 A.M. The king, in his formal dress uniform, stepped out. Then the queen appeared in a long green gown, her hair wrapped in the Spanish style around a silver comb and covered by a mantilla. Sofia had decided not to wear the antique cloak of the queens of Spain, a garment of silk, velvet, and gold with shields from all the Spanish provinces embroidered on it in silver thread. (Created in the early nineteenth century, in the days of Isabella II, the cloak is carefully preserved in the Escorial.) Nothing had been planned for the queen to do during the ceremony, so throughout the formalities of accession she simply stayed by the side of her royal spouse. The rites were simple, in perfect accord with Juan Carlos's and Sofia's concept of a twentieth-century monarchy. Felipe, the little prince, and his two sisters—all three blond with blue eyes—joined their parents, who were greeted by Cardinal Vincente Enrique y Caracon, archbishop of Madrid. Accompanied by the parish priest, the prelate led the royal couple into the chancel under a canopy bearing the crest of the Bourbons, where two tapestried chairs awaited them. The nave could accommodate only a thousand people, which put a severe strain on seating protocol. Eighty delegations in dress uniform or cutaways had been packed in facing the altar, which bloomed with gladiolas, camellias, and carnations. Behind, in a row of pews, sat relatives of General Franco, along with the dukes and representatives of the Bourbon-Dampierre family and the Greek royal family. Princes and members of other reigning families sat on one side of the transept, and on the other, members of the government and the queen's entourage. Less important guests found places in the recesses of eight lateral chapels.

Hailed as they left the church, the king and queen responded with smiles. They rode to Moro Park in their car—the convertible top down—moving very slowly, at the pace of the escort horses; it was a triumphal march punctuated by ovations and by blasts from the cavalry's trumpets. Back in the Palace de Oriente, the king received the homage of his people. Standing before the throne, he accepted the oaths of allegiance from dignitaries shimmering in their most opulent finery. The royal couple made a final appearance on the balcony where the crowd's ovation brought them back three times. The queen, smiling, thanked them by waving her hand. The day of enthronement drew to a close with jubilant military fanfares.

For Juan Carlos I, a twenty-seven-year apprenticeship had finally come to an end. He was born to be king, and he was king. "Among the Borbóns," he said, "being king is a career." Franco had also understood this. It was one of the reasons he had decided to take in hand the education of little Juanito. However, according to the Fundamental Laws of Succession, which he had drafted, to become king one needed only to be thirty years old, Spanish, in agreement with the laws and principles of the Franco regime, and approved by the Cortes. The caudillo could thus have chosen the first Garcia or the first Lopez who appeared, or else one of his faithful companions in arms. Doubtless, the name de Borbón, with its profound political and historical overtones, weighed heavily in the balance. If Franco had long dreamed of the Borbóns, which one, father or son, would he be tempted to choose? "It is better to have two open doors," he confided at the time to one of his intimates. In reality, he had already chosen the son. He was a young boy, malleable, a boy whose education he could supervise and who would always have the advantage, in the eyes of many Spaniards, of not having known the tragic period of the Spanish Civil War (1936–1939), and not being compromised by it. Above all, the choice of the son would give the caudillo a good twenty years to gain the time he needed to organize Spain on his own terms.

FRANCO WAS NO MORE, but would Juan Carlos be able to assume the overwhelming political heritage left by the caudillo? It was the question all of Spain was asking, and one that intrigued the international scene. In fact, nobody really knew the ideas of the prince, who for six years had had to make a profession out of not expressing any. It was vaguely known that he had a taste for liberty. Through various conversations held in private, he had led others to believe that he would favor the opening up of Spain to a more liberal democracy after forty years under a severe dictatorship. In 1969, during an interview with a journalist on the question of whether a monarchy might be considered an anachronistic institution, Juan Carlos had replied, "One must not forget that in Spain, throughout the centuries, the monarchy has been used to give the state continuity and a symbol of national unity. It can also be affirmed that the integrity of Spain has been in danger only when monarchy has been obscured. It is doubtless this that made Franco think of a monarchical institution to succeed him. When this plan is supported by the people, I believe it is difficult to speak of anachronism. It is a system strongly rooted in history but nevertheless perfectly introduced into the present."

The question about the monarchy's future also disturbed Juan Carlos's father, the count of Barcelona. "If you know how worried

I am, how afraid I am for my son," he exclaimed, "with the Falange who want to crush him, with the Basque terrorists, and now the Sahara. . . ." The legitimate pretender, with sixty-two years of life experience behind him, felt he was better qualified to take on this difficult role than his son, a young man of thirty-seven. During Franco's final agony, when Juan Carlos was shuttling back and forth between the Pardo and Zarzuela Palace, father and son kept in close communication by telephone. "Of course, I gave him advice . . . a father's advice only. But everybody knows we are not in agreement on the means for reestablishing the monarchy. My son believed that he could govern with the existing team—the Arias Navarros, the Solis, the Valcarcels—and slowly democratize the country. I believed otherwise. I said, 'It's necessary to move quickly, very quickly, to proceed to a referendum, to save the Constitution as rapidly as possible.' He would never have rid himself of the *camarillas*. It was necessary to surprise them with speed. He didn't want to understand that." As one of the count of Barcelona's associates said, "The young prince didn't like power, and it was he who was going to reign. The count was dying to reign, and moreover, he was slightly more popular than his son, yet the power eluded him. Life is unfair." Unfair, perhaps, but whose fault was it? As one of his other supporters noted, "He understood too late that the general, from the very first, had placed his chips with the son." But don Juan did know that exile would be a catastrophe for a future king, and for this reason he wanted his son to have a Spanish education in Spain. He did not wish this golden odyssey, this antiquated Spain stuck to the soles of his English shoes, these suitcases that were repacked every three years, this growing old in strange palaces (a Velasquezlike ambiance but without the brocade), and above all the inaction of exile inflicted on his son.

Franco knew exactly what he was doing in isolating the pretender, a mature man, not as easily influenced as his young son. In fact, Franco might have feared more than he wanted to acknowledge the popularity of the pretender.

Franco would periodically announce the restoration of the dynasty and emphasize that Spain was living under a monarchical regime; so don Juan's hope of recovering his ancestors' throne was perfectly justified. Although he was only the third son of Alfonso XIII, the last king of Spain, don Juan was the sole pretender to the throne. His oldest brother, Alfonso, the first prince of Asturias—

the title given to the heir to the throne—had renounced his rights and left for the United States, where he became an automobile salesman. A hemophiliac, he bled to death after an automobile accident in 1938 on a Miami street. The middle son, Jaime, was born a deaf-mute; his speech was an incomprehensible hoot. Encouraged by his father, he renounced his hereditary rights in 1939. Several years later sensationalist newspapers claimed that love had returned don Jaime's voice to him after all kinds of medical treatments had failed. The woman responsible for the miracle was Charlotte Tiedman, a German singer don Jaime met in Rome shortly after his divorce from his first wife. Charlotte Tiedman soon became Her Royal Highness Princess Charlotte de Borbón. Armed with great patience, Charlotte, a faithful and attentive teacher, succeeded in improving her husband's inaudible diction. Proud of the results, Charlotte urged Jaime to reclaim his right to the throne, if only for his descendants. Luckily this feeble attempt had no repercussions. The last son of Alfonso XIII, don Gonzalo, was also a victim of the hemophilia that weighed on the royal house. Only don Juan had escaped this terrible heredity. So the hopes of the monarchists rested with him, the count of Barcelona.

THE COUNT OF BARCELONA was big and physically impressive—six feet two and a half inches tall, muscular, athletic—who lived surrounded by his trophies for tennis, golf, swimming, and skiing, and cups won in international sailing regattas. Don Juan, who was born in the paternal residence of San Ildefonso, dreamed of being a sailor. He was enrolled at the Naval Academy of Cadiz when the coup d'etat of April 14, 1931, deposed King Alfonso XIII. At the time, don Juan was sailing in Saragossa with the cadets of the San Fernando Naval Academy. Brusquely, the instructor interrupted the lesson and called the infante aside. "Your Highness, I have some bad news," he said. The bad news was the victory of the republicans in the elections, the cries of "death to the king" under the palace windows, the flight of Alfonso XIII, the fall of the monarchy, and the exile. Don Juan immediately left for Gibraltar in a small destroyer. When the boat weighed anchor in the British port, the prince saluted the crew that was presenting arms, then walked down the gangplank to the dock and headed for the first store that he saw. Taking off his cadet's uniform, he said simply,

"Let me have a pair of gray flannel slacks and a blue blazer." It was the beginning of the rambling existence of a fallen prince. Faithful to his vocation as a sailor, the count of Barcelona went next to England and entered the Naval Academy at Dartmouth; because he was one of Queen Victoria's descendants (his mother was Princess Ena of Battenberg, great-aunt of the Duke of Edinburgh), he was welcomed with open arms.

Later, as a young officer of the Royal Navy on duty in Sri Lanka, he received a long missive from his father. His older brother don Jaime had renounced his right to succession. Thus, don Juan was heir presumptive to the throne. But he didn't give up navigating the world in the service of Her Gracious British Majesty, or collecting tattoos. (Only Christian X of Denmark, probably the only sovereign tattooed like a denizen of an Asian slum, could compete with him.) Don Juan remained at Dartmouth four years, and they would be the happiest of his life. Discipline there was light compared with the rigidity of Spanish etiquette. He himself once related that during his childhood he was authorized to see his father only twice a day, ten minutes in the morning, ten minutes in the evening, timed by the master of ceremony. After studying at the University of Brussels and then in Florence, he married his cousin, the Infanta Maria-Mercedes de Borbón-Sicile, in 1935. Like all exiled royalty, they roamed from city to city, from one capital to another, spending substantial amounts of time in Rome and Lausanne. In 1947, don Juan decided to move to Estoril, in Portugal, the classic retreat for exiled kings; Umberto of Italy lived in a nearby villa. Moreover, Estoril was only about 125 miles from Spain. The Comte de Paris, pretender to the throne of France, and the Prince Duarte Nuno, who was reclaiming his rights in Portugal, were the other two members of the team of four melancholy would-be kings who met occasionally for a hundred-meter freestyle swim or a game of bridge to pass the long nights. Of the four, don Juan had the best chance of one day regaining his crown.

That same year in Estoril, don Juan heard the caudillo's speech that would determine Spain's new status. However, considering don Juan's rash and inopportune reaction, he did not seem to realize the historical and political potential he himself possessed. "I refuse to associate myself with a false monarchy and to recognize a law voted in by the Cortes, whose members were chosen by Franco and who are not competent to make the decision. Franco's action is simply a face-saving maneuver destined to assure the duration of his power." At this point the tension between the two men was at a peak, and they were at the brink of an irreparable break. In spite of his increasing irritation, Franco made the first conciliatory step. He sent an emissary to don Juan to arrange a meeting. On August 25, 1948, a few miles off the coast of San Sebastian in the Gulf of Gascogne, Franco's yacht, the *Azor,* was approaching the open sea. It appeared to be an ordinary fishing party on a day's outing, the long fishing rods for tuna set out over each side of the rails. A few miles away another vessel, a small cutter called *El Saltillo,* was fighting the waves of the Cantabrian Sea. A strapping fellow, well tanned and well muscled, gripped the helm. When he noticed the Spanish chief of state's white yacht, he gave a curt order to one of his crew, and the banner of the Spanish royal house was hoisted up the main mast. Two men—the athletic prince in yachtsman's garb, the pudgy little general in a white alpaca suit—were soon to meet for the first time. (They knew nothing about each other except for their respective ages; each year the two men exchanged telegrams on their birthdays.)

The top-secret meeting lasted four hours. Although the rivals came to respect each other, neither would budge from his position. However, an accord was achieved which, in plotting the future of don Juan's oldest son, plotted as well the future of Spain: the Infante Juan Carlos would complete his schooling in Spain. Soon after the unusual meeting, don Juan asked his followers not to oppose or campaign in any way against the Fundamental Laws of Succession; for his part, Franco promised to familiarize the country with the dynasty.

Two months after this dialogue, young Juan Carlos de Borbón left his mother, his sisters, and his French governess. The little prince had known nothing but a life of exile. He was born on January 5, 1938, at the Anglo-American Clinic in Rome. Several hours later, he was baptized at the Church of the Master's Palace of the Sovereign Military Order of Malta by Cardinal Eugenio Pacelli, who later became Pope Pius XII. In 1942, the Spanish royal family decided to establish residence at Les Rocailles, an estate in Lausanne, on the shore of Lake Leman. Juanito attended his first school in Switzerland, and later, when his parents moved to Estoril, he was sent to study with the Marianist fathers in Lisbon. At the age of ten, after his father's encounter with Franco, Juanito discovered his country—Spain—for the first time. Accompanied by his "moral guide," Father Zuleta, by the duke of Sotomayer, by José Maria Oriol, and by his younger brother Alfonso, the child took the train from Lisbon to Madrid. A car took the party from the station to Las Jarillas, the property of the Marquis de Urquijo, transformed for the occasion into a strict and well-protected boarding school. Young Juan Carlos was welcomed by eight boys his own age, selected from among the most aristocratic families of Spain. The prince looked very British to them, with his blond hair, blue eyes, and pale complexion, dressed in short pants and a navy blue trench coat. The school schedule resembled that of a standard boarding school—up at 7:30, mass at 8:00, breakfast at 8:45, classes from 9:00 until the 1:00 lunch break. In the afternoon there were various sports activities, followed by classes until 9:30 P.M., when dinner was served. Lights were out at 10:30. Juan Carlos was showered with presents—candy, books, games—sent most often by Spanish dowagers faithful to the monarchy. These gifts were always divided up into nine absolutely equal parts.

Two years later, the young prince, along with his younger brother Alfonso, was sent to San Sebastian. Some people believed that Franco thought the enthusiasm of the monarchists was becoming too cumbersome in Madrid. Others, more practical perhaps, thought it may simply have been time to give the use of the house in Las Jarillas back to its owners. In San Sebastian, the palace lent to them had originally been given by the city to their grandfather. The large residence was soon turned into a school for the young highnesses. It was a strange school that had only two classrooms—one for each of the boys—and sixteen students in all. Five teachers and one priest were in charge of their education, and they were kept to the same sort of rigid schedule that they had grown accustomed to in Madrid: no distractions except for outside reading and sports. A leave from the school could be obtained only through the caudillo's authorization.

In 1952, Juan Carlos was once again living in Madrid at the home of the duke of Montellano and studying at the Institut San Isidro, where discipline was even more strict. His mail was carefully monitored. He was weak in math, stronger in history and languages. Deprived of his youth, Juan Carlos was never able to be a boy like other boys. (Even at the age of seventeen, Juan Carlos had never been to a movie. When Franco learned of this, he himself chose the first film the prince should see: *Bread and Wine,* a highly edifying film.)

An aura of sadness surrounded him, perhaps stemming from the solitude of a life far from his family, and perhaps also from his position as prince and chosen heir, which allowed no room for whims or fantasies. Nevertheless, he was a child who loved to laugh and have fun. It was only in the house in Estoril, where he spent all his vacations, that he discovered moments of true freedom.

The following year Juan Carlos returned to San Sebastian, then soon after went back to Madrid, where he passed his baccalaureate exams with honors. As a reward, the caudillo took him to visit his ancestors' palace, the Palace de Oriente, where don Juan had lived as a child amid the gilt paneling, the frescoes by Tiepolo, the family portraits painted by Goya. The old general served as the young prince's personal guide, giving a brief history of the palace as they went from room to room. Throughout his years of study, this would be the only time Juan Carlos would see Franco.

ON DECEMBER 28, 1954, the second meeting between the count of Barcelona and General Franco took place in the Spanish province of Caceres, near the Portuguese border, on the 123,000-acre estate of the aristocratic Ruisnada family, notorious royalists. The count of Barcelona arrived in Spain at the wheel of his own car. The Portuguese police had elected not to stop the well-tanned man, who was accompanied, as always, by a fox terrier and driving a black Bentley ninety miles an hour on the sunny, winding roads of Portugal. Nothing could slow down this devotee of intense sensations, not even the photographs of his family that his wife, Princess Maria, had stuck to the dashboard. At the border a special detachment presented arms; it was the first time that the head of the royal house had officially returned to his country since 1931. Franco awaited don Juan amid an extraordinary deployment of armored trucks, assault troops, and police. They discussed the further education of Juan Carlos. "A supplementary year of general culture would seem to me to be in order," the count suggested. "In my opinion," replied the general, "it is high time to introduce him to the military arts." "You forget," don Juan insisted, "that travel broadens the young. A stay abroad, at a modern university like

Louvrain in Belgium would give the training necessary to be a contemporary sovereign." Don Juan tried vainly to maintain a certain independence in the face of the caudillo, but the latter controlled the game from the beginning, and didn't intend to lose. "He's going to be seventeen years old. Nothing could be more valuable for him than the ambiance of his own country, given the position that he holds in the dynasty." The decision was without appeal and don Juan knew it. Checkmate to the pretender.

This historic meeting temporarily determined the fate of Juanito: a year of general studies in Madrid, two years at the General Military Academy in Saragossa, a year at the Marine Naval College, a year at the General Air Academy, a degree in economics and political science from Madrid University, traineeships in industry, and finally a training period in the government. Thus was the prince to be occupied until he reached the age of thirty, his constitutional majority. And then . . . then, only Franco knew. Juan Carlos would be king only if Franco wished it. In the meantime, in May 1953, under the command of Lieutenant General Carlos Marinez Campos y Serrano, duke of La Torre, a humorless, inflexible man, the future monarch began his apprenticeship as a cadet at the General Military Academy. His intense period of training would be capped on December 13, 1959, when the titles of infantry lieutenant, ensign, and air force lieutenant were conferred on the young prince.

Meanwhile, a drama that occurred on March 29, 1956, when he was vacationing at the family home in Estoril, would mark Juan Carlos profoundly for the rest of his life. Before dinner one evening, he and his younger brother Alfonso were in the arms room on the third floor of the Villa Geralda cleaning and oiling their guns. A bullet seemed to be stuck in the barrel of Alfonso's new .22 caliber pistol. With a striking lack of caution, he raised the pistol to his eye to see what was blocking the bullet, his fingers resting on the trigger. The gun went off. Alfonso was killed instantly, his head split open before his brother's eyes. The ambulance that was immediately called left empty.

Alfonso's body lay in a chapel set up in a small back salon of the villa. He rested on a bed of precious lace and wore the black outfit of Valencia's Order of St. Galicia. Surrounding him were his parents, his sisters, Maria-Pilar and Margarita, and his brother, Juan Carlos, prostrated with grief. Eighteen-year-old Juan Carlos, traumatized, seriously considered joining a monastery. But destiny had already decided for him.

On March 29, 1960, another meeting was held between Franco and don Juan. As a result a joint communiqué was made public. "Following the mistaken interpretations of Juan Carlos's stay in Spain, particularly from abroad, his excellency the chief of state and the count of Barcelona wish it to be known that the motives for this stay are educational and sentimental; it is natural that Prince Juan Carlos be educated in the atmosphere of his own country, which in no way prejudices the question of succession or the normal transmission of dynastic obligations and responsibilities." In the course of this meeting it was also decided to grant Juan Carlos, prince of Asturias, a house in Madrid: Zarzuela Palace. The choice was significant: the palace is situated in the domain of the Pardo where General Franco lived. But in fact Juan Carlos didn't live there until after his marriage.

On September 13, 1961, in Athens 101 cannons were fired from Mt. Lycabette. In the absence of his father, King Paul of Greece, Prince Constantine announced over the radio the engagement of his oldest sister, Princess Sofia, to the probable heir to the Spanish crown, Prince Juan Carlos de Borbón. General Franco was informed at the same time as the press: once again, don Juan wanted to flaunt his independence vis-à-vis the caudillo. From Lausanne, where the two families were gathered at the home of his mother, Queen Victoria-Eugenia, don Juan telephoned to Pazo de Las Meiras, the chief of state's summer residence. From there he was put in touch with the *Azor,* on which Franco was cruising. An aide-de-camp ran up to the bridge and told the general: "The count of Barcelona is calling you from Switzerland. It's urgent." The telephone connection was a poor one, but don Juan managed to explain that his oldest son was engaged. "Excuse me a moment," Franco replied. Somewhat surprised, the count of Barcelona waited. Ten, fifteen, twenty minutes passed with no one at the other end of the line. Exasperated, don Juan gave the receiver to his secretary. After an extremely long time, General Franco returned to the telephone. He recited, in a trembling voice, the congratulations he had left to compose. As a commentator at the time said, "It was then, for Franco, a historic moment, and for every Spaniard worthy of the name an historic moment means an historic speech."

THE FIANCÉS had met for the first time in August 1954, during what was called "the Cruise of Kings" on the 5,000-ton floating palace *The Agamemnon*. Organized by Queen Frederika of Greece, it was conceived as a sort of floating matchmaking service for the princes and princesses of Europe. Three hundred members of the top European aristocracy accepted; only Queen Elizabeth decided not to send a member of her family, even though her husband was born a prince of Greece. The "royal vacation colony" did not spawn a romance between Sofia of Greece and Juan Carlos of Spain. Both were only sixteen years old at the time and more interested in the extraordinary luxury of the boat and the thousand distractions it offered.

The years passed, and the two young people had grown up by the time they saw each other for the second time in England at the marriage of the turbulent duke of Kent. And who was Sofia's assigned escort? Prince Juan Carlos, naturally. Chiefs of protocol often have the skills of clever sleuths. People talked afterward of a thunderbolt, flashes of passion, intimate looks, lightly touching hands. The young prince was invited to Mon Repos, the villa of the Greek sovereigns in Corfu, so that he could sail in some regattas with his "friend" Constantine. Happily, Princess Sofia and Prince Juan Carlos, both good pupils with a profound sense of duty, adopted the attitude everyone expected of them and declared "their love."

The Greeks were deeply moved, since their little princess was going to leave them. The Spaniards were satisfied; the prince had made a good choice. Princess Sofia's family tree included two German emperors, eight Danish kings, five Swedish kings, seven Russian czars, a king and queen of Norway, a queen of England, and five kings of Greece.

At her birth in Athens on November 2, 1938, after a traditional twenty-one-cannon salute, the crowd surrounding Psychico Palace began chanting, "Sofia, Sofia"—the name of her grandmother, a Prussian princess and wife of Constantine I. The family yielded to the people's wish, and quite willingly, since the name Sofia means wisdom. In April 1941, when Sofia was two and a half years old, the Italians invaded Greece, closely followed by the Germans. Athens was bombed. Princess Frederika and her children, Sofia and

Constantine, then one year old, embarked for Crete to join King George II and their father, Prince Paul, the king's brother. They soon moved on to Egypt, then to South Africa. From 1941 to 1956, Princess Frederika, most of the time separated from her husband, changed her residence twenty-two times with her three children (her second daughter, Princess Irene, arrived to enlarge the family circle in 1942). In the autumn of 1946 they returned to Greece; less than six months later King George II died of a heart attack and his brother Paul mounted the throne. Princess Sofia became the daughter of a king. But family life hardly changed: the family moved to Tatoï, a large turn-of-the-century house constructed to George I's specifications in the middle of a pine forest.

For Sofia, these were the happiest years of her life. At thirteen she was sent to Salem, an esteemed German boarding school whose director, George of Hanover, was Frederika's brother. The discipline there was extremely strict. The similarities in the early lives of Juan Carlos and Sofia are striking: both experienced exile in early childhood, followed by a strict educational environment far from home. These circumstances are coupled with the fact that neither Prince Paul nor the count of Barcelona was first in line to reign; only death and illness changed the course of events for both. When she returned to Athens, Sofia was an accomplished young lady, ready to assume her responsibilities as a king's daughter. She was aware of her duties as a Greek royal princess, and she took on the role perfectly, as she would later on when she became the queen of Spain. Sofia's progress to this point was immensely satisfying to Queen Frederika, who did not like having her orders challenged or her long-term plans diverted.

THE DATE AND PLACE of the marriage were set. The ceremony would be celebrated in Athens on May 14, 1962. The only shadow over the marriage was that the princess was Greek Orthodox and the prince was Catholic. His Holiness Pope John XXIII granted them a special dispensation, lifting the ban on the union of a couple of different religions. (Sofia converted to Catholicism during her honeymoon, in a ceremony that took place in Corfu in the presence of the Catholic Archbishop of Athens. A future queen of Spain could only be a Catholic.) Meanwhile, wedding preparations were feverishly being made in Athens. The capital was transformed into a construction site since the Greeks (or rather the queen) didn't want to be ashamed of the city. Athens had a complete facelift, even though the government was less than happy with the drain on its funds. The Bank of Greece, situated opposite the Church of St. Denis, was requisitioned to serve as a grandstand for some three thousand Spanish guests. On the big day they would thus be in a prime position to watch the nuptial procession. Yachts moored in Piraeus were also requisitioned, since there was not a single hotel room left in the capital. King Paul chartered two Constellation jets to transport royal guests to Athens. There was no stinting on the quality of service; after all, in principle a daughter is married off only once. Since neither of the two planes was stopping over in Lisbon, the groom's father would disembark from his little sailboat in Piraeus after a voyage of several days.

On May 14, at eight o'clock in the morning, five cannons sounded, announcing the start of the ceremonies. Already, all along the main streets tens of thousands of people were gathered; Spaniards were in the majority near the Catholic church, while around the Greek Orthodox cathedral, the Metropolis, Greeks were predominant. One hour later, the first official limousines began arriving in front of the Church of St. Denis, preceded by white-shirted motorcycle police. Positions at windows along the parade route had been sold out months earlier. Places along the promenades, in the hours preceding the ceremony, were being sold for 1,000 drachmas apiece. Clusters of humanity clung to the tops of street lamps, while thousands of others, people who had been waiting since dawn, sat on folding chairs and benches, holding little flags and balloons—some in red and yellow, the colors of Spain, others in blue and white, the Greek national colors—that would be released as the procession passed.

The sun was hot. Before the ceremony had even begun, there were thirty faintings and one death. Then a murmur rippled through the crowd, "Natous, natous"—"There they are, there they are." Preceded by an officer and six buglers on horseback, a long car carrying Queen Frederika, resplendent in a gold lamé gown, and the count of Barcelona, slowly came into view. Consistent with her roles as queen and mother of the bride, both of which she truly loved, Frederika waved with one hand and wiped away tears with the other. Suddenly the crowd's murmur grew louder: the royal carriage was approaching drawn by six white horses mounted by equerries in navy blue uniforms and accompanied, also on horseback, by the Master of the Horse on the left and Crown Prince Constantine on the right. The palace marshal had almost had heart failure when Constantine expressed the desire to ride along with the royal team; it was a breach of protocol. The queen had begged him not to do it. The king had grumbled, but his son would not relent: "It's that or nothing. My sister is my teammate for regattas; she's my best friend. I am going to accompany her on horseback; it's my wedding present."

King Paul was in the dress uniform of the marshal of the Greek army. When the carriage approached the church, an immense clamor erupted under the Greek heavens; the cheers were endless. (The carriage had been constructed and designed for the triumphal entry into Paris, in 1875, of the man who would have been called Henry V, count of Chambord. But he never became king of France, and the Greek sovereigns had purchased the vehicle.) In front of the church the king stepped out, followed by the princess, smiling beneath her eleven-foot tulle and lace veil, which her mother had worn for her own marriage. Sofia wore a simple gown of white organdy designed by Greek couturier Jean Dessès. Her eighteen-foot train was carried by six maids of honor dressed in robes of silver silk gauze with pink, blue, turquoise, and yellow bodices. A few seconds after his fiancée appeared, Prince Juan Carlos, in the khaki uniform of a lieutenant in the Spanish army, arrived with his mother, who was dressed in salmon pink.

The interior of the church was blanketed with roses and red and yellow carnations. The Catholic Archbishop of Athens, Monsignor Printisi, wearing white and gold vestments and holding his miter on his head, moved toward the young couple waiting before the altar. He posed the ritual question in Greek to Sofia and in Spanish to Juan Carlos. Then, to the strains of Handel, the bride and groom left the church, passing under the arch formed by the swords of Spanish officers from three branches of the armed services, sent by Franco's government. The boom of twenty-one cannons from Mt. Lycabette proclaimed to the Athenians that their princess had become, before God, the wife of the "very Catholic" Infante don Juan Carlos de Borbón. This time the newlyweds were together in the gilded carriage that slowly retraced its earlier route to the sound of cheers and a barrage of flowers tossed from balconies. Back at the palace they rested for a short interval, and then it was time to leave for the long Byzantine ceremony.

The princess arrived at the Greek Orthodox cathedral on her

On her wedding day in Athens, Sofia waves to the cheering crowd from her glittering carriage. (Sygma)

father's arm, since in the eyes of the Greeks she was still not married. Monsignor Chrysostomos, primate of Greece, awaited her under the portal and presented her with a copy of the Bible. The princess bent to lightly kiss the holy book. The vast nave of the Metropolis was decorated from top to bottom with more than 30,000 red roses, which wound around the columns, filled immense vases, and covered the walls. The ceremony began with the couple exchanging their rings three times according to Greek ritual, with the *koumbaros,* or godfather—on this occasion King Paul—conducting the exchange. It was also the king who held the crowns of the Greek royal house above the heads of the bride and groom during the marriage ceremony. (These two crowns, usually exhibited at the George I Museum, are masterpieces of Russian goldsmithing; they have been in the Greek royal family for many years.) Finally came the traditional dance of Isaiah, which the newlyweds executed by three times circling a table full of candy that they would toss to guests; in turn the guests, as tradition dictated, showered the couple with rose petals and rice, symbols of happiness. Each guest had a small pouch of rice in his pocket. In all, 220 pounds of rice were scattered in the church and in the streets.

Already twice married, Sofia and Juan Carlos went on to one of the salons in the royal palace to sign the register for their third marriage, this one civil, in the presence of the mayor of Athens and the president of the State Council. Finally, a sumptuous lunch reunited the newlyweds and their 150 distinguished guests. The couple left the festivities before the dessert, and departed for Glyphaia. That evening they drifted peacefully aboard the luxurious black yacht lent to them by Greek shipper Stavros Niarchos.

Although this princely marriage made most of Europe's aristocrats happy, since they could all see and be seen at the event, the grandiose spectacle did not please everybody. Up to that point most of the Greeks had been fond of their queen, whom they nicknamed Friki, but some Greeks now felt that Frederika had overdone it in marrying off her daughter. It was she, they said, who pushed King Paul into asking Parliament to endow Princess Sofia, who was presented as a sort of Cinderella of marriageable princesses. Parliament needed heavy persuading, but making the best of a difficult situation (or in a gesture of good faith) the government finally agreed to part with 9 million drachmas, about $30,000. To Frederika, nothing seemed too fine, too splendid for the showcasing of the Greek court. She wanted her daughter's marriage to be as well executed and as spectacular as Queen Elizabeth of England's, which she had attended in 1947. It was indeed. Frederika was delighted, as evidenced by her extravagant description of her son-in-law shortly after the wedding: "Juanito is incredibly handsome; he has curly blond hair, which he doesn't particularly like, but which ladies 'of a certain age' like me adore. He has dark eyes and long lashes; he's tall, athletic, and plays on his charm at will. But what is more important: he is intelligent, he has modern ideas, he is full of goodness and kindness. He's proud enough to be a true Spaniard, yet at the same time he possesses enough tender understanding to pardon others their shortcomings." Here, then, was an ideal son-in-law, especially considering that he also had a kingdom at his fingertips.

Sofia and Juan Carlos did not move into Zarzuela Palace, once the hunting lodge of Philip V in the eighteenth century, until nine months after their marriage. It was first necessary to restore the building, which had been partially destroyed during the Spanish Civil War.

FROM 1962 TO 1969—a period of uncertainty—Sofia would bear three great trials and experience three great joys. In 1962, she underwent an emergency appendectomy during her second month of pregnancy and had to give up her hopes, at least for that year, of being a mother.

But on Sunday May 3, 1963, a communiqué from the office of the count of Barcelona announced what all of Spain had been hoping for: a happy event was anticipated before Christmas. Elena Maria Isabella Dominica de Silos was born on December 20 at Neustra Señora de Loreto Clinic. At her bedside Sofia had the joy of having with her not only Juanito, her sister Princess Irene, and Queen Frederika, but also King Paul, on what would be his last visit abroad. Three days later a Te Deum mass of thanks was celebrated at the Church of San Jeronimo el Real, where in 1906 King Alfonso XIII had married Princess Victoria-Eugenia of Battenberg. The baptism, significantly, was celebrated at the Zarzuela, in the presence of General Franco, Mrs. Franco, and the count and countess of Barcelona. The latter held her granddaughter during the baptismal rites.

The following March King Paul died of stomach cancer. Three years later, a military coup d'etat would force young King Constantine to abandon his throne for exile, and Sofia would be profoundly affected by her brother's defeat. In the meantime, when Juanito announced to her on June 13, 1965, that "God has given us another daughter," Sofia burst into tears. She had been hoping for a son; it seemed that Franco was only awaiting the arrival of an heir to the Borbón dynasty before he would make some important decisions. All the same, Christian Frederika Victoria Antonia de la Santisima Trinidad was well received.

The historic moment finally arrived on January 30, 1968, when baby Felipe uttered his first cry. Juan Carlos immediately called his parents, who were in Miami, and then dialed the Pardo.

On February 8, the day of Felipe's baptism, Sofia fully realized the still very important place that the Borbóns occupied in Spanish hearts. For this special occasion, Queen Victoria-Eugenia was authorized to return to Spain to baptize her great-grandson. She had not been back in her country since 1931. Her welcome was delirious. The count of Barcelona, who went to greet his mother at the airport, was overwhelmed by cheers of "Viva don Juan," while the queen was wildly applauded and cheered with shouts of "Viva la Reina." Felipe Juan Pablo Alfonso de Todos los Santos was baptized by the capital's archbishop, don Casimiro Morcillo. Present were not only the families of Juan Carlos and Franco but also those of the king of Bulgaria and the vice president of the government, Admiral Carrero Blanco, as well as other distinguished Spanish personalities. It was a national event that portended a royal future. Now it seemed that nothing would stop the ascent to the throne of Sofia and Juan Carlos.

Around this time, Sofia was deeply distressed by the waves of criticism breaking over Queen Frederika. The queen was reproached for acting as a behind-the-scenes adviser and for devoting all her efforts, since the death of King Paul, to her daughter's royal future. Queen Frederika had been closely linked with General and Mrs. Franco until problems of protocol arose between them, notably during baby Felipe's baptism. Her visits to Spain became so resented that Franco himself had to intervene to "advise" her to space her visits more widely apart and to shorten her stays at the Zarzuela. This polite but firm reproval and semibanishment seemed to change the former queen of Greece. Everything she once desired—honors, money, jewels, politics, power—no longer held any interest for her. Only the search for Truth helped her forget her disappointments. This mystic side of her led her to India. There she lived garbed in a cotton sari and sandals in a Calcutta ashram, ecstatic before the wisdom of a guru. Her young daughter Irene, controlled by her mother all her life, followed her in this same path for several years before returning to Europe. Frederika died in 1981 at Madrid Hospital, where she had been admitted for a simple eyelid operation, her life cut short by a bad reaction to anesthesia. Throughout her life, Frederika had been under the sway of her iron temperament and her need to talk too much. General de Gaulle is said to have remarked privately about her, "She's a pleasant person, not bad physically, intelligent, but what a blunderer!"

Juan Carlos was also having his problems: his father, as heir to Alfonso XIII, should legitimately have been the next king of Spain. But was it not Franco's will to ignore the father in favor of elevating his son to the first rank? Since the marriage of Sofia and Juan Carlos, his intention had been manifestly clear. In fact, just before his departure for his wedding in Athens, Juan Carlos had received from Franco the necklace of Charles III, an honor normally reserved only for reigning monarchs. Given their delicate situation, the couple led a discreet life, striving not to offend anyone's sensibilities.

On January 5, 1968, when Prince Juan Carlos celebrated his thirtieth birthday, the minimum age for assuming the throne, the familiar Spanish sky was once again cloudless. At the last minute, the princely couple decided to go off to Estoril, the Portuguese residence of the count and countess of Barcelona. Many found this action significant and believed that Juan Carlos wanted to demonstrate that he pretended to be nothing more than the heir to don Juan, his father, head of the Spanish royal house and unquestionably the titular head of the dynasty. Juan Carlos greatly admired and respected his father. He once declared to a journalist, rather imprudently as it turns out, considering the subsequent course of events: "There cannot be any problems between my father and me. Dynastic laws exist and no one can do anything about them. Never would I accept to reign while my father was still living: he is the king. If I am here, it is so that the dynasty can be represented in Spain while my father is in Portugal." In the dramatic moral crisis that faced Juan Carlos, when he had to choose between his filial love, his dynastic loyalty, and his attachment for General Franco, he opted for the throne out of the sense of duty his education had instilled in him rather than out of enthusiasm. His advisers and his entourage all contended that it was in the best interests of Spain.

For years Juan Carlos was the sole representative of the monarchy at the chief of state's side in Madrid. Nothing more. He played no official role. Nevertheless, he occasionally received up to thirty dignitaries a day from the worlds of politics, diplomacy, economics, and finance. "For a politician," explained Juan Carlos, "the craft of king is a vocation, since he loves power. For the son of a king, like me, it's another affair entirely. The question is not knowing if I like it or do not like it; I am born to it. And, since my childhood, my teachers have taught me to do the things I do not like as well as those I do. Among the Borbóns to be king is a profession." But, in private, the prince talked openly of the restraints. Princess Sofia, who had received a similar education, offered a parallel view: "The question is not whether he desired it or not, because, in any case, he was born to become king. His ancestors ruled over Spain for more than two centuries. How could he not have a dynastic sense?" In 1969, just before his nomination, Juan Carlos had a talk with his father in order to decide what position to take. "If you forbid me to accept the succession, I'll pack my bags and leave with Sofia and the children. I couldn't stay at the Zarzuela. I've never instigated any kind of intrigue so that the designation would fall to me. What should I do, refuse? It would have been better had it been you; but it's Franco who decides, so that's how it is." "Try to work it so that the decision is made later," don Juan replied. "This is not in my power, and if, as I believe, I am offered succession, what are you going to do? Is there another solution?" The discussion arrived at an impasse, and the prince could still not determine what his father's attitude really was.

On July 12, 1969, Franco received the prince and told him he was going to name him as his successor. Everything had been done in the greatest secrecy. Juan Carlos affirmed to Franco that he was there to serve his country. On July 23, his succession was announced at a public ceremony with no member of the royal family in attendance.

With regard to the enactment of the Laws of Succession, it is interesting to note the following points:

1. The monarchy was not being restored but newly established. The prince, descended from kings who had ruled over Spain for centuries, would be the first of a line. This Franco emphasized to him in the exact terms he had used since 1947, when the Laws of Succession were enacted: "The royalty that we are establishing owes nothing to the past. It is only when the crown has been set on the prince's head that the regular order of succession will begin." Don Juan was forgotten, and the new monarchy would begin with Juan Carlos I. "Thus we will put an end," Franco brusquely added, "to all the speculation and the vain intrigue of some political groups [the don Juanistes]."

2. As a consequence of Franco's solution to dynastic continuity, Juan Carlos took the unusual title of prince of Spain and not prince of Asturias, the traditional title in the Spanish royal family. The nuance was important. At his presentation to Parliament, the future king would swear fidelity to the chief of state, to the principles of the Movimiento, and to the Fundamental Laws as they had been established by the regime. But he also added, "I am part of the direct line of the royal house of Spain, and I aspire to be the worthy successor to those who have preceded me."

3. Franco did not intend to make Juan Carlos king until he himself was gone. "The prince will have the status of heir, which will permit him to round out his training at my side, and also to perfect his knowledge of national problems." From the Laws of Succession on, the prince would always be by Franco, but he would try to be as little noticed as possible.

4. General Franco felt obliged to stress many times over the absolutely legal character, according to him, of the proposal he submitted to the Cortes. The "traditional, Catholic, social and representative" monarchy—namely, his regime—had twice, with an interval of twenty years, been approved by referendum with a 90 percent majority. If the decision to name an heir was not taken earlier, asserted the chief of state, it was because the institutional structure had not been refined and because it had first been necessary for him to form a definitive judgment on the character and personality of his successor. It was because he was "aware of his responsibility before God and before history" that he was finally able to render his decision. One after the other, the members of the Cortes declared themselves either for or against the Laws of Succession. Results of the ballot: 491 votes in favor, 19 against, and 9

abstentions. Among those opposed were two Juan Carlists, a few monarchist supporters of don Juan, and many Falangists deeply hostile to kingship. Juan Carlos and Sofia were henceforth the second-ranked figures in the state. Speculation on succession finally came to an end.

FROM THIS DAY FORWARD the princely family was to live in the limelight, their daily activities part of the daily news. Everyone wondered what the future would bring. The prince and his family tried to remain as discreet as possible in order not to compromise this future. He used all the resources of his navigational art not to favor either the Opus Dei or the Falange; he did not want, later on, to be king of any political party. During an official trip to the United States he told a journalist, "During my reign, the military will have a less important role than they have had up to the present." He added, "I believe that the people want more liberties. The problem is to know at what speed we can accord them."

He wanted to be a twentieth-century king and to win the hearts of those who should have been closest to him and who were, in fact, his greatest adversaries: the students. On March 12, 1970, before an audience of young people, Juan Carlos forcefully affirmed, "I will never be a dam that contains, but rather a channel along which one can move forward methodically: it is a king of our times that I one day hope to be. If someone tried to reestablish the monarchy such as it was forty years ago," he went on, "it would be overthrown in two hours. I know that many Spaniards are not enthusiastic toward kingship. We must make them change their minds by showing them what it is, and what I am."

In fact, who was this man formed in the best military schools of Spain and constantly controlled by a strict and unforgiving discipline? What kind of personality was hidden within the man with the immobile features, this man laced into his military uniform, always photographed from the front, his head held high, the look steady? Some people thought that behind this imposing stature, behind this apparently empty blue stare, he was hiding nothing. Nothing he said or did betrayed the least bit of personality. He may have seemed indifferent, but in fact Juan Carlos wanted above all to remain in the shadows, unnoticed, to avoid compromising himself with General Franco and the orthodox Francoists. He limited his appearances in their company to the exigencies of protocol, all the while trying to avoid giving his actions the least significance or emotion. Never would he hold out his arm in a salute, never would he sing "Cara al Sol" (Face to the Sun), the Falangist hymn. He could not reveal, either, the basis of his true thinking—a monarchy, yes, but for democracy. During his long purgatory, everything incited him to caution. It was evident that the young prince did not believe that a king of Spain could ever be a symbol as in the Nordic countries or in England.

Personally he would prefer to stay in the background and govern through his prime minister and his government. In a conversation at the Zarzuela, the prince did not hide his liberalizing intentions: "It is all in the laws; everything is in the Spanish constitution. But the possibilities have never actually been exploited. At least not yet. It's possible to advance to an authentic liberalization starting from the Fundamental Laws. That, in any case, is my personal conviction. There is no reason, for example, to be afraid of the press. We should, in our situation, draw inspiration from our European neighbors . . . but it's also wise to be careful. Not everything can be done today or tomorrow. But I believe it's necessary to adapt oneself to circumstance, to march to the beat of one's own time, to listen to the youth. It is one of my principal concerns. I believe I am tuned in to the young Spanish generations who have never known civil war. I belong to this segment of society born after the conflict: so does 60 percent of the Spanish population. They are the majority. They do not want to concern themselves with the quarrels and rancors of the civil war. Their stakes are in the future. Modernize, that is the key word. I am still friendly with the captains and the majors that I knew throughout various stages of my military training in three armed services. I see them from time to time, or they call me. They advise me, encourage me, spur me ahead. . . . The colonels, the generals, they're another matter. . . ."

And then, on November 22, 1975, the prince was king. Juan Carlos I realized that time was not necessarily working for the monarchy. Some people predicted a split-second regime, uprisings, and an abdication without glory. But in just a few months Juan Carlos, with the support of his people and the political parties, would bring back democracy. Today, for a majority of the Spanish

Felipe is ready for a pony ride while Elena (*left*) and Christina (*right*) wait their turn. (Spanish Embassy, Paris)

Opposite bottom: A quiet evening at home playing parlor games. (Embassy of Spain, Washington, D.C.)

Juan Carlos I became king solely at the will of General Franco and is now one of the most powerful monarchs in Europe. (Spanish Embassy, Paris)

Sofia, the daughter of former King Paul and Queen Frederika of Greece. She and Juan Carlos first met when they were both fourteen years old. (Spanish Embassy, Paris)

youth, the king now represents "the only true democrat in the country." On the European scale, what happened in Madrid was very important. Behind the Sadat-Begin meetings were aspirations. Behind the accords of Juan Carlos with the opposition were realities.

In 1976, when Juan Carlos replaced Arias Navarro, the old Francoist at the head of the government, with a young centrist, Adolfo Suarez, disapproval was widespread, as much among the conservative old guard as among the liberals. Abroad, the majority of opinion wrongly interpreted this decision as the death knell for Spain's democratic hopes. "Everybody was against me," the sovereign recalled. "One of my childhood friends telephoned me that same day to tell me, 'You just chucked the monarchy out the window.'" In response, the king asked his friend to give him twenty days to prove him wrong. "Even my best friends often mistook my intentions."

At the end of twenty days, he had already redeemed himself with the reestablishment of the political parties and the syndicates, the announcement of general legislative elections for June 1977 (the first in forty-one years), and the proposed policy of regional autonomies. The reason for his success? Juan Carlos explains it by crediting the political maturity and wisdom of the Spanish people. But the king also recognizes the value of decisiveness and rapid execution. He doesn't play on "the solitude of power," but he knows how to skillfully protect the independence of his power. Juan Carlos believes not in repression but in reforms; he believes not in revolution but in democratic evolution.

TO SUCCESSFULLY CARRY OFF this democratic evolution, of which, as sovereign, he holds himself to be the trustee, the king works twelve hours a day. Every morning, he arises between six and seven o'clock. After half an hour of exercise, followed by a bath, the king dresses. English-style breakfast is taken with his family between 7:00 and 7:30: fried eggs with sausages and ham, orange juice, toast, and light coffee. At eight o'clock, the king is in his office, situated in a private annex of Zarzuela Palace. There, his press attaché hands him a résumé of the day's news and a pile of newspapers with articles or passages of interest circled or underlined in red. The king receives all the Madrid and Barcelona newspapers as well as the most important papers from each of Spain's major cities. He reads French and English papers in the original. (Juan Carlos is extremely gifted in languages: he speaks French and English fluently, gets along well in Italian and Portuguese, and has a working knowledge of German and Greek.) He then spends about half an hour signing important papers and urgent letters. At ten o'clock, the parade of ministers begins. Disliking the barriers of protocol, his majesty always welcomes his visitors standing up and cordially shakes their hands. He has the sincere simplicity of the Bourbons in his relations with others, and always appears affable and attentive.

Lunch never takes place before two o'clock. In general, the royal couple take this light meal *à deux* since the children eat at school. The menu varies little from day to day: steak or other red meat, a salad and fruit; in the evening, the repast is hardly more exciting, with fish or an omelet replacing the grilled meat. Wine is almost never served, and the coffee after the meal is never strong. When the king is not in one of his periods where he has resolved to give up smoking, he delights in lighting up a Celtas (a brown cigarette, the only kind he likes), after carefully removing the filter, to his friends' great amusement. Sometimes in the afternoon Juan Carlos and Sofia take a short stroll in the gardens accompanied by their dogs, or if the weather is not accommodating, they watch some television before returning to their duties.

At four o'clock, the king is back in his office, where every day a few more papers, a few more petitions, a few more complaints arrive. If he has an official meeting or trip on his schedule, he writes his own speeches. His workday extends to the evening news at nine o'clock, which he never misses, thanks to a small television installed next to his desk. Later in the evening he is still answering the ever-abundant mail that arrives at the palace every day in two huge postal sacks. The mail runs the gamut from official letters to solicitations, to demands for audiences or money, to complaints or congratulations. All requests are transmitted by his office to competent organizations in order to verify their legitimacy. It is also in the evening that the king prefers to hold less formal audiences and private visits, since the mornings are given over to more thorny problems. Dinner is called for ten o'clock, with the children and the queen. Often the family reunion stretches out to eleven o'clock, when the children retire. Once the children are in their beds, the parents go up to kiss them good night. Returning to the living room, the king indulges in some reading, always very serious works on law, history, economics, or politics—or almost always, since the king doesn't disdain an occasional good novel, especially when it's a best seller. Sofia listens to music, her passion. The queen is so fond of music that a network of loudspeakers has been installed all over the palace, even in the kitchens. She is president of the National Orchestra of Madrid, and she herself plays the piano.

In spite of his extremely heavy schedule, the king, for whom sports are extremely important, always sets aside an hour during the day, in addition to his morning exercises, to play squash. Saturdays and Sundays are devoted to the family, to horseback riding, to tennis, and to skiing in the winter, in the mountains of Guadarrama, a few miles from Madrid, where the whole family lines up for the ski lift right along with their subjects. Juan Carlos is also a fine shot, and hunting remains one of his favorite pastimes. Often when he has the time he gets into his helicopter and goes to hunt near Toledo at the estate of his cousin, the duke of Calabria. In the summer, Juan Carlos and Sofia take a month's vacation at Marivent, a palace near Palma de Majorca, where they love to sail.

Queen Sofia spends a great part of her time answering the numerous letters she receives. She is involved, like other queens, with the Red Cross and with various charitable organizations, including one for the handicapped. Beyond her official and domestic obligations, the queen takes courses in philosophy and contemporary culture at the University of Madrid. Sofia is also a familiar figure in the Madrid boutiques. She never buys her dresses from the major foreign couturiers, preferring the simplicity and low prices of the Spanish designers.

Daily life at the Zarzuela might resemble the life of any family of the Spanish upper-middle class if it were not for the heavy surveillance and security that surrounds it. To enter into the "park" of the Pardo, where the Zarzuela is located, it is necessary to cross two barriers set up by extremely vigilant police before arriving at the palace. The area is thick with military, civil, and police troops, and the entire park is enclosed by high fences topped with barbed wire. A king's security is not to be taken lightly, yet the royal couple are sometimes seen dining in a restaurant or strolling in the street with no protection whatsoever.

People even remember that the lone motorcyclist who sometimes appeared in Madrid dressed in black leather with matching boots and gloves and full helmet, and who gunned the motor of his large Japanese motorcycle on the Calle José Antonio, was none other than his majesty Juan Carlos. At the time, the government and the politicians frowned on this sort of escapist fantasy. The stakes were much too high—the whole future of Spain. "Everything is secured, and well secured," the caudillo used to say regarding his succession. But a sudden, accidental disappearance of Juan Carlos would plunge Spain into a grave constitutional crisis. Juan Carlos had never been able to convince Franco to name an heir to follow him. "Baby Felipe," the prince confided bitterly then, "is not the official heir of the dynasty."

Herein lay a great weakness of the Constitution: Juan Carlos, named by Franco, and confirmed by the Cortes, had no officially designated heir. At that point, no one in politics could ignore the fact that the republican concept was still very much alive. Juan Carlos knew it. On May 15, 1977, during a private and very moving ceremony at Zarzuela Palace, the count of Barcelona, the only legitimate heir of Alfonso XIII, renounced his rights to the crown, thus permitting, according to the Laws of Succession, the oldest of his grandsons to be officially named prince of Asturias—heir to the Spanish throne—on November 1 of that year. Poor Franco. The only failure in his career was not being able to obtain in his lifetime don Juan's abdication. And although the generalissimo had done everything he could to separate father and son, these two, in spite of appearances of total discord and in spite of several very real cool periods, were no less Borbón or less in league with each other because of it.

Madrid political circles used an incisive formula in discussing Juan Carlos: "The army wanted him, the people accepted him, the parties acknowledged him."

As time went on, the king asserted himself without hesitation, when necessary, all the time conserving the role of arbitrator that he deemed his own; occasionally he descended into the arena to show that he was on the side of those who wished for a rapid but controlled democratization of Spain. This was notably the case during his trips to Catalonia and Andalusia, and later to Asturias. Contrary to General Franco, who was always isolated from the public by his guards during official visits to the provinces, Juan Carlos willingly gave himself over to the crowds. The Spanish were impressed by his physical courage; his open and approachable attitude had paid off.

Juan Carlos seemed to have won the match—all the more convincingly too when, on June 15, 1977, the first elections in forty-one years were held, a striking accomplishment for the king. A referendum approved the setting up of a bicameral parliamentary regime. It was a total and dazzling victory, particularly since observers throughout the world had given the monarchy almost no chance of success, let alone survival. "The sad prince," "the great booby," "the good boy," "Juanito," "the caudillo's heir," "Juan Carlos the Brief"—Juan Carlos Alfonso Victor Maria de Borbón I, eighth king of the Borbón dynasty, thirty-seventh king of Castille, thirty-sixth king of Aragon, fifty-second king of Navarro, thirty-eighth king of Granada, twenty-eighth king of Valencia, Galicia, and Toledo, had borne all these nicknames with a stoic and very Borbón silence. Today Spain is no longer scorned by Western nations, including those that had been notably cool to Juan Carlos's accession.

ON JANUARY 29, 1981, Adolfo Suarez, the head of the government chosen by the king, resigned. Scarcely one month later, on February 23, at around 6:30 P.M., a long and rather gloomy session of Parliament suddenly turned chaotic when soldiers burst through the chamber brandishing pistols. A right-wing faction of the military was attempting to topple the government. Armored tanks were on their way to the capital with orders to invade all the ministries, the radio and television stations, and the newspaper offices. And only one man among all the Spanish had the resources and the prestige to end this coup d'état: the king. All through the night Juan Carlos was on the telephone calling his forces together, relying on their loyalty to him and to the regime to help restore democracy to Spain. By dawn, the situation was well in hand: all military personnel had returned to their barracks and the Cortes resumed its session. Juan Carlos had once again saved the democracy.

Nothing illustrates better the diversity of the royal function than Juan Carlos's brilliant career. He is one of the few monarchs to have been invested with real power and yet he renounced most of his prerogatives. Nonetheless, the king of Spain is still one of the most powerful in Europe. By his courage and by his refusal to align himself too closely with any party, he continues to remain above the fray and in doing so strengthens his position as arbiter. If Juan Carlos succeeds in holding on to his position as the "great mediator," and if he manages to eliminate the terrorism that is sweeping his country, his son don Felipe may indeed fulfill his destiny as the king of Spain.

7

HOLLAND

◆

Through Mystics and Scandals,
a Monarchy Endures

The monarchy of Holland is full of paradoxes. With its well-kept streets, its charming houses with flower-filled window boxes, and its precise, melancholy canals designed by a romantic surveyor, Holland is a land of decency and tranquillity, and above all of self-control. Yet its sovereigns have sometimes shown a sad lack of the three attributes. The reigning family, the Orange-Nassaus, is more popular today than ever, despite a century of scandals, calamities, quarrels, rocky marriages, angry antimonarchical demonstrations, and endless misalliances.

Created by William of Orange (William the Silent) in 1544 to be ruled by "wise and strong men," this dynasty has produced, since the death of William III in 1890, only women. Holland is an austere country where the home, with its strong family ties, is the cornerstone of existence; yet the marriages of its sovereigns, from Queen Wilhelmina's pathetic alliance with Duke Henri of Mecklenburg-Schwerin to Queen Juliana's hardly less disastrous marriage to Prince Bernhard zu Lippe-Biesterfeld, have been marked by chronic misunderstandings and bitter disagreements and have frequently come within a hair's breadth of official separation.

Henri openly complained more than once about the hard lot of a prince consort. On the birth of his daughter Juliana in 1909, he commented to the prime minister, after hearing the cannons fire fifty-one times, "What a shame it's a girl!" When the prime minister assured him that the Dutch people would be happy to see another woman succeed Queen Wilhelmina, Henri answered, "I wasn't thinking about that, but rather about the poor man who will one day become the prince consort." This "poor man" was to be Prince Bernhard, who would stretch the limits of unorthodox royal behavior to undreamed-of dimensions.

The paradoxes of the monarchy extend as well to its most eminent members—the queens themselves. (Only in fairytales, it seems, do queens exhibit all the virtues.) In this conformist country where the Protestants and Catholics unfailingly attend church every Sunday morning, Queen Juliana was for many years devoted to strange, ritualistic practices conducted by Greet Hofmans, a sort of female Rasputin. Several years after the Hofmans episode, the queen took up with another eccentric, this one from the United States, who, with a vocabulary evolved from gangster films, recounted his dealings with the inhabitants of Venus and his flying-saucer flights to Jupiter, while the queen listened wide-eyed and beaming with admiration.

In a land whose tradition of patriotism is one of the oldest and staunchest in Europe, whose citizens opened the dikes to flood the territory about to be conquered by the Nazis, three successive queens were married to Germans—nationals of the neighbor that was their most bitter enemy. The first, Wilhelmina's husband Prince Henri, was denigrated by Hitler as "the poor royal imbecile come to borrow money from me." The second, Prince Bernhard, who married Juliana in 1937 on the eve of World War II, was a former member of the German Secret Service, and the third, Claus Von Amsberg, who in 1965 became the husband of Juliana's daughter Beatrix, was a living, bitter reminder of the war and the Nazi occupation, a man who had belonged to the Hitler Youth and had worn a Wehrmacht uniform. When he was approaching the church with Princess Beatrix for their wedding ceremony, tens of thousands of demonstrators shouted their disapproval, and a dead chicken, marked with a swastika, was hurled at the footman of the majestic golden carriage in which the bridal couple were riding.

In this ardently democratic country, and in this ardently Protestant royal family, Princess Irene, Queen Juliana's second daughter, married a man who was a combination of the three attributes most detested by the Dutch: he was Catholic, Spanish, and Fascist.

Most paradoxical of all, in this thrifty, Calvinist country where the level of personal savings accounts is the highest in the world, where most of the inhabitants are content to dine on cheese sandwiches and coffee, and where government ministers travel by bicycle, the queen is one of the highest-paid sovereigns in history. The labor unions and the government fight long and hard over the merest salary readjustment, even 1 percent; yet these same people uncomplainingly accept their queen, with her luxurious palaces and fine jewels, and a personal fortune somewhere between $1 billion and $4.5 billion—making her perhaps the richest woman on all five continents.

The spirit of egalitarianism is probably stronger in Holland than anywhere else in Europe, yet the 14 million Dutch are content with a sovereign figure as their leader. The queen is known in all quarters as the citizen-queen, and her popularity is unquestioned. Even the leftist political parties, who deep in their hearts favor a republic, do not dare to refer to these liberal ideas in their campaign programs, since they would probably be ousted during the elections. For certain contemporary historians, the paradox of Holland and its monarchy is linked to the mysteries of monarchy in general. Not only is this antiquated system of government maintained in the most highly developed and democratic country in the world, but it seems to flourish above all in the richest and most egalitarian countries on the Continent as well. Other, more skeptical historians explain the Dutch paradox by citing the very nature of the people from the Low Countries, who lead exemplary lives of faith, austerity, and thriftiness but who are, at the same time, happy to see at least one among them living the way they would love to live.

DURING THE REIGNS of Wilhelmina (1890–1948) and Juliana (1948–1980) there were few changes or innovations; the monarchy remained firmly fixed in the nineteenth century. But when Beatrix mounted the throne in 1980, the Dutch monarchy smoothly entered the twentieth century under the influence of this young, modern, and curious woman who ardently wished to learn and to do well. As headstrong as her grandmother, whose tenacity and pugnaciousness she also shared, Beatrix, of all the European monarchs, was probably the most well prepared for her career. After attending the state lycée and supplementary private classes, she studied law and political science at the University of Leiden (Holland's Oxford). At eighteen, she became a member of the Council of State, religiously attending the weekly meetings, taking notes like the good student that she was and listening attentively to the best minds in the kingdom. She traveled around the world, from the depths of Asia and Africa to America, and after several early, headline-making gaffes, she demonstrated a seriousness and application that impressed her future subjects.

It was Beatrix's personality that disturbed her people. Willful and impatient, she often publicly expressed her desire to succeed her mother and mount the throne. The Dutch were equally shocked by her class consciousness. On the subject of her sister Margriet's marriage to Peter van Vollenhoven, a member of the upper-middle class, she commented publicly, "She would have done better to marry someone from our class." She made another disturbing comment after the "Sovereigns' Cruise" in 1962, organized by her mother to celebrate the twenty-fifth anniversary of her marriage: "It's nice to take up again with one's own people." She meant that it was pleasant to rediscover her family, since the Oranges were related to almost all the kings of Europe. But her reputation for arrogance led most people to assume that she was expressing her pleasure in being surrounded by others of her own rank.

From the beginning, Beatrix's personality has been the subject of violent controversy throughout Holland. Never, it was said from the time this impetuous, often rebellious girl could walk, never would she be like her mother, never would she be as popular. Little Beatrix herself would often repeat, with an air of humility very likely put on, "Never would I know how to do what my mother has done; I would try to do something else."

Throughout Holland Queen Juliana personified all the virtues, and for some reason she especially enchanted the inhabitants of the Low Countries; perhaps it was the charm of her mediocrity. What was so marvelous, after all, about this ungainly woman, overweight even before her first pregnancy? About this speaker whose simplistic oratory—which galvanized the crowds—betrayed her inability to conceive thoughts with any depth? About this royal creature, dominated by a Rasputin in a skirt, who would have been written off as a slightly daft woman if she hadn't been queen? Yet her subjects saw in Juliana their mothers, daughters, and sisters; she was a queen whose destiny cruelly resembled that of thousands of other women betrayed by unfaithful husbands, struggling to raise their children, or intrigued by mysticism.

But who could identify with Beatrix? Few possessed the rare talents or profound egotism to look at this exceptionally strong personality, this high intelligence, this uncompromising honesty, this indomitable energy, this uncommon vitality, and say to themselves, "It's me, it's me, exactly!" The Dutch, not surprisingly, did not see themselves in Beatrix and regarded her with suspicion from her infancy onward, through her modest childhood pranks and her first careful steps as queen.

Beatrix would have been a great success in any walk of life. But her destiny was already sealed on the night of January 30, 1938, when Juliana's labor pains began. The night was stormy, but the icy air did not hinder a crowd from gathering beneath the lighted windows of Soestdijk Palace. Dawn was breaking when Prince Bernhard's private secretary announced to a few court intimates in one of the salons that a child would be born at any moment.

It was 9:47 A.M. when she finally came into the world. Eight minutes later, upon hearing the fifty-one cannon shots, the Dutch knew that a crown princess had just been born and that, if they remained faithful to the monarchy and the dynasty of Orange, a third woman would one day mount the throne of Holland—Juliana succeeding Wilhelmina, then still queen, and Beatrix succeeding Juliana.

Souvenir vendors proliferated, offering myriad objects marked "January 1938." Beatrix had arrived at a propitious moment to save the industrious Dutch merchants from severe economic losses—hardly a bad beginning for a crown princess.

On Tuesday February 2, Beatrix made her first appearance in the family salon, in the arms of her father, who carried her on a cream-colored pillow. Prince Bernhard announced, "I had hoped for a boy." He and Juliana had decided to call her Beatrix, which means *happy* in Latin, since they wished happiness for their daughter. The family friends present, some drinking anisette, others chocolate, raised their glasses and cups in a first toast to the newborn child.

Beatrix Wilhelmina Armgard (named for her two grandmothers)

was baptized in church on May 12, a brilliantly sunny day. She wore the dress of precious lace ordered by her great-grandmother Emma for the baptism of her grandmother Wilhelmina. Juliana and Bernhard rode from the palace to St. Jacobskerk in The Hague in a majestic gilded carriage. Throughout the city, festooned with banners, people wore orange ribbons and boutonnieres in honor of the house of Orange-Nassau. An astrologist had charted the horoscope of the little princess and discovered an impatient character, a lack of simplicity and modesty, a taste for change, and a large dose of rectitude.

In August 1939, Juliana gave birth to a second girl, Irene. Less than a year later, in May 1940, troops of the Third Reich destroyed Holland's tranquillity, and the royal family fled to England; from there Juliana and the children went to Canada, crossing the Atlantic on a Dutch ship. Bernhard remained in England where, refused admittance to the secret service, he joined a division of Dutch airmen.

It was an odd early life for a crown princess. What is a child to think when her mother says to her, as Juliana said again and again to little Beatrix during their Canadian exile, that she is exactly like everybody else, no more, no less, but that in time she would have a special and unique destiny? When the war ended, Beatrix and her two sisters (Margriet was born in May 1945) returned with their mother to Holland, and the family, who had been living in large, middle-class homes in Canada, moved into the icy splendor of Soestdijk Palace. A long, white structure built in a semicircle, Soestdijk comprises a hundred rooms with marble floors and walls. In the shadow of magnificent paintings and gilded furniture, Beatrix was greeted by ministers and servants with equal formality. Journalists pursued her endlessly, and if she stuck out her tongue, a cardinal sin at seven years old, she was severely reprimanded.

Beatrix later described her impressions of this period: "I still remember very well my astonishment when I discovered my unique position as princess and that, indeed, I was not completely like the others. It was on our return from Canada in 1945. I was seven years old. I still didn't really understand what a palace was, or why other children were so poorly dressed, most of them not even wearing shoes, but rather, wooden clogs. Perhaps it was at this time that, unconsciously, my interest in the third world was born.

Teen-age Juliana in the native costume of the southern province of Zeeland.
(Consulate General of the Netherlands)

Soestdijk Palace, Juliana's favorite residence, was home to Beatrix and her sisters when they were children. (Royal Embassy of the Netherlands)

After spending World War II in exile, Queen Juliana and her daughters are reunited with Prince Bernhard in Holland in 1945. Left to right: Margriet, Beatrix, and Irene. (Royal Embassy of the Netherlands)

"I had arrived from Ottawa, where life was very simple. Everybody called me 'Trix,' even the domestics. My mother had given strict instructions that I not hear the word 'princess.' I lived like a little savage, but I got to learn a lot about the outside world, since the house was always full of officers—Dutch soldiers who were welcomed with open arms."

Rejoining Juliana and his children at Soestdijk, Bernhard did not restrain his criticism. His daughters had received a lax education, he said. He was also indignant because Beatrix called his private secretary by his first name. She committed still another error when she told a journalist, whose profession she didn't understand, that she loved chewing gum. Life to Beatrix seemed to be a forest of prohibitions.

Against Bernhard's advice, Juliana decided to send Beatrix to the Werkplaats School, whose director believed children should play in great freedom. Every day a chauffeur drove Trix and Irene to school, with two detectives in the car. Since Juliana wanted her children to receive a "normal" education, the girls joined a scouting organization, went to dancing school, and were required to keep their rooms straight and to clean up after their pet rabbit. Juliana also had her girls take cooking lessons. Beatrix, she proudly related, could prepare a very respectable little meal. (In fact, Beatrix always hated to cook, and throughout her college years always ate her meals in town rather than prepare the merest omelet at home.)

At school, Beatrix was treated exactly like the other children. One day her teacher telephoned Juliana to say that Beatrix refused to sweep the room. "In that case," said the queen, "she will come back home on foot." It was a two-hour walk. The time when she should have arrived home came and went. Bernhard and Juliana were worried; their daughter was only ten years old. Bernhard took his car and looked for her along the road, in vain. When Beatrix finally came in she was in great spirits. "I hitchhiked," she said.

In 1950, under pressure from her father, Beatrix quit the Werkplaats School. When she entered the Baarn Lycée, her teachers discovered that her penmanship was poor, her spelling weak, and her knowledge of grammar and arithmetic worse than mediocre. She was also an extremely high-strung little girl. She needed discipline, said her teachers, and the perfectly realistic Beatrix agreed completely.

The other children were not at all impressed by their royal class-mates. "My little sister Pietie [Margriet]," related Beatrix, "con-fided one day to her friends at the school in Baarn, 'My grandmother is queen.' To which one of the girls responded, just as proudly, 'My grandfather is a baker and I eat cakes every day. Do you?' This shut us both up immediately."

Beatrix soon caught up in school. She had no further academic problems, she made friends, and when she passed her baccalaure-ate exams in 1956 she was a tall and extremely elegant young woman.

The year of her eighteenth birthday, 1956, was a milestone for Beatrix. She had reached her constitutional majority. The third Tuesday of September, she climbed into a gilded carriage beside her mother to attend her first official ceremony, the opening of Parliament. It was also the year of her religious confirmation, mak-ing her a full member of the Dutch Reform Church. And in the fall, in the city of juniper trees and white carnations, she began her studies at the University of Leiden, created in the sixteenth century by William the Silent to thank the inhabitants of the city for their bravery. (During the Spanish siege the burgomaster of Leiden of-fered his own body to feed the trapped and starving citizens rather than capitulate to the enemy.)

A serious student, Beatrix majored in law, modern history, and sociology. Like her classmates, she lived in a rented apartment in the city. She formed many lasting friendships during her stay at the university. Several years later, at the time of her marriage to Claus, her old classmates managed to slip between a crowd of angry stu-dents and the royal couple, forming a solid wall of protection and support. (While attending the university, Beatrix herself once par-ticipated in a demonstration, albeit a nonpolitical one, against the police, who had removed parked bicycles from a prohibited area.) The princess passed her university exams in 1961 and celebrated her success on the yacht, The Green Dragon, given to her by the Dutch navy.

Beatrix drew an annual endowment of 300,000 florins a year, some of which helped fund her official travels throughout the world, from Dutch Guiana to Hong Kong, from Finland to Mex-ico. She was a good ambassador and a very hard worker who studied in depth each briefing dossier before every trip, even before every inauguration or ceremony. In delicate situations, such as in her conversations with Indonesians on the brink of independence, she managed to be extremely diplomatic, never making the slightest gaffe. In Guiana, where she was warmly received, she was dubbed with the nickname Princess Smile.

The time was long past since Beatrix had envied Irene, her younger sister, who was not only prettier and more elegant, but also more clever, more adroit at dealing with people. For many years Beatrix was incapable of skillfully relating to others. She would blurt out everything she thought or felt, at the risk of shocking her listeners, and it was a long time before she could, with an extreme effort of will, temper the spontaneousness of her character and hide her true thoughts. (Many years later, during a trip to Asia with Claus, she responded with irritation to questioners who were denigrating the Soviet Union, "Why do you always say that the Russians are responsible for all the evils?" For this she was roundly criticized. The question of whether she was perhaps pro-Soviet was raised.)

BEATRIX WAS A YOUNG WOMAN ripe for marriage. Newspapers and gossip sheets, with great joy and imagination, had her engaged to a wide variety of available suitors. Such is the fate of any princess, but Beatrix took the situation rather badly: "If a young man is polite enough to accompany me to my car, he is suddenly persecuted by trivial questions and telephoto lenses." But the Dutch press did nothing to improve the crown princess's temper.

In all, Beatrix was linked with 215 suitors. But her friends knew that only one man counted in the life of this fiery woman. From her earliest encounters with him, Beatrix knew she had been right to wait for a man she could truly love. This man was Claus von Amsberg.

Beatrix was twenty-seven when she met Claus, a German career diplomat eleven years her senior. He soon became, and has been ever since, the most important person in her life. Beatrix was too intelligent to marry someone who would allow himself to be reduced to the role of straw man, or who would be eternally absent from the family circle. Claus brought a new image of male humanity to the Dutch royal family. Beatrix had conquered the curse of the Oranges—conjugal failure among Dutch queens. She would not be a wife like Wilhelmina, who humiliated consort Henri, nor like Juliana, whose husband made a career of romantic adventures and maintained almost publicly a titled mistress and an illegitimate child in Paris.

Beatrix's sister Irene was already married. In 1964, after converting to Catholicism, she had married Prince Charles-Hugues de Bourbon-Parme, pretender to the Spanish throne. She did not obtain Parliament's authorization and had to renounce her title and her rank as well. (She has since left her husband, causing yet another scandal.) But Irene was only the second daughter. Nothing she did could matter as much as the activities of Crown Princess Beatrix. The rumors of an engagement between Beatrix and Claus that began to circulate around Holland had the effect of a battle cry, clearing the ground for action.

The couple met in 1964 in Gstaad, the celebrated Swiss-German ski resort, where Beatrix was staying with friends. The press at the time had linked her with a new "fiancé," Richard zu Sayn Wittgenstein, and he made an ideal smokescreen behind which Beatrix could hide the true object of her affections. Claus could appear on the scene without anyone paying him the least attention. The press, taking vague note of him in Beatrix's entourage, established that he was unknown to international jet-set society, after which he disappeared for several months from the papers.

During this period, Juliana tried everything she could think of to convince Beatrix to give up Claus. She even tried to have him transferred by the minister of foreign affairs in Bonn to an obscure post in Africa. Beatrix got wind of the effort and went on a hunger strike. The tender Juliana gave in after three days.

The drama centered on the fact that Claus was German. This might seem somewhat curious, since Bernhard, the prince consort, was also German, as was his predecessor and father-in-law, the unfortunate Henri. But the country had suffered the occupation of Hitler's troops during the war, and twenty years later the Dutch were still violently anti-German. Not only was Claus German, but he had worn a Nazi uniform in 1945 while he was serving in Germany's 90th Panzer Division.

The royal family opened an inquiry into Claus's military background and determined that he was absolutely innocent of all war crimes; not even the slightest misdeed could be attributed to him. Even the president of the Labor party, who thought little of Juliana and nothing of Beatrix, had to admit that Claus came through as white as snow. Still, Juliana begged her daughter to capitulate, emphasizing the fact that the monarchist segment of the population had shrunk somewhat and might grow even smaller if she persisted. Beatrix defended her fiancé with all the tenacity of an authoritative woman desperately in love. Summoned by the prime minister, the presidents of all the political parties approved the marriage. Claus would become a naturalized Dutch citizen.

Tempers were just beginning to cool when Beatrix tossed another bombshell. Breaking from the royal family tradition of marrying in The Hague, she decided that her wedding would take place in Amsterdam. The city at the time was under the siege of squatters, who were called "provos." Leftists, anarchists, nihilists, they were hardly favorites of the police (who pitilessly clubbed anyone with long hair), or of any political party, or of the Dutch royal family. A royal marriage in their territory meant a concentration on their turf of everything they most hated. "I could marry in The Hague or in Rotterdam," Beatrix explained, "and I would win everybody's heart in either of the two cities. But if I win Amsterdam, it is the whole country I will have conquered." However, the general population was not convinced that Beatrix wanted to do anything more than show what little regard she had for public opinion. The head of the provos, rather admiringly, declared, "Beatrix is more provo than all of us."

The crown princess had once visited incognito the hot spots of this hot city—first, the famous red-light district, then the bars where the young rebels gathered. She felt she understood them, these rebels. But they didn't take kindly to her little tour. One anarchist paper published some practical advice: how to make your own little bomb for Beatrix's marriage. A student paper published a list of "wedding presents" covering several pages: bombs on the procession, nails under the wheels of cars, white mice under the horses' legs, a swastika projected on the church wall, and other little kindnesses.

Beatrix remained unshaken. Parliament was on her side; the cabinet had given its benediction. Her mother, finally won over to her cause, publicly declared, "I can assure you it's for the best."

But Pastor Kater, who was to celebrate the ceremony, had been threatened with assassination, arson, and even castration.

The day of the wedding, March 10, 1966, was cold and rainy. Beatrix and Claus took their places in the gilded carriage, hiding their anxiety under brave smiles. They crossed the city, erupting with smoke bombs, to the cries of "Claus, *raus*" (Claus, get out) and even a few shouts of "Long live the republic." Later, Beatrix addressed her people with soothing words: "We understand that many of you cannot share with us the joy of this day." Claus added, "I know that for some among you, our marriage recalls painful memories of the past. But I would like to ask you to give us a chance to build a new future with you."

On this day of ceremony, snubbed by European royalty, a day on which she saw her daughter crying from tear gas, Juliana doubtless remembered her own wedding, when 100,000 Dutch girls, gold ribbons in their cotton caps, surrounded the big church to greet her and celebrate her marriage. And perhaps she wished from the bottom of her heart that her daughter, whose wedding day was so different from her own, would have a different private life, and a happier one, as well.

One year later, in order to escape the journalists who waited in front of her residence in Drakensteyn, Beatrix was transported to the University Hospital in Utrecht in an armored car. At 7:57 on the morning of April 27, 1967, after a labor complicated by a Cesarean section, the first crown prince of Holland in 116 years was born. For the first time in as many years the cannons sounded 101 times.

The country was overjoyed. The Dutch sang patriotic songs until the early hours of morning in bars that usually closed precisely at 1:00 A.M. Ten thousand people came to sign the register at Soestdijk Palace, while at Drakensteyn, a gift arrived every minute. If Beatrix's marriage had threatened to undermine the foundation of the monarchy, the birth of her son did much to reinforce it. Today Holland's crown prince, Willem-Alexander (nicknamed Wimpie), attends Beatrix's alma mater, Baarn Lycée, along with his two brothers, Johan Friso and Constantijn (born in 1968 and 1969 respectively). He has a reputation for being fiery and excitable. He skis, sails, and plays soccer with a ferocious will to win. He loves animals and displays an outgoing character and a certain arrogance. It is said that he resembles his mother and his grandfather, Prince Bernhard, but that he shows his father's stubbornness as well as his high spirits. Beatrix allows her sons as much freedom as possible but is afraid of "criticisms to which they are more exposed than other children, even though they have the same characteristics and the same pranks." Prince Bernhard pretends that his grandsons are the "worst-raised children in Europe."

FOR MORE THAN A DECADE after Beatrix's marriage, the overriding question in Holland was when Juliana would cede the throne. It was said that the sweet, maternal Juliana was afraid to send her daughter into the jungle of modern royalty. But Beatrix feared nothing and for years had been fidgeting with impatience, ready to mount the throne. When she was only eighteen, during the period of her mother's involvement with the mystic Greet Hofmans, there already was talk of Juliana's abdication in favor of Beatrix. But after Beatrix's marriage to Claus, the Dutch were in less of a hurry to replace Juliana. In 1980, however, Juliana had finally had enough, her strength, if not her authority, undermined by the terrible scandals that had marked her reign, and even her childhood.

She had often seen her mother, Queen Wilhelmina, humiliate her father, Prince Henri, in public. Although he was born duke of Mecklenburg-Schwerin, one of the families of the high German aristocracy, Henri never attained the title of prince of the Netherlands, or an endowment of any consequence. The queen treated him with such contempt that even President Theodore Roosevelt, on an official visit to Holland, was deeply struck by it. In a letter to one of his close advisers, he described Wilhelmina verbally dragging her husband through the mud in front of him—the president of the United States—because he did not understand something she said to him. Prince Henri spent long nights on the town, after which he was usually brought home drunk by taxi drivers who had gathered him up from the bawdy houses of Amsterdam or The Hague. Even the palace gardeners pitied this man who had the unfortunate honor of sharing the bed of the queen, a prince who did not even receive the kind of respect due a valet. Although Juliana was very close to her mother, this pathetic situation must have left its mark on her. Her childhood could not have been a very happy one.

When it came to beauty, intelligence, and charm, Juliana was not overly blessed by Mother Nature. Nevertheless, when she reached a marriageable age there was no lack of eligible candidates. The crown princess would inherit not only a throne and a crown but also one of the most fabulous fortunes in the world. Among her suitors was one who found special favor in her eyes, a young man two years her junior, rather handsome and elegant, and a daredevil who loved fast cars and competitive skiing: Prince Bernhard zu Lippe-Biesterfeld.

Bernhard's family had once reigned over a pocket-sized principality, much larger, with its 130,000 inhabitants, than today's independent sovereignty of Liechtenstein. His father had served in the Kaiser's army during World War I and twice received the Iron Cross with palms for bravery. Juliana first met Bernhard in 1936 in Bavaria. The young prince had just arrived from Paris in his Mercedes convertible, and the heavy young girl, tightly controlled by a dictatorial mother, was dazzled by this personification of masculine charm. They saw each other again many times, and Juliana increasingly hoped to marry this young man who opened up to her a world of adventure and romance, a world she never before knew existed. That same year, Bernhard asked for her hand and entered into an arduous negotiating session with her parents that resembled a contract discussion between two banks rather than a discourse about love. Queen Wilhelmina and Prince Bernhard discussed the marriage agreement point by point. Bernhard's daily activities, his responsibilities, the honors that would be due him, the money that would flow to him, were all covered. Later, he would refer to his engagement as "the Treaty of Weissenburg," the name of the hotel near Gstaad where the memorable sessions took place. These preliminaries could not have been very pleasant for the young princess, who sat in on them as a silent observer.

A few days after his engagement, Bernhard asked the Führer, Adolf Hitler, to authorize his renunciation of German nationality so that he could become a Dutch citizen.

JULIANA AND BERNHARD'S MARRIAGE, on January 7, 1937, gave rise to a few demonstrations of anger, but the great majority of the Dutch showed joy and even enthusiasm, since the succession of the House of Orange was thus assured.

The long honeymoon trip was an enchantment for the young Juliana, but things began to spoil almost as soon as she returned. Queen Wilhelmina increasingly interfered in the life of the young couple, and her royal authority tyrannized the prince consort, who had become her new target since her favorite victim, Prince Henri, had departed to a better world to recover from his early misadventures. Even the birth of Princess Beatrix, on January 31, 1938, did not improve the stormy relations between Bernhard and his mother-in-law. Queen Wilhelmina never refrained from criticizing Bernhard for his bad habits—drinking and smoking in public, sailing or skiing on Sundays. Usually Juliana maintained a prudent silence, but once in front of several members of court, she took her mother's side against her husband. Throughout the years their misunderstandings grew progressively worse. Even Juliana's exile to Canada during the war did not improve matters. Bernhard made a few brief visits to Canada, during which it became increasingly apparent that the couple had nothing in common.

On May 12, 1948, Wilhelmina announced her intention to abdicate. On September 7, she and her daughter appeared on the balcony of Dam Palace in Amsterdam. Wilhelmina, wider, heavier, and more aggressive than ever, announced her departure to her people; then, raising her fist and swinging it in a big circle around her head, she cried out with a power that astounded everyone present, "Long live the queen!" "Long live the queen!" the crowd responded. Wilhelmina repeated the gesture and the cry a good dozen times, as if she wanted to incite the passion of the crowd and create an emotional bond between the subjects and their new queen —a bond that, for Wilhelmina, was an integral part of the hereditary mystery that is monarchy.

Having removed herself from power, Wilhelmina nevertheless continued to counsel her daughter on her activities as queen as well as on her private life, and until her death she personally managed her own colossal fortune. She was the largest single shareholder in Royal Dutch-Shell, the largest oil company in the world outside the United States, as well as a major shareholder in Exxon, in Unilever, and in Phillips. Even after her retirement, she continued to receive her personal friends, among them the Rockefellers, who certainly helped her profit from their financial advice. But her administration of the family fortune did not keep her from playing an increasingly active role in her daughter's life. During the great crisis provoked by the appearance on the scene of the faith healer Greet Hofmans, Queen Mother Wilhelmina supported her daughter against Bernhard and Beatrix.

Nothing shook the Dutch monarchy quite like the Hofmans affair. It began in November 1947, when Bernhard himself invited the faith healer to the palace. Bernhard scarcely believed that this skeletal woman with peasant features could save the sight of his fourth daughter, Marijke, born ten months before, but he undoubtedly hoped that she would have a calming influence on the very legitimate anxieties of Juliana. The queen was instilled with a terrible feeling of guilt, since Marijke's blindness was caused by the German measles Juliana had caught during her pregnancy. To everyone's astonishment, Hofmans, who at fifty-four had difficulty expressing herself and who had read fewer than a dozen books in her life, rapidly took almost complete control over the queen's personality; she was soon accused of playing a role comparable to that of Rasputin, in court and even in Dutch politics. But then Juliana had always had a weakness for astrology and occultism. Greet Hofmans organized prayer sessions around the baby's bed, acted as the queen's confessor, gave her courses in theology, and explained to anyone who would listen that the truest relationships of this world could be diagrammed on "a vertical plane," meaning between man and God. "Horizontal" relationships—between man and woman—were of no value.

After Bernhard physically ejected her from the royal palace, Hofmans set up shop in Het Oude Looe, Queen Mother Wilhelmina's castle, where she continued to give courses every day. She now had two royal followers—Juliana and her mother. The two women brought all their important visitors to listen to Greet's sermons, and Eleanor Roosevelt, upon whom this little pilgrimage was imposed, heard Greet Hofmans preach that sickness did not exist and that "cancer was a manifestation of the world's spiritual disorders, caused by militarism and war. For this reason I can't cure cancer before war is eliminated."

Among Greet Hofmans's faithful was a descendant of one of the most illustrious Dutch families, Baron van Heeckeren van Molecatan, who, during the growing war between Bernhard and Juliana, brought to the faith healer's cause the talents of a fine diplomat. Bernhard, supported by his eldest daughter, Beatrix, believed that the queen was losing touch with reality and that she would soon be incapable of handling the responsibilities of the crown. Beatrix had been particularly horrified to learn that the participants in the Het Oude Looe séances not only prayed but engaged in dialogues with extraterrestrials who honored them with their visits.

Beatrix and Bernhard were in favor of Juliana's abdication. For years, and to this day, historians have tried to analyze the real motivations for this offensive led by Juliana's husband and daughter. Did they truly believe that Juliana was incapable of carrying out her responsibilities? Or did Beatrix, impatient since the age of eighteen to accede to the throne, want to attain it more quickly, and did Bernhard want to play the role at her side that he never had the chance to play next to his wife? These were dark days at the royal palace, interminable scenes during which husband and daughter badgered their wife and mother: she had to abdicate, and in so doing she could concentrate full time on her mystic activities.

Wilhelmina entered the fray and backed Juliana. She kept her daughter from yielding under this joint attack. But it was the Dutch government that finally intervened to end the crisis.

The majority of the Dutch population was not exactly kept abreast of what was happening at Het Oude Looe and of the influence Greet Hofmans exerted in affairs of state through her control over the queen. But in political circles everyone—the parliamentarians, the councillors, the judges, and all those connected with the Binnenhof, the Dutch seat of political life in The Hague—was indeed aware of the problem and decided to put a stop to it. According to the Dutch Constitution, the queen is inviolable and cannot be held responsible for anything she says or does. Her ministers and the prime minister must assume total responsibility for her actions—and in this case they didn't want any more of it. The government dissolved, and though new elections took place in the winter of 1956, no political party would agree to form a government as long as the Hofmans affair remained unresolved. Baron van Heeckeren van Molecatan, who had become the privileged adviser to the two queens, negotiated furiously, but to no avail. No Dutch parliamentarian wanted to accept the power and thus, constitutionally, the responsibility for the queen's actions. Wilhelmina and Juliana were obliged to bend to the exigencies of the parliamentarians and accept the formation of an investigative committee, without which the principle of monarchy itself would have been drawn into question. The commission, composed of three "sages," decided that Greet Hofmans had to go and that Baron van Heeckeren van Molecatan must leave court. Princess Beatrix was sent to the University of Leiden to complete her studies.

The queen did not agree with the findings of the commission, and rejected all the recommendations. She wanted to address the people directly to explain her point of view. Wilhelmina was also ready to address the nation in support of her daughter. Prime Minister Willem Drees clearly demonstrated where the real power lay. He prohibited all radio and television stations from letting the two women speak. From that point on, the crisis was over. The prime minister formed a permanent government and ceased asking for the abdication of Juliana, or the abolishment of the monarchy. In return, the queen muted her prayers at Het Oude Looe. Soon the faith healer's influence diminished, and she died destitute and forgotten in 1968.

THE HOFMANS CRISIS was resolved, but Queen Juliana's family problems remained intact. The most serious was Prince Bernhard himself. Everyone who knew him emphasized his charm, his intelligence, his curiosity, and his spirit of adventure. Although born into the high German aristocracy, he was quickly confronted by the realities of life. Sent to a "plebeian" school, he was regularly beaten up by his classmates, who found it amusing to ridicule a prince. When he complained to his parents, his mother, Baroness Armgard, advised him to defend himself with punches to the stomach. He studied law at the Universities of Lausanne and Munich and obtained his doctorate of law with excellent grades. He also attended the University of Berlin and became a member of the Air Club. The sport was only a cover for what was in fact a training school for the German Luftwaffe. (The Treaty of Versailles still prohibited Germany from having an air corps.) He resigned after an airplane accident and joined a motorized SS squadron which he left after his final exams. Shortly thereafter, he left for Paris, where he worked in the French office of I.G. Farben, one of the largest German industrial enterprises and a power close to the Nazi government.

A man of Bernhard's stamp who, in spite of his young age, had experienced life in all its forms, from its most exciting to its most dangerous, would understandably find it difficult to play an obscure role beside a rather lackluster wife. During World War II, Bernhard tried to aid the Allied cause at high levels. But the English were suspicious of him. The Royal Air Force's high command refused to accept him into a top post, and the directors of British intelligence blanched in horror when King George VI asked them to work Bernhard into their ranks. He diverted his abundant energy into the world of business, all the while trying to lead a merry life away from the austerity of Holland, where he returned as seldom as possible. He was Dutch industry's best representative abroad, traveling constantly to interest American financiers and industrialists in economic projects in the Netherlands. He rightly claimed that he knew the cream of the international financiers, as well as most of the great statesmen throughout the Western world. It was Bernhard who, in 1954, created the annual Bilderberg Conference, named after the hotel in an isolated corner of the Netherlands where the meetings took place. For one weekend, this unique conference assembled the world's top financiers and the best minds in government and academia for forty-eight hours of secret meetings, the purpose of which was not to discuss concrete economic projects but rather to examine the world philosophically in an attempt to understand where it was going.

Bernhard presided as well over the International Wildlife Association. After spending many years of his youth hunting tigers and elephants, he put all his efforts into trying to preserve the specimens that had once been the objects of his hunter's eye. Participation in Bernhard's committee—composed of 1,001 contributors— required a donation of $10,000. The donation might have seemed considerable, if not excessive, had the members been simply animal lovers with no ulterior motives. But the amount became relatively insignificant in view of the fact that it also opened the doors to the gilded salons of Soestdijk Palace. Bernhard had set a rule: all contributors would be invited to the royal palace, where they would meet other contributors, among them the world's top financiers. Dr. Tibor Rosenbaum, owner of a small Israeli bank in Geneva, had never hunted down anything larger than a fly, and his interest in wildlife was even less passionate. He was one of the first subscribers. He managed to gain the confidence of the prince, who reportedly lost a large sum of money when the bank failed after a major scandal involving Rosenbaum in 1975.

Another contributor, Robert Vesco, gained worldwide notoriety by reputedly pulling off the swindle of the century. He was charged with appropriating more than $200 million from mutual fund investors by pretending to bail out the failing Investors' Overseas Service, founded by Bernie Cornfeld, another great friend of Bernhard's. The queen was not at all pleased with the prince's new companions. She forbade them to enter Soestdijk Palace, but they nevertheless remained part of Bernhard's life as he traveled from one continent to another, dancing the tango with Evita Peron or the samba with a creole beauty. (He did stop to relax from time to time while on the road vaunting the merits of Dutch industry.) Between Juliana and her husband, not even a shred of their former conjugal relationship remained. And between Bernhard and his son-in-law, relations were hardly in a better state. Claus, now in his forties, was impatient to assume the top-flight role of Prince Bernhard, who in middle age was more flamboyant than ever.

IT WAS IN THIS strained family atmosphere that the Lockheed scandal erupted, probably the most serious royal scandal mixing money and influence-peddling since the cardinal of Rohan tried to bribe Marie-Antoinette with a diamond necklace, although in Bernhard's case the consequences were less serious: Marie-Antoinette eventually lost her head on charges of treason while Bernhard lost only his presidency of the Red Cross, his position in the Wildlife Association, and his post as inspector general of the Dutch armed forces.

The affair began in Washington, D.C., in 1975. A Senate subcommittee had heard the testimony of the vice president of the Lockheed Corporation, which was then being investigated for paying bribes. The executive stated that close to $1 million had been paid to an eminent Dutch personality. Shortly afterward, the committee discovered that the personality was Prince Bernhard himself. As soon as Bernhard was implicated, the first hint of his downfall, all the participants in the upcoming 1976 Bilderberg Conference canceled. The conference was never reconvened.

The Senate commission and a Dutch commission of three sages created by Prime Minister Joop den Uyl established that Bernhard had accepted $300,000 in 1960, $300,000 in 1961, and $140,000 in 1962 in payment for his effort to persuade the government to equip the Dutch Air Force with the Starfighter, a jet fighter plane manufactured by Lockheed.

The Dutch population was deeply shocked. A member of the royal family, the queen's husband, a man who had finally won the love and admiration of the citizens, had been willing to squander public funds in order to fill his own pocket! In addition to testimony from people directly involved in the affair, the investigators found a letter that the prince had written to a former vice president of the Lockheed Corporation. He wanted a commission of $4 to $6 million in exchange for persuading the Dutch government to buy Orion aircraft, used in antisubmarine warfare. The sum was never paid.

By now Prince Bernhard's endowment from the Dutch government had reached $300,000 a year, and thanks to judicious investments his personal fortune had grown to $12 million. But apparently this was not sufficient to allow him to live according to his tastes.

The scandal was a blow to the country, the government, and the queen. Juliana struggled to keep her husband from being subjected to the humiliation of legal proceedings and, worse still, from being sent to prison for violating common law. Prime Minister Joop den Uyl was pulled by two opposing forces: by the furious population demanding that the affair be pursued to its natural end, which would have had grave personal consequences for Bernhard, and by the queen, who was threatening to abdicate. The Socialist party, which had just formed a government thanks to a delicately balanced coalition, did not want to hear any talk of abdication, since that would most likely mean the fall of their government and new elections.

Joop den Uyl was a small man, with a deferential, even unctuous, manner. But in the course of his confrontations with Queen Juliana, he exhibited firmness as well as imagination, tirelessly repeating to her that, as queen, her person was inviolable and that her husband could profit indirectly from the situation. He cautioned her that if she were to abdicate, she would be simply a Dutchwoman like any other, and Prince Bernhard would no longer have any protection against the judiciary police heading the investigation.

Such an investigation, with every imaginable consequence, would besmirch the House of Orange to such an extent that four hundred honorable years of history would be wiped out with one stroke. Juliana continued to stonewall the situation. But the accusations against Bernhard were growing very serious and precise. Every day brought its share of details on parties he had given during his trips abroad, for which he had requisitioned local Dutch

embassies and their stock of wine, alcohol, and cigars; on his ro-
mances and his mistresses, scattered, according to the press, in
more than twenty countries; and on his not altogether honest personal and business relations. Finally the problem was resolved:
Bernhard resigned from all his official functions, forfeited his annual endowment, and agreed to stay quietly and unobtrusively in
the background. The government called off all judiciary proceedings and, for the moment, the queen was not to abdicate.

Throughout the drama, Juliana was supported by Beatrix, who
had been her father's ally during the Greet Hofmans crisis but who
was now firmly at her mother's side. Beatrix had certainly been
disappointed by the father she had so much loved and admired, but
perhaps she also understood that the future of the dynasty and the
honor of the House of Orange compelled her to face the crisis with
her mother and against her father—who in the final analysis was
an intruder into this line of women who ruled the Netherlands. To
some degree it was history repeating itself: mother and daughter,
both solid Dutchwomen, aligned against the prince consort, the
German aristocrat. Four years later, in 1980, Juliana abdicated and
Beatrix mounted the throne.

"OFTEN, over the last few years, when I suffered increasingly
from a sense of uselessness in my role as heir to the Dutch throne,
I showed impatience. But on this day I better understand my mother's words at the time of her accession: 'I have been called to a task
so arduous that no one who has given it a moment's thought would
wish to do it, but also so splendid that I can only say—who am I
to be permitted to perform it?' "

Thus Beatrix expressed her sentiments on the night before her
enthronement. Juliana had chosen to abdicate on her seventy-first
birthday. Some said that she had attached one string—she wished
to retain the power to advise her daughter and to continue, with
Beatrix as go-between, to influence the life of the nation. Others,
to the contrary, maintained that the characters of Beatrix and Juliana were hardly compatible, and that Juliana was no longer involved. The new queen had her own advisers, members or former
members of the government, and her husband Claus, the one person, it was said, she respected above all others.

The day of Beatrix's coronation seemed almost a repetition of her marriage. The "provos" had been replaced by the "krackers," the new name for the squatters and rebellious youth, and the theme of their demands was also new. The problem was no longer Claus, but the coronation itself—too expensive, they claimed, for a country whose shaky budget was insufficient for such a display. The ceremony would cost $12 million according to the newspapers, $70 million according to the banners of the demonstrators. One slogan, referring to the housing shortage in Amsterdam, proclaimed, "Accommodation instead of coronation," while graffiti appearing a few days later declared, "Trix is nothing at all." In addition to local agitators, Dutch security feared the appearance of an IRA contingent from Ireland in response to the presence of Prince Charles of England. But only the tear gas bombs that made helmeted military forces weep, the humming police helicopters that drowned out the church bells, and the black smoke that rose up from torched cars obscured the famous sun of Orange.

Inside the New Church of Amsterdam (which dates from the sixteenth century), the pomp, the dignity, and the emotion were all present for Beatrix's solemn installation as queen. As tradition dictated, the full complement of heads of state, representatives of the European monarchies, ministers, secretaries of state, and members of the Council of State were seated in the church. Then, Beatrix entered with her procession, wearing an ermine-lined purple cape embroidered with gold lions over her long white dress. Claus, solemn and staying ever so slightly behind, escorted her. As she walked slowly down the long aisle holding firmly to Claus's arm, choirs sang "The Wilhelmus," the national anthem.

When the ceremony was over, Beatrix and Claus left the church by the main door and were greeted by the applause of the crowd gathered outside. Soon another ovation rose, this one louder and more rousing: it was an homage to former Queen Juliana, who was leaving through a rear door with her other children, on her way back to the palace on foot.

As time went by, Queen Beatrix gained more and more esteem, both from her subjects and from successive Dutch governments. Her private life was an outstanding success. "I know what good fortune it is to have at my side a husband who supports me, who completes me, and who corrects me," she often said. In 1978, after serving in several public service posts, Prince Claus was made special adviser to the Minister for Development Cooperation. After Beatrix became queen, he also received chiefs of state from the

Third World and participated in international conferences on aid to undeveloped countries. But his most important role was that of counselor to his wife. At the end of 1982, a great misfortune struck this model couple: Prince Claus was afflicted with an extremely serious neurological disease, in which the face or various parts of the body are suddenly seized by paralysis. The queen was devastated, and it was between crises of despair that she fulfilled her royal duties.

She still holds a certain influence over the business affairs of her country, but her role is shrouded under the Rule of Palace Secrecy, a secrecy so jealously guarded that remarks made by the queen to her ministers remain forever unknown to the public. Juliana had little theoretical knowledge of politics and economy, but she made it a point to know well the heads of the principal political parties, their strong points, their weaknesses, even their relationships with other politicians. Beatrix replaced this high-level, interpersonal experience with a thorough theoretical knowledge of the sovereign craft, garnered from her solid studies, her many years of participation in the Council of State's weekly sessions, her numerous trips abroad, and her studious reading of thousands of documents. In their dealings with her, government officials are struck by the fact that they are speaking not only to their queen but to a woman above party lines who represents a whole generation and who is also well informed and open-minded.

Apart from these privileges and duties, Beatrix and the other members of the royal family are citizens like any other—though considerably richer and much more luxuriously lodged. A new law will soon take effect which provides a greatly narrowed definition of the royal family. Beatrix's sons will still be royal highnesses, but the children of her three sisters will not be. Parliament will no longer be responsible for their actions. This law was not drafted to penalize the family, nor did it arise from a spirit of republicanism. Its only purpose is to permit these future men and women to live normal lives and to integrate fully into society, although numerous professions are still prohibited to members of the royal family. Two of Beatrix's sisters, Irene and Marijke, have already opted for this "normal" life by not asking for Parliament's authorization to marry. Juliana's grandchildren, almost all boys, will be able to work and take on all sorts of responsibilities, even if they are not compelled to do so by material considerations.

For the last dozen years the queen of Holland has been a full

Queen Beatrix with Claus, the most important person in her life. (Royal Embassy of the Netherlands)

Prince Constantijn, Prince Johan Friso, and Prince Willem-Alexander, the first crown prince born in Holland in 116 years. (Consulate General of the Netherlands)

  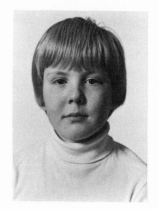

citizen who pays taxes on revenue and capital. It was during Juliana's reign that a commission of three sages, presided over by a professor of constitutional law from Rotterdam, studied the family's finances and came to the conclusion, supported by Parliament, that they were taxable like the finances of all other Dutch families. When the commission delivered its report to Queen Juliana, a report that in the long run would cost her hundreds of millions of dollars, the old woman thanked them for the interest they had taken in her affairs and their kindness and served them coffee herself. It was certainly more than most taxpayers would do for their tax inspectors.

The queen's annual endowment is not taxed, since the legislature considers that most of the money goes into professional expenses in the course of the queen's duties. (The palaces used by the royal family, excluding Drakensteyn, which is Beatrix's personal property, are the property of the state, and the family pays rent to the state.)

The country's economic crisis during the past few years has required all Dutch workers to tighten their belts. Even the royal family has not escaped the general cut in salaries; the queen's endowment and the endowments of Claus, Juliana, and Bernhard have decreased by several thousands of dollars since 1981 and are expected to drop further.

A recent public opinion poll revealed that 89 percent of the Dutch favored the institution of monarchy, 5 percent were for a republic, and 6 percent had no opinion. The majority of Beatrix's and Juliana's most devoted admirers are women. A certain feminism mixes neatly with royalism, and it is difficult to determine where the emotional ties between ordinary women and their queens end and where the satisfaction of seeing someone of their sex occupy the throne—symbolically the supreme power—begins.

Today, although the land is a kingdom, it is a kingdom where the middle class of Amsterdam, Leiden, and The Hague holds all the power, and where the queens and the princes are citizens like any other.

8

BELGIUM

◆

How a Timid Young Man Saved a Monarchy in Peril

O n July 16, 1951, a serious boy with a long, straight profile and an anxious look behind his glasses put an end to the monarchical and constitutional crisis that was destroying Belgium. Few contemporary kings have acceded to the throne in an atmosphere of such tension. At the oath-taking ceremony several days later, few could believe that the Belgian monarchy would last. In the middle of the ceremony a deputy cried out, rattling the windows as well as the assembled guests, "Long live the republic, down with the king!" Baudouin I was twenty-one years old.

He is now celebrating the thirty-third year of his reign. In Europe his record for longevity on the throne is second only to that of the prince of Liechtenstein, and in the rest of the world only the emperor of Japan has reigned longer than he has. He has more prerogatives than any other constitutional monarch and more possibilities to enter into the intricacies of political gamesmanship, of which he is a master. He has met almost everyone in the Belgian political system, made up of twenty parties. The linguistic, cultural, and economic subtleties at the root of the perpetual hostilities between the Flemish and Walloon communities are familiar to him. Confronted with numerous crises in the course of his career, the king has become an experienced politician.

Physically, Baudouin has changed little since his accession. He still has the wise and slightly retiring air of a studious young man. But his assurance shines through the reserve, and the Belgians who see him travel through the streets of the capital several times a day in his black Mercedes sense it. Once he would sit back in the depths of the car as if he wanted to escape the glances of the curious. Now he sits straight up and even leans out of the window occasionally to wave to passers-by. This, for him, is a major accomplishment. He has earned the acceptance of all the diverse ethnic and political elements in the population, managing to become the symbol of his country and to assume to the fullest his function as monarch. He plays the fundamental role of "national cement," as the Belgians like to say, and likewise maintains a life style as dull and gray as cement, one that purposely attracts no attention. If it is true that a monarchy flows from one man alone—the king—then this man must be adaptable to circumstance and to the needs of his people. Baudouin has succeeded, perhaps better than any other European monarch, in endowing himself with a style that marries grandeur and simplicity, a style developed doubtless in part after a bit of market research but also out of his own personal inclinations.

Of this discreet and effective king, the man in the street often remembers only his self-effacement. Accustomed to the personalization of power and to seeing chiefs of state announcing their projects and decisions on television, the population does not always understand the role of the Belgian king. The display of the English royal court and the curiosity aroused by Queen Elizabeth's activities create the impression that the queen plays a much more active role than she actually does. The English monarchy could disappear, as could the thrones of Scandinavia, without affecting the institutions and the functions of the country. Baudouin, on the other hand, plays a fundamental role, not only as a symbol of national unity but also as a rudder in steering the course of his country's politics during times of crisis. The Constitution cloaks the king's political activities in something close to secrecy, and what the law doesn't do, he does himself. Quite retiring and secretive, with no taste for pomp and ostentation, he doesn't arouse the people's interest with a lavish life style or extravagant expenses. Yet if the

Belgian monarchy disappeared, the country's political life would be plunged into a state of despondency which it would have a hard time overcoming.

Grandeur and simplicity also define the style of Baudouin's court. Antiquated protocol dating back to the Spanish Court of Philip II, according to some, and to the Hapsburgs, according to others, has been abolished. Cutaways have been replaced by three-piece suits, and chamberlains of the old school have been superseded by efficient civil servants, former judges, or diplomats. But the correct way to address the king is still, "Hello, Sire, how is the king?" The king, however, does not consider it an affront if certain people neglect to speak to him in the third person. Occasionally he leaves his office to drop in unexpectedly on one of his colleagues if he needs information or the answer to a question. It happens rarely, but when it does, it is the gravest possible infringement on the spirit of order and organization by which the palace functions.

Like a good civil servant, the king arrives at his office every morning at nine, and for the next hour he receives his staff one by one. He's briefed on the day's news, reads dispatches sent over from the Belgian Ministry of Foreign Affairs, and scans governmental documents—orders of the day from the counsel of ministries, deliberations and decisions—supplied by his administrative director. He also looks over documents submitted for his signature, such as bills, treaties, and international conventions. In principle, the king's initials are only a formality; he is bound by the Constitution to sign all bills and acts that the government presents to him. But having his own ideas about the craft of being king, Baudouin has managed to give this formality real dimension.

His civil cabinet, composed of a dozen officials, meticulously studies the bills and acts submitted to him. Their task is to verify that there is no contradiction between a new bill and an old law, and to make sure that no requisite formality has been overlooked by the minister directly responsible. They are also concerned with fuzzy wording or poor editing. Baudouin has thus developed the symbolic royal signature into a sort of final filter and a bulwark against carelessness. Often the king himself will call for further clarification before signing a decree or send it on to the State Council if he thinks it may be incompatible with an existing law.

After working with his team, the king holds private audiences with three or four people a morning, chosen from among members of government or from the opposition, with whom Baudouin maintains excellent relations. Around one o'clock the king returns home to his palace in Laeken. Ordinarily he lunches privately with Queen Fabiola and then spends his afternoons receiving visitors in his private office or studying dossiers. The two major subjects that intrigue Baudouin are Africa, where his grandfather's uncle, Leopold II, built an empire, and Europe. But not the Europe of kings; he actually seems to disassociate himself from his "brothers and cousins"—reigning or deposed European monarchs—and rarely participates in events where the royal jet set gathers. He is passionately interested, on the other hand, in the European economic community—the Common Market—which symbolically chose to install one of its most important seats in Brussels; and he appears to favor a supranational Europe, albeit a limited one.

Such is the scheme of the king's "normal" day. But everything is turned topsy-turvy in moments of governmental crisis.

THE BELGIAN KING constitutionally has the right to recall his ministers, but there has been no instance where a ministerial departure was related to the king's initiative. Most often a government coalition is upset by a parliamentary vote, or else a minister simply hands in his resignation. It is here that the king can intervene. He accepts the resignation, or tries to prevent it by asking the existing prime minister to reconsider his decision. Then he tries to raise the country out of the new political quagmire. A whole ritual has been established during which the king meets with the principal political figures one by one, as well as with representatives of various social and professional groups and organizations who had a part in precipitating the crisis or who might be capable of resolving it. The king tries to keep himself informed on three points: the general situation, the rapport between the political powers, and the name of a future prime minister who would be able to restore a coalition government.

Belgian political life is of an unparalleled complexity, since the numerous traditional political groups are further divided by the ethnic division between the Flemish and the Walloons. Baudouin is the one personality, not only level-headed but imperturbable, who knows how to control the stormiest discussions without giving either side cause to doubt his impartiality. It is a unique situation difficult to imagine in most other countries; the fact that the reigning monarch is of foreign origin, outside the fratricidal quarrels of the Belgians, adds greatly to the effectiveness of this royal mediation.

Once the government is formed, the royal palace announces the news to the country, and a date is set for the new prime minister to take his oath of office before the king at Brussels Palace. It is a simple administrative formality which, since Baudouin's reign, is bereft of ceremony.

There is no doubt that Baudouin's attitude since his accession stems in part from the months of his adolescence lived in prerevolutionary conditions. The day of his coronation more than 40 percent of the Belgians were violently hostile to the return of a monarch. Throughout their history, Belgians have always exhibited two distinct traits. Whether they are miners or farmers, merchants or lawyers, doctors or industrialists, they are all basically middle class, and a demanding middle class at that, famous for their critical and rebellious spirit. At the same time, they are fond of material comforts and like their lives to be peaceful and easy, endowed with physical security and abundant meals. (The fourteenth-century inhabitants of Brussels were called Kiekenfretters, which means, in Flemish, chicken guzzlers, or gluttons.) Baudouin knows how to reconcile these two characteristics—the rebellious spirit and the love of well-being. Since his accession, Belgium has had, in spite of internal tensions, an unprecedented era of economic development.

THROUGHOUT THE YEARS of Baudouin's reign, the monarchy has become ingrained in the land and has become, as well, a symbol of material prosperity. Still, the king is not universally admired or supported. When on extremely rare occasions he is booed, the perpetrators are a small minority of the extreme right, unhappy that this son of a king accused of collaboration during World War II refused to give wholesale amnesty to other collaborators. If this postwar crisis linked to the crown has dimmed over the years, it is due in part to the Belgian belief that the king and only the king can assure the country's union. But it is also, and more important, due to the character and intelligence of the man

Baudouin's mother, the beautiful and gracious Astrid, had been queen for only eighteen months when she was killed in an automobile accident in Switzerland. (Belgian Institute of Information and Documentation)

who was once a sad prince, then a solitary king, before evolving into the king of today who has made such a success of his career and his life. His childhood, his youth, and his reign reflect the vicissitudes of his country, shaken by the currents of history, murderous wars, and internal passions.

In 1934, little Baudouin was only four years old when his grandfather, the person he was closest to in his whole family, was killed in an accident. On the afternoon of February 16, King Albert I, an avid mountain climber, had been attached to a piece of rock that pulled loose, and he fell straight down into the void. Everything changed for Baudouin. His father became King Leopold III, and Baudouin became the duke of Brabant and heir to the throne. For the next several months Baudouin's mother played a dominant role in his life, trying to alleviate the loss and bewilderment he felt after his grandfather's death. Then, on Thursday August 29, 1935, Leopold III, on vacation in Switzerland at the villa Halishorn, proposed to his wife, Astrid, that they take a mountain drive in his sports car. The queen was reading the road map, and the king leaned over to take a look as well; in the next instant the car struck a tree. Astrid, thrown from the car, broke her skull and died almost instantly. At the royal palace of Brussels, where her body lay in state, 2 million people over the course of four days filed past her coffin to pay their last respects. Her death would weigh heavily on the history of the Belgian monarchy.

Baudouin passed the next four years in the lugubrious atmosphere of Laeken Castle. His only company was his older sister Josephine-Charlotte and his younger brother Albert.

Meanwhile, at the Belgian border, and even within the country, major problems were incubating. The worldwide economic crisis of the 1930s struck Belgium heavily; bankruptcies were innumerable, and unemployment grew every day along with the poverty and destitution of the workers (neither social security nor unemployment benefits existed at the time).

Even more serious was the German threat which was growing more sharply defined daily. Hitler's army occupied the Rhineland. Europe seemed irrevocably on the road to war, and Belgium, neutral as a result of the Accords of 1831 upon which the country was established, did not know which way to turn, or how to react.

Meanwhile, King Leopold's relations with his ministers and with Parliament were foundering. On February 2, 1939, Leopold III called his ministers together to express his dissatisfaction. Addressing experienced politicians, ambitious and concerned about their political prerogatives, he adopted the tone of a schoolmaster scolding his disobedient students. A few months later, the king refused to approve the list of honors proposed by the government and submitted for him to bestow. This act was yet another affront to the ministers and parliamentarians.

In spite of appearances, Leopold III was ill-equipped to handle the crises that were striking him and his country. He had certain qualities that harmed rather than helped him. Serious and conscientious, he followed rules to the letter. Shy and inhibited, he had no idea how to create personal links with the middle class, the bedrock of Belgian society.

During his father's reign, Leopold had had few responsibilities, and he had become one of the most popular men in the country. His handsomeness, his romantic air, and his marriage to the beautiful Princess Astrid of Sweden had touched the Belgians. Leopold was like a legendary prince and he had found the perfect bride. Princess Astrid seemed to have stepped straight out of a fairytale, so beautiful, gracious, charming, and gay was she. Her uncle, King Gustav V of Sweden, called her *un cadeau du ciel*—a heavenly gift. Brought up in the casual atmosphere of the Swedish court, she knew, from her first moments in Belgium, how to mix with the people—running her own errands, often on a bicycle, and insisting on standing in movie lines like everyone else—and how to make her family and husband happy. At Stuyvenberg Castle, where the royal couple and their three children lived, Queen Astrid served the meals herself. Her subjects could watch her swim, play golf, ski, or mountain climb. As long as she lived, something of her grace reflected on her husband. After her death, the king's sadness and melancholy moved the Belgians, especially the women, who were not insensitive to the charm of this young and apparently inconsolable man.

But because of his clashes with the government and with Parliament, as well as the economic problems plaguing Belgium, his popularity had already begun to erode when the German army, without warning, invaded the Netherlands and Belgium on May 10, 1940. It was a tragic month for the Belgian king. His army was shattered, German bombs were destroying the cities, and his quarrels with his ministers had become more and more frequent and violent. The success of the German attack convinced Leopold that France was lost and that all of Europe was soon going to be under Nazi domination.

The ministers, especially Prime Minister Hubert Pierlot, urged him to order a Belgian retreat toward France. But as commander-in-chief of the armed forces, Leopold ordered, to the contrary, a retreat toward the Belgian coast, moving further away from his allies. More serious yet was the major dispute about his own role. The government wanted him to follow the lead of Queen Wilhelmina of Holland, who, at the moment of her troops' retreat, expatriated herself in order to become a national symbol of resistance. Pierlot wrote Leopold several letters to remind him that "it is the government, and the government alone, which assumes the responsibility of chief of state," and to beg him to leave the country.

On May 25, two weeks after the invasion, the dispute deepened into disaster. The king received the prime minister, the minister of foreign affairs, and the ministers of defense and the interior at Wynendael Castle. The four ministers stood, because the king did not invite them to sit down. Pierlot once more repeated his demand: the king must leave the country and continue the fight. In spite of Leopold's refusal, the forthcoming rupture might yet have been avoided, had Paul-Henri Spaak, the minister of foreign affairs, not tried to convince the king man to man to change his mind in the final moments of their audience. Spaak, exhausted, asked if they could sit down, and he continued to set forth his arguments, but in a more relaxed manner. Once seated, the king also seemed to loosen up, to speak in more confidence, and his words, Spaak later wrote, amazed and terrified them. They realized that he wanted to continue to reign in Belgium and that, moreover, he intended to replace their democratically elected government with a government named by him and to reign as a sort of vassal to Hitler. Spaak recalled, "We told him what all this implied: dishonor, desertion, treason." Pierlot warned him that they were going to take a stand against him, but no argument seemed able to sway the sovereign's decision. Leopold concluded the audience with these words: "I understand you; you have your convictions and I know they are sincere. Do what they impel you to do." He then rose, shook their hands, and left the room. The rupture between the king and his government was complete. While Leopold remained in Belgium, his government fled to England.

To the Belgian population itself, which was living under German occupation and was virtually uninformed about the virulent accusations leveled by the Allies, Leopold's position was more understandable; the people even felt a certain sympathy toward the king, who had chosen to share his woes with his subjects. But the affection of the Belgians for their king vanished with the arrival of his new love.

King Leopold had met Liliane Baels in 1938, three years after the death of Queen Astrid. Her family, of Flemish origin, had not a shred of nobility in its background. She herself offered nothing that pleased the Belgian people. Her father had made a fortune during his years as a politician. Her grandmother, it was said, was a shrimpmonger at the Ostende fishmarket. This was nothing more than slander, but it created a disastrous impression.

When Leopold first met Liliane, on a golf course, she was twenty-one years old. She was tall, brunette, and exceptionally beautiful. At first they saw each other occasionally, but with the war and the king's voluntary exile to Laeken Palace, she was with him more often. Their morganatic marriage was common knowledge among most Belgians when Liliane Baels, who had been given the title Princess de Rethy, became pregnant. At the king's request, Cardinal Van Rouy ordered that a pastoral letter be read in all the churches of the kingdom informing the faithful of the king's new matrimonial situation. The Belgians took it poorly. The man whom they had considered as the symbol of their suffering under the occupation, on voluntary retreat in his castle, and still mourning the death of his wife, was in reality concerned only with his own happiness. An editorial in a Belgian paper took him to task: "Your Majesty, we had thought that you had turned toward us in your bereavement, and we have just learned that you are leaning on the shoulder of a woman."

Liliane's family didn't help ameliorate the situation. Her father seemed to be living, if not royally, at least like a duke from his politically gained capital stashed in southern France. Her brother evaded his military service. In spite of a draft notice sent to him, he had refused to join the Belgian troops that were serving with the English army, an act that caused him, at the end of the war, to be tried and condemned. Worse still, Liliane's marriage to Leopold was not legal, since the Constitution stipulated the consent of the government for sovereign marriages, and that the king obviously had not obtained.

Princess de Rethy, to her credit, at least created a warm and tender home environment for her husband's three children. But even this was turned against her when the Belgians learned with indignation that Queen Astrid's children were calling "the adventuress" *maman*. The court spokesman tried in vain to explain that it was the children themselves, against the advice of Princess de Rethy, who insisted on calling her so. Nothing worked. The Belgians attributed all sorts of evil and treachery to the king's wife.

During the war, the king met with Hitler at Berchtesgaden, in the Bavarian Alps. The Allies, as well as the Belgian population, interpreted this as tangible proof of Leopold III's political collaboration with the Germans. The king was spurned by his government-in-exile and rejected by most of the population as the war drew to a close.

On June 6, 1944, after the Allied troops landed in Normandy, the Germans informed Leopold that he would have to leave the next day for Germany. He was detained at first at the Castle of Hirschstein-sur-Elbe, then, early in 1945, at Strobl in Austria. Shortly after the liberation of Belgium, the king himself was liberated by the American Seventh Armored Division on May 7, 1945. Demonstrations broke out all over Belgium against his return. On May 10, the prince regent, Leopold's younger brother Charles, and four ministers representing the four major segments of the country, presented themselves to the king in Austria to inform him that the Belgian population, and particularly the political parties, were categorically opposed to his return to Belgium.

For five years Belgium was torn by an internal battle over the subject of the king. Finally, on March 12, 1950, the Belgians went to the polls. Fifty-seven percent of the voters favored Leopold's return, but the majority of those in favor came from the Flemish provinces, while in Walloon areas the king received substantially less than half the votes. The king returned on July 22, but ten days later, during an anti-Leopoldist demonstration, the police opened fire on the crowd. This time the government was determined: the king had to abdicate. If he did not comply, the government would resign en masse and the political parties would refuse to form any other government as long as Leopold sat on the throne.

On July 16, 1951, the abdication ceremony took place in Brussels Palace. Pale and drawn, Leopold addressed his eldest son: "My dear Baudouin, it is with pride that I transmit to you the noble and heavy mission of henceforth wearing the crown of a Belgium still, in spite of the most terrible of wars and the upheavals that followed, territorially and morally intact, free and faithful to its traditions." In the palace's large reception hall, the kings, both in uniform, stood erect behind a heavy oak table. The ministers, the chamberlains, and the court officials who surrounded them all wore expressions suitable for a funeral, but nobody looked more unhappy, more at a loss, than the new twenty-one-year-old king, who had attained what should have been a joyous milestone in his life.

DURING THE MIDDLE AGES a common malady struck the German principalities: *Kronprinzen-Krankheit,* or crown prince disease. It attacked young, and sometimes not so young, heirs to the throne who wanted to usurp the rights of their fathers, overthrow them, or kill them to take possession of their crown and power. Baudouin IV the Bearded, who died in 1035, was a victim of the "disease." But almost a millennium later Baudouin the clean-shaven, new king of the Belgians in 1951, far from coveting his father's throne, would happily have given it back. He was a shy and affectionate son who had lived his whole childhood at his father's side—a marvelous father who skied, who swam so well, who had taught him so much, who stood head and shoulders above anybody else. King Leopold spoke many languages, he knew everybody, and even during his exile he had kept his dignity and remained master of his destiny. Baudouin loved his mother, whom he remembered more and more dimly, but he also loved his stepmother, Princess de Rethy, whom he infinitely admired. Baudouin insisted that his father, Princess de Rethy, and his brothers and sisters continue to live with him in Laeken Castle. There the dethroned king presided over meals, led conversations, organized games, and occupied the royal bedchamber. Baudouin, the new king, continued to occupy his study on the second floor, adjacent to the room of his younger brother Albert. He still had his old bookshelves filled with scientific magazines and algebra and trigonometry textbooks. When anyone asked him questions during semiofficial dinners at Laeken, he would turn to his father to answer for him. Invariably, Leopold said to him, at least in public, "It's for you to answer." If the young king hesitated, Leopold added, "You have your advisers." Nevertheless, some Belgians were heard to remark, "Baudouin reigns over Belgium, but Leopold reigns over Baudouin."

In the evenings, Baudouin could relax in the warmth of his family, but he spent his days practicing his new trade. Every morning at 8:45 he left for his office at the royal palace in a black Cadillac that displayed a banner of black, yellow, and red silk embossed with the lion of Flanders. During the short ride, he read his files on pending legislation and the brief commentaries his father had scribbled during the night. Baudouin almost always wore the beige uniform of lieutenant-general. On his desk he kept a photograph of his father and a bouquet of fresh flowers that Princess de Rethy gave him every morning.

The king devoted himself to his new career with characteristic seriousness. He meticulously studied his files, met with his advisers and ministers as often as possible, and even visited incognito the squalid workers' quarters that surrounded his capital. He was scandalized by what he saw: dilapidated apartments where people slept three or four to a bed or even on empty bags, courtyards full of garbage, seven-story buildings with toilets long broken. In one garret children were fighting over their parents' only chair. Baudouin was furious, especially after he heard from the local parish priest that people were paying hiked-up rents for these miserable lodgings.

As soon as the press reported his visit, his popularity took a giant leap forward. But a few months later it precipitously fell back. An unusually violent storm had devastated the Netherlands and the north of Belgium. Tens of thousands of people found themselves without a roof over their heads in the rain. In Holland, Queen Juliana visited the damaged areas, setting up an emergency-aid fund, soliciting donations from banks, and even canvassing the city streets herself. But Baudouin was away with his father and Princess de Rethy in Antibes, where press photographers caught him lying on a lounge chair by the sea, laughing joyously. Several days after the catastrophe, he returned to Belgium but stayed only a few hours before rejoining his family in southern France. A court spokesman tried to explain that the king had left again to "care for an attack of tonsillitis," but the press, along with the members of Parliament, was outraged. They blamed Leopold and Princess de Rethy, this time probably rightly so, for inviting him to rejoin them. Devoted and obedient son that he was, he didn't know how to refuse. The people's anger turned once again against the father, and Baudouin, whose popularity was certainly diminished, fared much less badly as a result of this incident than he might have expected. But it was a salutary warning and the last time he made such a grave error.

BAUDOUIN tried to modernize the workings of the court, which had been one of the most liberal and contemporary in Europe in the nineteenth century but which seemed antiquated and backward compared with the Scandinavian courts with which Baudouin was allied. For example, after an official audience, a visitor still had to take one hundred steps backward before he could turn his back on his sovereign. With Leopold still presiding over family affairs, modernizing the court was extremely difficult. However, the dethroned king had promised to leave the palace, and even the country, as soon as Baudouin took a wife. The problem was that the king, a stern and rigid young man, didn't look at women and had never even learned how to dance. Nothing could entice Baudouin to lead a more worldly life, not even the quest for a wife. He didn't seem ripe for marriage, but the Belgians could be patient, long unaccustomed as they were to having a real queen.

Astrid had been queen of Belgium for only eighteen months, and the Belgians had known only one other queen, Elisabeth, in more than half a century. Elisabeth, a sophisticated sovereign, interested in the world, in the arts, in new political ideas, was the only woman who played a significant role in the life of the Belgian dynasty. Queen Louise-Marie, wife of Leopold I (1790–1865), was a sad and lonely drudge. Marie-Henriette, wife of Leopold II (1835–1909), was a merry, smiling Austrian archduchess when she mounted the throne, but she grew into a neglected and ridiculed cipher. Leopold III's wife, Princess de Rethy, never played a public role and tried to appear as seldom as possible. Marie-José, Leopold III's sister and the former queen of Italy, lived in Switzerland and rarely returned to her native country. Baudouin's older sister, Josephine-Charlotte, left Belgium in 1953 to marry Prince Jean of Luxembourg, the future grand duke, and had her own national obligations.

So Queen Elisabeth, wife of King Albert I (1875–1934), stood alone as the most prominent and enduring of Belgium's royal women. While she was queen she carried out her duties perfectly, her sense of discipline holding sway over her imperious character. But after Albert's death in 1934, her personality seemed to grow more and more capricious and eccentric.

She filled her house with artists, painters, and musicians, and spent hours each day playing the violin. One morning at exactly six o'clock the members of her court discovered her at the bottom of an old bombshell crater in the castle park playing away on her violin. She explained to her chamberlain and her ladies-in-waiting, stunned to learn she wasn't asleep in her bed, "The night was marvelous, all starry. This morning is splendid. What's more, the acoustics in this hole are better than in any auditorium."

Elisabeth often astounded the Flemish and Walloon middle class with her political opinions far to the left even of the Belgian Socialist party. She regularly visited the Soviet Union, the last time at age eighty-seven, and was enchanted by everything she saw. She confided to her friends that the Communist system was far from perfect, that it needed many generations to achieve its goal, but that it was the system most concerned with the individual. She was also a great admirer of Israel and, to the great displeasure of successive Belgian governments, supported most Israeli political decisions.

Thus, while the Belgians were fond of Elisabeth, she was not a queen quite to their tastes. They had great expectations for Baudouin, whom they knew would not fully assume his role until he married and his father left the family castle of Laeken. Everyone hoped for a fairytale princess, beautiful, young, royal, Catholic, who would personify all the women of Wallonia and Flanders, instill in the king the confidence he lacked, and bring a smile to the face of this unhappy young man. The press regularly "engaged" him to the most beautiful princesses in the world, and just as regularly his spokesman denied the speculations. Then on September 16, 1960, Prime Minister Gaston Eyskens announced in a radio bulletin the engagement of the king to an "unknown," the only woman the sentimental press had failed to mention: doña Fabiola de Mora y Aragón, a slim Spanish aristocrat, thirty-two years old, two years older than her husband-to-be.

The future queen participated in many sports, but she particularly enjoyed tennis and horseback riding. She played the guitar, the piano, and the accordion. Above all, she was extremely pious.

Albert I and Elizabeth at their villa in 1916. (Belgian Institute of Information and Documentation)

She never missed a religious ceremony, and those close to her long believed she would eventually become a nun. In Madrid, where she had her own apartment—although she dined and slept at her mother's palace—she occasionally attended parties and celebrations frequented by the aristocratic Spanish youth, but she was always extremely reserved at these events and no one remembers ever seeing her dance.

Fabiola's father, don Gonzalo de Mora y Fernandez, had, in 1894, been accorded the title count of Mora by Pope Leon XII, much to the dismay of the authentic Spanish Mora counts, ennobled in the sixteenth century under the reign of Philip II. Her mother, doña Bianca de Aragón, was not a descendant of the illustrious kings of Aragón: "Aragón" was simply a surname. Don Gonzalo died in 1954 from complications resulting from a broken thigh bone, and doña Bianca, who possessed one of Spain's greatest fortunes, henceforth spent most of her time occupied with charitable institutions, notably the Society for the Prevention of Cruelty to Animals in Spain.

Most of Fabiola's life was spent in the enormous Mora castle that the family acquired in 1921 and enlarged over the years. Today it is surrounded by a middle-class neighborhood with numerous high-rise apartments.

Fabiola was never a spoiled child. In her large family she was neither among the oldest nor the youngest of her six brothers and sisters: Maria, Gonzalo, Anna-Maria, Alejandro, Maria-Luz, and naughty Jaime, the enfant terrible of the family. Order and discipline reigned over the household. During the Spanish Civil War (1936–1939), the family went into exile in Switzerland, moving into a grand-luxe hotel in Lausanne. The children lived two to a room, with a governess in each room. Fabiola learned German and English from her governesses and French from the Sisters of the Assumption.

In 1944, at the age of fifteen, Fabiola was deemed old enough to have a room of her own in the Madrid palace, but she was still obliged to make her bed and clean her room. Since she was very fond of her youngest sister, Maria-Luz, who did not take well to domestic chores, Fabiola also made up her room. Early on she acquired a taste for impeccable order. It upset her to see the smallest object out of place. The Mora house was not a cheery one: after the father's death, no music, no radio, and no television were permitted; the household remained in deep mourning. A television set that had been delivered two days before the count died was sent back immediately after.

Until her engagement, Fabiola followed a strict daily routine: she woke up at 7:30, and after less than half an hour devoted to her personal toilette and breakfast, she attended 8:00 mass at the Church of Santa Barbara. Right after mass she went to the Madrid military hospital, where she worked as a nurse in general surgery; she never missed a single day of work. She returned home for lunch and then, in the afternoon, visited "her poor," driving her car from house to house.

At the time of her engagement, Fabiola was the only child still living at the palace with her mother. She submitted to a daily timetable that was rigid and unalterable: the household staff dined at nine o'clock and then served dinner at ten o'clock sharp for the countess and Fabiola, who were seated at opposite ends of a long table; thirty minutes later the whole staff had to appear in front of the dining room table to recite the rosary, led one night by the mother, the next night by the daughter. The seventeen-member staff, on their knees, murmured the prayers in low voices. Two candles supplied the only lighting in the enormous room. At eleven o'clock, all the lights in the house had to be off.

THE MORA FAMILY learned almost accidentally that Fabiola was engaged. The countess and her tribe of children and grandchildren gathered as was their custom in the large family vacation villa in Zarans, on the Basque coast. They were posing in the garden for the village photographer, who at least twice a year captured on film this family infatuated with the idea of tradition and memories. As soon as everyone was lined up, Fabiola announced, laughing, "This is my last photo without my fiancé." Her mother, her brothers, and her sisters stared at her, agape. The countess was indignant that a suitor had dared ask for her daughter's hand without consulting her. Who was this poorly brought up young man? she asked. Fabiola apologized. "It's Baudouin, the Belgian king. He certainly wanted to ask you for my hand directly, but it appears that protocol prohibits it." Two days later Belgian Prime Minister Eyskens announced the king's engagement over the radio.

At first the Belgians were shocked that the king had chosen a

Spanish girl whom nobody knew anything about, then quickly became enchanted by the idea that their sorrowful bachelor king, who, it was thought, would eventually join a religious order, was not only going to marry but perhaps be happy as well. On September 22, 1960, Brussels welcomed Fabiola. Hundreds of thousands of people waited along the avenue to have a glimpse of the young stranger who would become their queen.

The engagement was brief; barely three months elapsed between the announcement and the marriage. On December 15, a civil ceremony was conducted by the burgomaster in the throne room of Brussels Palace. Afterward, the king, the queen, and their families left for the Cathedral of Saints-Michel-et-Gudule for the religious ceremony. To the accompaniment of organ music, Baudouin and Fabiola entered the sumptuously decorated cathedral. The walls were draped with purple and gold tapestries, flags from nine Belgian provinces hung from the balconies, and 12,000 carnations, the Spanish national flower, decorated the altar. The couple were wed by Cardinal de Malines, who thirty-four years earlier had married Astrid and Leopold.

A conservative man to the end, Baudouin sent a message to his people just before leaving on his honeymoon: "To truly love is not to look at each other, but rather to look together in the same direction. Our eyes and our hearts are turned toward you, my countrymen. May your homes always know the joy born of self-forgetfulness and of duty accomplished." The queen added her own personal message, ending with, "From now on my heart and my life are shared not only with my husband but with all of you."

The Belgians wondered about this new family, which resembled neither the Belgian middle class nor the local aristocracy they were accustomed to. For several months there was incessant talk about one of the new queen's brothers, don Jaime, marquis of Casasiera, called Jimmy by his friends and Fabiolo by the world press. Jimmy personified the classic Latin American playboy. His attire was startling—often a gold cape and red pants. He spent millions of dollars carelessly, played the piano in nightclubs, hunted lions in his spare moments, and passed the major part of his time seducing women. At the time of the royal wedding, he was married to a twenty-four-year-old Mexican starlet, Rosita Arena, who would have become a striptease artist, gossips said, had she not become instead the sister-in-law of an extremely austere king. Although married,

Jimmy continued to collect young and beautiful companions from all over the world. Jimmy's activities notwithstanding, neither he nor any other member of the Mora y Aragón family played a role in the life of the royal couple, in the Belgian court, or in Belgium. They rarely came to Brussels and never appeared in the local scandal sheets.

SHORTLY AFTER Baudouin and Fabiola's honeymoon, a wave of strikes rolled over Belgium. The mines, the factories, even the port of Anvers, were paralyzed. In the streets of Brussels, strikers stoned the display windows of movie houses showing as a "spectacular" a color film on the royal marriage. The popularity of the monarchy barely missed plunging once again to ground zero. But, unexpectedly, it was Baudouin and Fabiola themselves who brought Belgium back from the brink of disaster. The king, serving as an intermediary between the left and the right—that is to say, between the Walloons and the Flemish—used his unobtrusive political clout to avoid a major schism in the country's social and political life. Fabiola, who eventually learned Flemish, proved herself not to be intimidated by a few hostile crises. Alone at the wheel of her little car, she visited destitute families, exactly as she had done in Madrid, earning the admiration of Belgians in all political camps.

This crisis had barely been resolved when two new catastrophes struck Belgium at the end of 1960. First, a village was buried in a landslide. A few hours later, in the middle of the night, while it was still extremely dangerous to drive in the area, the queen, her head covered by a scarf, arrived without guard or lady-in-waiting, to help organize first aid. She was there not only as queen but also as a former nurse, who bandaged the wounded and consoled children on her knee. A few days later, floods struck Wallonia. Once again, the queen arrived on the spot. It was a far cry from the February day in 1953 when, under the influence of Leopold and Princess de Rethy, Baudouin remained in Antibes while storms ravaged the north of his country.

The queen has disappointed her people on only one major point: the continuation of the dynasty. For months, for years, the country awaited the happy news that an heir would be born. Finally that day arrived and the pope himself announced that the royal couple were at last expecting a child. But, sadly, the queen had a miscarriage.

Every day without exception, Fabiola performs her queenly duties. She visits hospitals, schools, nurseries, and often drops in on people who have written the palace asking special favors. Well organized, she employs a secretary and six other assistants who handle questions on mental hygiene and on the handicapped, as well as on musical training—all projects to which she devotes much of her attention. She knows how to listen to complaints and how to resolve them. The Belgians believe that she often dips into her personal fortune, which is considerable, to come to the aid of her subjects. It is customary to say that queens are good, but with Fabiola it's more than simple goodness: a royal and fraternal devotion to the whole of her people seems to govern her entire life.

Fabiola has no titled ladies-in-waiting, as did Queen Astrid and Queen Elisabeth before her. On each of her journeys she is accompanied by a woman who has some familiarity with the subject. She takes along an expert in the medical field when she visits a hospital, or an art expert when she attends an exhibition. She was accompanied by the Polish wife of a Nobel Prize winner when she visited Poland. The queen's ladies-in-waiting are thus chosen on their own merit, or on that of their husbands', and not, as was formerly the case, by virtue of their birth. This highly democratic practice, instituted by Fabiola, permits thousands of Belgian women to be briefly honored with the title of Lady-in-Waiting to the Queen. But it allocates an extra chore to the royal secretary's office, charged with contacting the woman selected, and requires an effort on the queen's part as well, since she is often unacquainted with the woman who, for a few hours, will be her lady-in-waiting.

Fabiola also does not have a titled hairdresser. The hairdresser who comes to Laeken and who accompanies her on trips is also chosen on merit, and is often a prize-winning stylist. She is not loyal to any one person.

Fabiola has tried to make the king's home as warm as possible, and to share all his tastes. Their day begins at seven o'clock, and an hour later they breakfast together, usually on coffee and fruit. Deeply religious, they attend mass three times a week in the chapel of Laeken Palace. Fabiola rejoins her husband for lunch. On the large oval mahogany table in the Laeken dining room, they rarely set out tablecloths, which are more time-consuming to care for,

King Baudouin and Queen Fabiola attend a gala performance at the Royal Monnaie Theater in Brussels. (Belgian Institute of Information and Documentation)

but use placemats instead. Accustomed since early childhood to a large house and a large staff, the queen scrupulously oversees the workings of the palace, and no detail, no matter how insignificant, escapes her attention.

In the evening, if the king is not busy with an official function, the royal couple enjoy having friends over for dinner. One of the guests most often in attendance is Cardinal Suenens, former primate of Belgium. Baudouin and Fabiola love to organize dinners on a theme—musical, artistic, or scientific—with food prepared by their French chef. For cocktails, the couple prefer fruit juice to the sherry they offer their guests. Occasionally they go out on the town together, to a restaurant or to the theater. Sometimes, between nine and ten o'clock at night, they can be spotted browsing or shopping in a self-service bookstore in Brussels. At home, they listen to music on their state-of-the-art stereo. Baudouin particularly loves Bach and Mozart, while Fabiola prefers Chopin.

For short doses of rest and recreation, they spend an occasional incognito weekend in London or Paris. They also own two vacation houses. One is on the Dutch border in Op Grimbie, where they stroll among the huge trees and around the two ponds that give the park a melancholy charm, or they walk in the nearby mountains accompanied by their dogs—the queen's dachshunds and the king's Hungarian pointers. The other house is in Motril, south of Granada in Spain, where they spend part of each summer. The king, passionately interested in astronomy, has installed a telescope in this house and he spends entire evenings with the queen observing the stars. He also goes fishing and occasionally brings home decent-size tuna.

Because of sciatica Baudouin is no longer as active as he once was. He has had to give up tennis and horseback riding, and more importantly, driving fast cars, formerly one of his greatest pleasures.

Baudouin maintains close relations with his sister Josephine-Charlotte, wife of the grand-duke of Luxembourg, and with his brother Albert, the heir to the throne. Albert is in charge of Belgian economic missions abroad and lives with his family at Le Belvedere, their estate. His wife, Paola Ruffo di Calabria, doubtless one of the prettiest women in all of the European aristocracy, is involved in many charitable activities; among her favorites is a child-care program called The Cradle. Elegant, she frequently attends the fashion shows in Paris. Since Albert is only four years younger than Baudouin, it is likely that he will never be king, so the role has every chance of falling to Albert's oldest son, Philippe. The latter does not carry the title of duke of Brabant, normally reserved for heirs to the throne, but since his eighteenth birthday, the age of constitutional majority in Belgium, he has been, by law, a senator even though he was never formally installed in that office.

Philippe's education reflects the double culture of the country over which he will likely reign: he spent nine years in a Jesuit school, St. Michel de Bruzelles, then attended classes at a Benedictine school, Lapham Abbey, where instruction was given in Flemish. Like his uncle the king, he has always shown more of an interest in scientific subjects than in literature. Another step in his training was at the Royal Belgian Military Academy.

Philippe loves to travel. He has already visited Italy and the United States frequently. When he spends weekends at the family property in Fenffe, in the Ardennes, he loves to take walks and listen to jazz or electronic music.

Baudouin and Fabiola have always had a soft spot for Albert's children. When Philippe's sister Astrid turned eighteen four years ago, the royal couple broke away from their customary austerity and reserve and threw an enormous birthday party in the greenhouse of Laeken Palace, world famous for its flowers.

Since his accession, Baudouin has given only one ball, and that was more than twenty years ago. But he has hardly been idle. During the first twenty-five years of his reign he has made 36 official visits abroad, organized 555 receptions and held 360 luncheons and dinners. He has attended, in all, thirteen concerts and eleven lectures or movies, at the end of which he has always said a few words to the artists and organizers. And he has given 215 speeches.

It was not very long ago, under the reign of Leopold III, that most of the king's colleagues were counts or barons, at the very least knights—in any case noble. Today the king does not have one aristocrat in his political cabinet, and although aristocrats make up 50 percent of the grand marshal's department, the entire department consists of only four people. In spite of these statistics, which would seem to indicate a diminished aristocracy, the Belgian nobility has never been quashed by opposing regimes and has never known the burden of a republic in the course of its history. There

Top: The sovereigns in one of the greenhouses on the royal estate of Laeken. Both take a great interest in botany. (Belgian Institute of Information and Documentation)

Bottom: A family dinner at the castle. From left to right: Princess Paola, the king, Princess Margretha (the king's niece), Princess Astrid, Prince Albert, the queen, Prince Philippe, and Prince Laurent. (Belgian Institute of Information and Documentation)

are currently a thousand noble families in Belgium, including eight princely families, three ducal families, and ten families of marquis, one of which has a rare privilege—all the children, not only the eldest son, inherit the title. (Since 1815, with one exception, practically no new grants of these three titles have been made.) There are, as well, 77 families of counts, 33 families of viscounts, 274 families of barons, 85 knights, and a few hundred other noble families who carry no title. And all today feel like orphans, because, since Baudouin's accession, they have lost the "magnetic pole" fundamental to all aristocracy—their king. Baudouin appears uninterested in them. He treats them like one social class among many, remaining faithful to his commitment not to become the pawn of any group, class, or party, be it the aristocracy or the unions.

Since the beginning of history, kings have always accorded noble titles for services rendered and were surrounded by nobles who had the run of the court. While the first practice is still in force, the second is on its way to becoming obsolete. In Belgium, the aristocrats as a group are no longer invited to the royal palace. And, as far as anyone knows, it is not from among them in particular that the royal couple choose their friends. At the only ball ever given by Baudouin, the aristocrats were lost in a sea of politicians and notables.

The monarchy is not a great expense for Belgium—in 1980 the total cost came to about $3 million. This is the amount of Baudouin's annual endowment, out of which he deducts his personal expenses; he reimburses the state, as well, for the salaries of court officials. He has no private airplane, no yacht, and only a few cars whose maintenance he covers personally. Although Leopold II was reputed to be one of the richest men in the world, his grandnephew, the current king, is probably one of the world's poorest sovereigns. He has almost no personal fortune, no collections of any great value, no family jewels. His only private residences are the house in Op Grimbie and the Spanish villa in Motril. His office consists of a few rooms on the first floor of Brussels Palace, offered for his use by the state; the rest of the huge building serves as state reception rooms and guest rooms for foreign chiefs of state on official visits. Laeken Castle, the king's residence, also belongs to the Belgian state.

From the moment he abdicated in 1951, Leopold III, once the

center of his country's political storms, faded from public view. He left the traditional royal residence of Laeken after Baudouin's marriage and retired to the smaller castle in Argenteuil where he devoted the last twenty years of his life to scientific research and anthropology. He also traveled extensively and became, like many an elderly pensioner, an avid golfer.

It was during this period that some of his harshest critics and most violent political opponents became occasional associates and sometime friends. Former foreign minister Paul-Henri Spaak, who during World War II had led the campaign against Leopold's remaining in Belgium and had subsequently asked for his abdication, became a regular dinner guest. Sometimes on summer evenings, the tall figure of the former king could be seen strolling with visitors on the castle grounds, perhaps rewriting Belgium's history in the light of the stormy postwar years.

When Leopold died, in September 1983, he was given a national funeral; many of his former subjects were surprised at the grief they felt and suddenly displayed. To some political commentators, it seemed as if he had been granted a new legitimacy after he was chased from the throne.

This renewed warmth toward a man once heartily detested was in part due to the close and occasionally friendly personal relations that Belgium's kings, past and present, have always maintained with the political establishment. In most monarchies, there is a symbiosis between king and nation from which political intermediaries are generally excluded. In Belgium the contrary is the rule. Baudouin, like Leopold before him, is rarely seen or heard in public, but he maintains close and regular contacts with ministers and parliamentarians. The throne may be less spectacular in Belgium than it is in the other monarchies, but its day-to-day working relationship with its political leaders is unique. It will be up to Baudouin's successors to try to preserve this privileged link between sovereign and government in a rapidly changing world.

9

LUXEMBOURG

◆

A Grand-Duke's
Comfortable Preserve

Luxembourg is so small (1,600 square miles and 380,000 inhabitants, 90,000 of whom are foreigners) that the monarchy is omnipresent. It is impossible to traverse the capital without noticing the rooftops and slender watchtowers of the grand-ducal palace in the center of the city. The grand-ducal crown appears everywhere, even on signposts and road maps.

In this fiercely egalitarian country where no one, not even the prime minister, is interested in calling attention to himself if it means risking the esteem of his fellow citizens, the grand-ducal family plays by an entirely different set of rules. It is readily accepted that the family needs a magnificent park and some two hundred rooms in the castle of Colmar-Berg. Their extreme privacy is respected to such an extent that nowhere else, it seems, does a monarchy arouse so little passion. Luxembourg's grand-ducal family stirs up a calm admiration in some and a profound indifference in others. No national vote, no opinion poll, has been taken in over sixty years to measure its popularity. It has no adversaries in the Parliament or in the government. Schoolchildren read in their history books that Grand-Duke Jean is "the personification of the Luxembourgian national soul." But most people would rather identify themselves with Gaston Thorn, the undisputed national hero, a former prime minister who at one time was promoted to the presidency of the Common Market, membership in which has made little Luxembourg the equal of her big sisters in Europe and beyond.

Luxembourg was geographically dismembered three times in its history and was governed, at various times, by Burgundy, France, Spain, Austria, Bavaria, Hesse, Holland, Belgium, and even by Russia and Italy. Almost every European country has, at one time or another, aimed its sights on this territory.

In 1815, after four hundred years of foreign domination, Luxembourg was made a grand-duchy by the Congress of Vienna and united with the crown of the Netherlands. By virtue of the "Family Pact," formed in 1783 and ratified by the Luxembourg constitution of 1848, no female succession would be possible in Luxembourg as long as there were still male representatives of the House of Nassau, which ruled in Germany and the Netherlands. Thus when Wilhelmina mounted the Dutch throne in 1890, Duke Adolphe of Nassau became the first grand-duke of an independent Luxembourg.

Arriving from Germany at the age of seventy-three, Adolphe, who was unfamiliar with the affairs of the country, left most of the major decision making to the prime minister. However, he promised the Luxembourgers that he would work with them toward "the development of autonomy, free institutions, and the consolidation of autonomy and independence in relation to Europe."

When Adolphe died in 1905 he was succeeded by his son Guillaume. But Guillaume was a man already marked by death, and he passed away in 1912 having exercised no more power in his seven-year reign than his father did. He left six daughters from his marriage to Marie-Anne de Bragance, Infanta of Portugal. Before dying, to ensure his succession, Guillaume had promulgated a new family statute, exactly the opposite of the 1783 pact, authorizing women to inherit the Luxembourg throne.

His daughters were extraordinarily beautiful. The most beautiful of all was the eldest, Princess Marie-Adelaide, who mounted the throne in 1912 at the age of eighteen. A few years after her succession, she attempted to unseat the leftist majority in Parliament with

her own rightist coalition. The plan failed. Exercising the prerogative sanctioned by law, the extremely authoritarian young woman
dissolved Parliament and ordered new elections, but once again the
leftists were victorious. Marie-Adelaide's actions did not make her
popular—nor did the rumors, during World War I, that she sided
with Germany. With public opinion growing more and more
against her, she abdicated in 1919. She was succeeded by her sister
Charlotte, who won the support of 75 percent of the population
through a national referendum which asked Luxembourgers to
choose among a republic, continuation of the dynasty, or union
with Belgium.

SINCE THAT TIME, no country in Europe has centralized all the
currents, all the ethnic groups, and all the languages of the old
continent better than this minuscule state. The lineage and education of the present grand-duke reflect the rich, diverse, and international character of the family's past. Grand-Duke Jean retains the
crown of the ancient Nassau-Weilbourg family, of German origin,
and related to the Orange-Nassaus, reigning in the Netherlands.
His father, Felix de Bourbon-Parme, was descended in direct line
from Louis XIV. His grandmother, the Grand-Duchess Marie-
Anne, born Princess of Bragance, was descended from the kings of
Portugal. And his wife, Grand-Duchess Josephine-Charlotte, has
Swedish, French, and German ancestors among others in her family tree.

Luxembourgers take little interest in the day-to-day activities of
the reigning family. When Grand-Duchess Josephine-Charlotte
does her errands in the city, few heads turn her way. When Grand-
Duke Jean opens a local meeting, the applause from a few dozen
participants is more polite than enthusiastic. In Luxembourg, unlike most of the other European monarchies, there is no passionate
current of opinion for or against the mnonarchy. It has become just
another of the country's institutions, one that has no great practical
use, perhaps, but that served to reinstate the independence Luxembourg had lost for over four centuries.

In the court of Luxembourg, the number of dignitaries are few.
Grand-Duchess Charlotte, Jean's mother, has her own personal
chamberlain; Grand-Duchess Josephine-Charlotte has four ladies-
in-waiting. The house of Grand-Duke Jean counts fifteen other

royal positions. Court Marshal Guy de Meyser presides over the houses of the grand-ducal couple. Thanks to this relatively small team, whose expenses are equally small, Luxembourg prides itself on maintaining the least expensive sovereign family in Europe. The total cost of royal endowments in the grand-duchy is around 67 million Luxembourgian francs, a modest sum to pay in exchange for the honor of having a sovereign and belonging to the exclusive little club of ten European monarchies. Yet the amount is not exactly negligible when compared with the royal finances of Belgium, whose king, charged with important political functions in a country ten times as large and twenty times more populated, has an endowment only 50 percent higher.

"HE REPRESENTS CONTINUITY," Luxembourgers readily say of the grand-duke, "and saves us from having to organize elections every five years. What's more, he's a charming and remarkably well-bred man." Exercising his monarchical role since 1964 without mistakes but at the same time without real brilliance, Grand-Duke Jean has helped to transform the workings of the Luxembourg monarchy into something resembling the presidential function in a parliamentary regime.

Every morning at approximately 8:30, the grand-duke leaves his residence, Colmar-Berg Castle, by car—a Rover or a Jaguar, which he usually drives himself—and heads for the grand-ducal palace in the center of Luxembourg, twenty-four miles away. Notified of his departure, the sentry at the grand-ducal palace stands ready to salute his sovereign when, around 9:00, he drives through the large open gates. The grand-duke quickly gets out of his car and disappears through the heavy palace doors. He ascends the great marble stairway, passes the enormous Russian malachite vases set on pedestals on the landing, and arrives in the audience salon. Here, the grand-duke receives ambassadors from more than one hundred countries who have come to present their credentials to him. (Fourteen ambassadors reside permanently in Luxembourg, among them representatives from the Common Market as well as from the United States, the Soviet Union, and Bulgaria.) Jean also receives his prime minister once a week (usually on Wednesdays) and his minister of foreign affairs approximately once a month.

At noon he returns to Colmar-Berg Castle to join the grand-duchess, whose mornings are taken up with visits to charitable institutions or with meetings of the numerous cultural organizations she sponsors. They have an informal lunch, either alone or with those of their children who happen to be home. The meal usually consists of a light appetizer, a meat course with vegetables and a salad, sometimes some cheese, and a dessert or fruit.

Afternoons are sometimes spent on other official activities, but it often happens that the grand-ducal couple are free. Grand-Duke Jean takes advantage of the time to read, preferably books on ancient or modern history, French or German literature, or even books in English, a language which the prince speaks fluently and particularly appreciates. In the office he maintains in Colmar-Berg Castle, he also pursues the subjects that are closest to his heart— the management of Luxembourg's natural and human resources, the preservation of its ecological and historical heritage, and its industrial development.

Grand-Duchess Josephine-Charlotte, who maintains excellent personal relations with numerous painters and sculptors, both Luxembourgian and foreign, grants an annual prize, established by her husband's great-grandfather, to reward a Luxembourgian artist. The winner is selected by a jury, but it is the grand-duchess herself who bestows the prize.

In the evening the grand-ducal family again dines *en famille,* unless they are receiving personal friends. Among the most regular visitors are King Baudouin and Queen Fabiola of Belgium, who come by train or car and are welcomed without ceremony at the station by the grand-duke. The grand-ducal couple are also regular visitors to King Baudouin's Laeken Castle.

Josephine-Charlotte is the sister of the Belgian king, and the daughter of King Leopold III and the radiant but short-lived Queen Astrid. Josephine-Charlotte's youth was marked by her mother's tragic death in an automobile accident, then by the German occupation and a long, difficult period under SS and Gestapo surveillance after her deportation to Germany.

During her youth the princess had met Prince Jean frequently at weddings and official ceremonies. (Jean's mother, Grand-Duchess Charlotte, was the princess's godmother.) The two also got to know each other during vacations spent with their families in France and Italy. They became engaged in September 1952, but the news was not officially made public until November, confirming the rumors that had begun to circulate. Their marriage took place on April 9, 1953. Josephine-Charlotte was twenty-five years old.

Her husband, Jean, who sported a dapper, thin black mustache, had led an exemplary life as a prince and a soldier. Godson of Pope Benedict XV, the prince had just completed four years at Ampleforth College in Yorkshire, England, when the German invasion of Luxembourg compelled him to flee with his family, first to France, then to Portugal, where President Roosevelt had arranged for the battleship *Trenton* to carry them to the United States. Soon after their arrival, the grand-duchess, her husband Prince Felix, and the children left for Montreal. Luxembourg's prime minister, Pierre Dupong, who was in Canada with the sovereigns, wrote to Joseph Bech, minister of foreign affairs, who had taken refuge in London along with most of the Luxembourg government: "The grand-duchess must not learn that we want her to remain in Montreal because of the London bombardments, because if she did she would go immediately to the British capital."

Despite these efforts to keep her safe, the grand-duchess rejoined the government in London in 1940 and remained there for the rest of the war. Her husband meanwhile had gone off to join the British army. Prince Jean remained in Canada to pursue his studies in law and political science at the University of Quebec. At the end of 1942, the twenty-one-year-old prince joined up as an anonymous Luxembourgian recruit in a British regiment of the Irish Guards. He went on to attend Sandhurst, the British military academy, won his lieutenant's stripes in 1943, and attained the rank of captain in 1945. After participating in combat following the Normandy invasion, he entered Brussels with his unit, the 32nd Brigade. A week later he crossed the Luxembourg border, arriving in the grand-ducal capital the same day his father as well as the American Fifth Armored Division entered Luxembourg.

Prince Jean, decorated several times during the war, was named a colonel in the new Luxembourgian army. He would become a general when he acceded to the throne.

After the war Joseph Bech, now prime minister, set the example for European reconciliation. Although it had lost three-quarters of its territory during successive dismemberments in its history, Luxembourg had no intention of trying to recover its lost lands. On the contrary, it hoped for the creation of a supranational Europe.

It was Bech, the representative of this minute country, who in

1950 laid the foundations of the "new Europe" alongside France's Robert Schuman, Italy's Alcide De Gaspari, and Germany's Konrad Adenauer. Grand-Duchess Charlotte set her power and position in favor of the creation of what would possibly be a European superstate. Luxembourgers still remember the joy and pride they felt back in 1952 when the first European coal-steel accords, today universally known as the Accords of Luxembourg, were signed in the capital.

In 1961, Grand-Duchess Charlotte named Prince Jean her representative as head of state. It was a delegation of powers designed to pave the way for her abdication, which took place on November 12, 1964, after forty-five years of reign. She was sixty-eight years old, still beautiful, slim, and remarkably majestic. She could look back on a reign that between the two world wars had coincided with a period of prosperity, peace, and economic expansion.

WHEN THE GRAND-DUKE mounted the throne in 1964, he and Josephine-Charlotte moved from Betzdorf Castle, their residence for eleven years, into the newly decorated Colmar-Berg Castle. They now had five children: Marie-Astrid, born in 1954; Henri, the crown prince, born in 1955; the twins, Jean and Margaretha, who arrived in 1957; and Guillaume, born in 1963.

The vast castle is maintained by a staff of fifty. Official banquets are served by footmen in deep blue and orange livery, the colors of the House of Nassau. Following special dinners, there is often musical entertainment. Every member of the grand-ducal family is a music lover, and the sovereigns like to treat their guests to an evening with either a Luxembourg musical group, such as a chamber orchestra or a choral society, or a soloist. Today white tie and tails are no longer de rigueur for large receptions, having been superseded by the less formal black tie and tuxedo. And although custom still dictates that women curtsy to the grand-duchess, it has not been obligatory since Juliana, the former queen of Holland, forbade that particular homage to herself during an official visit.

The grand-ducal family, whose taste for a relaxed and family-oriented life is renowned throughout the royal and aristocratic circles of Europe, likes to refrain from everything that smacks of the ceremonial. Parents and children speak to each other in the familiar rather than the polite forms of address. When there are no official

Opposite top: The grand-duke and grand-duchess meet with Pope John Paul II in Rome in 1980. (Fabian/Sygma)

Opposite center: The grand-ducal family prefers relaxing together at home and on vacations in the outdoors. From left to right: Guillaume, Henri, Grand-Duchess Charlotte, Grand-Duke Jean, Marie-Astrid, and Jean. (Sygma)

Opposite bottom: A summer holiday in the south of France. From the right: Crown Prince Henri, his wife, Maria-Teresa, son Guillaume, sister Margaretha, and brother Guillaume. (James Andanson/Sygma)

Little Prince Guillaume celebrates his second birthday on his rocking horse. (Raymond Reuter/Sygma)

receptions the staff is reduced to minimum, and during vacations Grand-Duchess Josephine-Charlotte sometimes does her own cooking. Luxembourgers often see members of the royal family (including the dowager Grand-Duchess Charlotte, still extremely active despite the fact that she is now in her eighties) calmly going about their errands like any other citizens or going to the hair salon in town if a hairdresser can't come to them.

Sports provide the best relaxation and diversion as far as the family is concerned. They all love the outdoors, and if the grand-duke goes hunting from time to time in Grunewald Forest, it is mainly to keep the wild boar and deer populations from growing too large. Water sports are a special passion. Every year, in either July or August, the family goes to their villa in lower Provence. There they swim, water ski, and sail. They also own a chalet in Crans-sur-Sierre, in Switzerland, where they go every winter to ski. At times they visit various ski resorts in Switzerland, France, and Austria, usually by the invitation of friends. Princesses Marie-Astrid and Margaretha enjoy horseback riding, while Crown Prince Henri is a fencer.

Grand-Duke Jean has a reputation for being an affable and easily approachable man. He has the opportunity to meet many Luxembourgers, not only the ministers and the members of Parliament he receives at the palace, but also the ordinary citizens he encounters in less formal circumstances during the many local ceremonies he attends. He formulates ideas and opinions from these occasions that he transmits to his prime minister during their weekly meetings. Never in his twenty years of reign has he overstepped the powers conferred on him. With regard to almost all the country's political ceremonies he delegates his powers. For example, he is represented every year at the opening of Parliament by his prime minister.

AFTER THE ILL-FATED REIGN of Marie-Adelaide, and after the dynastic question resolved by referendum in 1919, the Luxembourg Constitution was amended to restrict the sovereign's prerogatives. In theory, they are still considerable: the grand-duke alone exercises executive power. Every law voted by Parliament has to be approved and signed by him, and if he does not sanction a law within three months, it becomes null and void. The grand-duke is commander of the armed forces and makes all appointments to civil and military posts. Among his other prerogatives are the royal rights—the right to pardon, the right to confer noble, military, and civil titles, and the right to order the coining of money. Every session of Parliament is opened in his name, justice is rendered in his name, and he has the right to defer or reduce sentences pronounced by the courts.

Between the two world wars, Grand-Duchess Charlotte still largely influenced the choice of prime minister. Today, the role of the grand-duke is only a formality. In the course of negotiations which the grand-duke does not attend, the various political parties agree on a choice for the future candidate. The grand-duke is then notified when he receives the various contingents, and he has only to follow the recommendations of the political parties to confirm the choice. Respecting the letter of the law, the grand-duke stays within the limits of the powers conferred on him in exercising his sovereign constitutional right "to be informed, to warn, and to encourage." He has never granted one noble title; in fact, no Luxembourger has been ennobled since 1815.

Thus there is no local aristocracy in Luxembourg, and the few aristocratic families who do live there, most of them of Belgium origin, are indistinguishable from the upper middle class. The royal family, however, maintains close relations with all the crowned heads of Europe. The grand-ducal couple's silver anniversary celebration, in 1978, was attended by many representatives from other royal families as well as by several deposed kings, including the former kings of Greece, Rumania, and Italy.

All, of course, were invited to the biggest Luxembourgian event of 1981: the marriage of twenty-six-year-old Crown Prince Henri to Maria-Teresa Mestre, a young Swiss commoner born in Cuba. It was not the first time that a European crown prince chose to marry a commoner. Nor was it the first time that a member of the grand-ducal family had done so. Charles, the brother of the reigning grand-duke, was married in 1967 to Joan Dillon—daughter of Douglas Dillon, the former U.S. ambassador to France—after her first marriage was annulled by the curia in Rome.

Henri, a wise young fellow, had given no hint that he would marry a commoner, the worst folly that a royal highness, especially an heir to a throne, could commit. In 1975, just after taking his baccalaureate degree, he was commissioned as an officer at Sandhurst. Three years later he accompanied the great Luxembourgian politician Gaston Thorn to the United States to study the economic policies there. He earned a degree in economics at the University of Geneva in 1980.

Like Silvia of Sweden and Sonja of Norway, Maria-Teresa did not immediately receive the blessing of her future in-laws. As a matter of fact, Grand-Duke Jean had asked his son to seriously reflect on what he wanted to do before committing himself. Prince Henri waited four years, until he finished his studies, before confirming his wish to unite with his heart's desire. He had the support of his mother, who intervened in his favor, persuaded that Maria-Teresa would be a perfect grand-duchess for the times. Wasn't it said that Silvia of Sweden, the commoner of German origin, had largely helped to strengthen her husband's throne?

Besides, what fault could be found with this cultivated and beautiful young woman, born to an upper-middle-class Catholic family? Maria-Teresa was three when her parents moved from Cuba to Switzerland, where her banker father was able to transfer most of his large fortune. She was educated in the United States and in Switzerland; in 1980 she obtained a degree in political science from the Institute of Political Studies in Geneva. Very athletic, she liked to ice skate, play tennis and swim, and she spent vacations every year in Gstaad, where days of skiing were followed by nights of dancing. She spoke Spanish, French, and English fluently, and was interested in music, literature, and painting. The prince could not have met a more accomplished young woman.

When Prince Henri presented his fiancée to the government the reaction was unanimously favorable; his choice was perceived as a democratic act in tune with the times. Grand-Duchess Charlotte, Henri's grandmother, who was so intransigent about the marriages of her own children, kept silent. But the Bourbon-Parmes, cousins of the family, haughtily proclaimed their disapproval. And among the Luxembourgian people there was some disappointment. "If the prince is going to marry a commoner, why not a Luxembourger?" a young office worker wistfully wondered before the marriage.

Nevertheless, after the wedding ceremony a small crowd gathered in the street to cheer the newlyweds, who dismayed everyone —especially the conservative grand-ducal family—by kissing longer than was considered decent.

Henri and Marie-Teresa now live with their baby son Guillaume at Heisdorf, their country villa. The shy young prince conscientiously carries out many official duties, preparing for the day he becomes grand-duke of Luxembourg.

THE SANGUINE LUXEMBOURGERS did not seem disappointed when it became more and more apparent that Marie-Astrid, the oldest of the grand-ducal children, would not marry England's Prince Charles, contrary to rumor that for years was fodder for gossip magazines. The thought that a princess of Luxembourg would become queen of England was, early on, quite agreeable. But Charles, whose amorous adventures were related in a particularly detailed fashion in local papers, seemed unworthy of the virtuous Marie-Astrid, a stranger to scandal.

At twenty-seven, Marie-Astrid was so timid and reserved, so nervous in her smiles, and so unstylish in her dress, that many feared she would remain a spinster. Others whispered that she would take the veil. When her engagement was finally announced —to His Imperial and Royal Highness Archduke Christian of Austria, also twenty-seven and a friend since childhood—European aristocracy breathed a collective sigh of relief.

They were married in February 1982 and lived their first few connubial months in New York, in an apartment overlooking Central Park. The archduke was a trainee in a New York bank, while the archduchess revived her career as a nurse. She left every morning for the hospital and came home every evening to her husband and three-room apartment, where she created admirable cheese soufflés, her favorite dish. They now live in Brussels, where Christian is a banker and Marie-Astrid looks after their first baby, Marie-Christine, born in 1983.

Six weeks after Marie-Astrid's wedding, her youngest sister Margaretha married Prince Nicholas of Liechtenstein. Although eclipsed by the earlier celebration, the marriage was also an important event: for the first time in decades, and for perhaps the last time in the history of European monarchies, the children of two reigning princes married each other. Today petulant, brunette Margaretha and Nicholas, Liechtenstein's permanent representative to the Council of Europe, live in Strasbourg.

The wedding of Marie-Astrid to Archduke Christian of Hapsburg. Directly behind the newlyweds are Beatrix and Claus of Holland. (Ledru/Graham/Sygma)

MOST OF THE EUROPEAN MONARCHIES assure the unity and stability of their people, but they add other important dimensions as well. Pomp and spectacle attract millions of tourists to London to watch the changing of the guard at Buckingham Palace; the British royal family seems to endow everything that is "made in England" with an air of majesty. The prince of Monaco, in his small domain, procures economic advantages for his country which are gigantic and incontestable. King Baudouin is the guarantor and upholder of Belgium's political unity. Juan Carlos of Spain founded and attempts to preserve a new political democracy.

The grand-ducal family of Luxembourg brought independence to the country a hundred years ago. Today, the family continues to ensure the continuity of Luxembourg's narrowly defined, but nevertheless quite real, constitutional powers. Moreover, the family helps maintain its country's presence in the heart of Europe as much through its personal alliances as through its close contacts with all the heads of state and a great number of international figures of the first rank.

In spite of these functions, which are shared by almost all constitutional monarchs, today's grand-ducal regime is somehow lacking in charisma and purpose. The grand-duke no longer enjoys the same popularity that his mother, Grand-Duchess Charlotte, did. In theory, his prerogatives and powers are the same as those of his brother-in-law King Baudouin, but since political life in Luxembourg is infinitely less complex than in Belgium, Grand-Duke Jean doesn't have Baudouin's opportunity to play the role of mediator. And finally, since most Luxembourgers are perfectly indifferent to the grand-ducal family, the family would not be able to produce the kind of spectacular monarchy native to England or Holland, where the strength and the popularity of the royal families are linked to, among other things, their acceptance of living under the scrutiny and sometimes indiscreet attention of the public. Not knowing how to evolve into the present to give itself new vigor, the sovereign family of Luxembourg seems content to limit itself to maintaining the past.

10

LIECHTENSTEIN

◆

Land of the Patron Princes

If a public relations agency were to promote the institution of monarchy, it would undoubtedly anchor its publicity on Liechtenstein. This tiny principality, nestled in a valley between Switzerland and Austria, is about as close to utopia as a sovereign state can get. Numerous countries on all five continents might today still be kingdoms had their monarchs been as wise and benevolent as the princes of Liechtenstein.

Just sixty-one miles square, with a population of only 26,000, Liechtenstein is nonetheless large enough to function as a truly sovereign state. The landscape is Alpine, the air crystalline, the streets impeccably clean. Liechtenstein enjoys one of the highest standards of living in the world, even though it possesses no raw materials—no oil, no coal, not even a powerful central source of electricity. Almost all the inhabitants are employed in industry, and yet there is no pollution. Physically pure, this little pristine land is spiritually pure as well, staunchly maintaining its neutrality through two world wars. Although every Liechtensteiner is expected to participate in the country's defense in the event of war, there has been no need to do so since 1868, when the country disbanded its army.

The principal industries are the production of lavish postage stamps (designed by local artists and prized by collectors), the processing of metal, and the production of false teeth (Ivoclar-Vivadent, is the second-largest manufacturer of false teeth in the world, exporting 65 million sets a year). The capital, Vaduz has three enormous banks and dozens of stores that sell the best of everything—the most expensive photographic equipment in the world, the most elaborate refrigerators, and the most luxurious cashmeres. There is one car for every three people, and most families have two or three in their garage. Cultural activities, however, are minimal: one amateur theater which presents operettas and three movie theaters make up the local entertainment. Residents say they are too busy working and earning money to do much of anything else.

Prince Franz-Josef II, sovereign of Liechtenstein, lives in a castle surrounded by moats perched high above Vaduz. The castle's electrically controlled drawbridge serves to protect him, not from enemies, revolutionaries, or terrorists, but merely from hordes of tourists eager to invade his private property. The prince and his wife, Princess Gina, and their five children cost the principality not a penny. They collect no annual endowment; even the token amounts the prince receives compensating him for official expenses are plowed back into his charitable works. What's more, in time of crisis, the people know they can count on the generosity of the Liechtenstein dynasty, whose princes in the past dipped into their own purses to supply whatever was necessary to ensure the survival of the country. What president of a republic could boast of having brought such advantages to his electorate?

His Serene Highness Prince Franz-Josef is one of the richest men in Europe, even though he lost 80 percent of his fortune in 1968 through the nationalization of his properties in Czechoslovakia. (In Moravia and Bohemia alone he once possessed millions of acres of land and 360 villages.) Franz-Josef still owns six palaces (two in Vienna), agricultural lands, hunting preserves, and an extraordinary collection of paintings considered by many, in terms of the number and quality of the canvases, to be the best private collection in the world. Works include masterpieces by Rubens, Brueghel the Elder, Van Dyck, and Dutch masters of the eighteenth century.

Franz-Josef is the last surviving sovereign of the Holy Roman Empire, created in 972 when Pope John XII crowned the duke of Saxe Emperor Othon the Great. The empire set out to gather hundreds of kingdoms, principalities, and free city-states under its umbrella, and for almost nine hundred years was all-powerful. Then Napoleon I appeared on the European scene and conquered the empire's armies in 1805, dispersing the 343 member-states. When, one year later, Napoleon created the Confederation of the Rhine—a league of German states—little Liechtenstein remained one of the rare survivors of the defunct empire. Since that time the other surviving member-states have vanished, including the great dynasties of the Hapsburgs in Austria-Hungary and the Hohenzollerns in Germany, and many thrones have collapsed. Yet counter to all logic, one prince managed to survive this imperial demolition and to reign today over a country purchased by his ancestors with their own funds three hundred years ago. Here, in this tiny Alpine domain, the last remaining star of the Holy Roman Empire discreetly shines on.

The name Liechtenstein could be a synonym for benevolent and enlightened government. With unselfishness and vision extremely unusual among princes, this dynasty is responsible for raising its subjects from ignorance and squalor. In the history of sovereigns, the Liechtensteins occupy a separate place, one in which they are to the art of governing what patrons are to pure art.

The Liechtensteins took their name from a castle to the south of Vienna, their original family seat. In 1608, Charles of Liechtenstein, former governor of Moravia and a member of the imperial court of Prague, was made a prince in recognition of his meritorious service to the Hapsburgs. From the moment of the promotion, the Liechtensteins began scouting for a territory to call their own, preferably one within the province of the Holy Roman Empire so they would be able to join the empire and reign as one of its sovereignties.

During this period, a little valley lost in the Alps was mired in misery and violence; the few thousand inhabitants survived with great difficulty. War was only one of the misfortunes that struck them regularly. At the beginning of the seventeenth century, in the valley of Vaduz, which belonged to the counts of Hohenem, the plague was rampant. Weakened and diminished by disease, the villages were successfully plundered by the Souaves, the Austrians, and the Swedes. But an even greater calamity was to befall the defenseless peasants. For thirty years the evil Hohenems instituted a witchcraft purge, bringing up charges of sorcery against the

The hilltop castle at Vaduz houses 1,600 paintings, which is only a small part of Franz-Josef's vast collection. (Press and Information Office of the Government)

Franz-Josef and Gina have been happily married for forty-one years. (Press and Information Office of the Government) tiny population of their territory. The peasants' lives were comprised of the village warning bell, bonfires, and the murderous insanity of their sovereigns. In the course of three decades of madness more than three hundred of the three thousand inhabitants were executed, most of them burned alive.

Serenity was restored when Jean Adam André, the son of Charles of Liechtenstein, bought the domain of Schellenberg in 1699 and, thirteen years later, the neighboring county of Vaduz, sold by the abominable Hohenems. In 1719 Charles VI, sovereign of the Holy Roman Empire, united the two domains under the name of Liechtenstein and elevated the newly created country to the status of a principality of the empire. The first reigning prince was Anton Florian, second cousin of Jean Adam André, who died shortly after his purchase of the lands.

The new princes of Liechtenstein had never seen their valley principality, but it hardly mattered. What was important was that their new status in the empire conferred on them a seat and a voice in the Council of Princes and further extended their influence and fortune in Austria-Hungary, where they possessed lands ten times more extensive. Through the eighteenth century, the princes distinguished themselves as field marshals and ambassadors at the service of the Hapsburgs, and fully enjoyed the uninihibited showiness of the Hapsburg court, a temple to the waltz and to elegance, to celebrations and to the good life, where all in attendance dressed in white stockings and court dress.

The Liechtenstein princes launched their country first along the path of sovereignty and independence, then on to modernization and prosperity. Aloïs II (1805–1836) established the Austrian civil and penal codes and abolished serfdom. Jean II (1858–1929) laid down the foundations of a modern economy and in the course of his reign gave Liechtenstein and Austria a total of 75 million Swiss francs, a fabulous sum drawn from his personal fortune.

Franz-Josef II, the current prince, was born in 1906 at Frauenthal, one of the family castles in Austria. He was named for his godfather, Emperor Franz-Josef I. An important part of Franz-Josef's childhood, from 1911 to 1914, was spent at the castle of Gross-Ullersdorf, one of the most beautiful royal residences in the world, situated on a site of incomparable splendor in a park larger than the country of Liechtenstein. (An ardent nature lover, the prince dates his passion for the outdoors from this three-year period.) He attended high school in Vienna with the children of the local middle class and, after passing his final exams, enrolled at the Institute of Agriculture in Vienna, where he studied forestry and was graduated as a forestry engineer in 1929.

In 1938, on the eve of World War II, Franz-Josef, thirty-two years old, succeeded his great-uncle Franz I as sovereign of Liechtenstein. The trying years of war further solidified the bonds between the country and its prince. With only fifteen thousand inhabitants and four policemen, and no army whatsoever, minuscule Liechtenstein was the extremely vulnerable neighbor of Adolf Hitler's Third Reich and its helmeted storm troopers and armored regiments. Liechtensteiners knew that their independence depended greatly on the reigning dynasty. Prince Franz-Josef, whose liberal and democratic spirit was well known, witnessed with undisguised pain the German takeover of Austria, his country of origin. The first of his line to live full time in Liechtenstein rather than in Vienna, it was perhaps the shock that he suffered on learning of SS troops stomping through the streets of the Austrian capital that spurred him to identify more completely than any of his predecessors with his tiny principality. To maintain neutrality, he cut most of the ties between Liechtenstein and Austria and tightened his bond with Switzerland.

Five years after he inherited the throne, Franz-Josef married Countess Georgina de Wilczek, an aristocratic young woman from Silesia who was fifteen years his junior.

The young prince had known Georgina, whom he called Gina, for years; their families had been friendly for more than a century. (In fact, around 1900 Georgina's grandfather had been in charge of restoring the castle at Vaduz, without having any idea, of course, that he was transforming the setting where his great-grandchildren would grow up.) The courtship of Franz-Josef and Georgina was a long one, blooming from a simple friendship. They appeared often in Vienna at balls and cocktail parties and frequently attended the theater. Georgina was regularly invited to the great hunts that Franz-Josef gave in the fall at his properties in Czechoslovakia.

Georgina arrived in Liechtenstein only two days before her marriage. She still remembers her amazement of coming from battle-scarred Austria during the middle of the war to enter the little mountainous country where nobody stinted on lights, dinners, fruits, and chocolates. Under Hitler's regime Gina had been obliged to work at a "social service." She had the choice of becoming an aide to a large family or joining a farm operation. She chose the stables and the fields, and in addition to farmwork helped care for prisoners of war.

On March 7, 1943, her life changed dramatically. In a tranquil country carefully maintained outside the conflict, Gina married Franz-Josef in a frosty landscape where the sky was as white as the earth and the branches of the trees were covered with snow. She wore a simple bridal gown created from a remnant of low-grade silk obtained with great difficulty because of wartime rationing. The marriage festivities were kept to a bare minimum. Only twenty family members and friends were able to attend the ceremony; not one member of the Hapsburg family, all refugees in the United States, was present.

Just before the end of the war, their first child was born: Crown Prince Hans-Adam Pie, named in honor of his godfather, who was an ancestor of Pope Pius XII. Philippe-Erasme was born a year later, then Nicolas-Ferdinand in 1947, Nora-Elizabeth in 1950, and finally the youngest—considerably younger than his sister and brothers—François-Joseph Wenceslas, born in 1960. The children shared a happy childhood, secure in the cocoon of a particularly harmonious family life. All five attended primary school in Vaduz, Franz-Josef and Gina believing that their children should receive a normal education.

TALL, with gray hair and mustache, Prince Franz-Josef bears a striking resemblance to the Hapsburgs, to whom he is related on his mother's side (Archduchess Elizabeth). The prince leads a tranquil life in his castle in Vaduz, amid the splendor of his paintings, tapestries, and lavishly sculpted wood-paneled rooms. Until recently, when Crown Prince Hans-Adam moved into the east wing, the royal family occupied only about 40 of the 115 rooms of the castle. Although still largely unoccupied, the entire structure has been renovated. With great pride in his huge residence, Franz-Josef supervised all maintenance and restoration work. It took fifteen years to install central heating and electricity, since the prince was insistent that all the pipes and wires be perfectly invisible so as not to mar the beauty of the medieval and Renaissance decor. In one concession to modern creature comfort, he allowed two elevators to be set into the ancient stonework.

Usually dressed casually in a turtleneck, sports jacket, and suede shoes, Prince Franz-Josef attends 8:30 mass in the castle chapel several times a week, has breakfast, and then begins his workday. He reads the newspapers and then, with the aid of his secretary, attends to official duties as well as his private affairs. Late in the morning, he gives a number of audiences for members of the government.

During his free afternoons Franz-Josef jogs through the countryside; in the summer he swims in the castle pool and, of course, in the winter skis on nearby trails, always accompanied by a guide. He loves the long, difficult slopes and prefers to ski outside the marked trails. He is very proud that his children are better skiers than he is, noting that "they started very young and I only at twenty-five." His life style is unpretentious and low key—he travels throughout his country without an escort and even has his telephone number listed in the directory.

A bit of a Renaissance man, Franz-Josef is deeply interested in botany and zoology and in art history. He is a specialist in the Romand (French-Swiss) period of twelfth- and thirteenth-century art. He is also an expert on rugs and tapestries. As Princess Gina has noted on several occasions, "He dedicates all his time to the principality, but he could have been a beaux-arts professor." Franz-Josef keeps only a small part of his collection of paintings—1,600 canvases—at the castle. His two favorites are by Rubens: a portrait of the artist's daughter and another of his sons. Many paintings in his collection are exhibited in the state museum, which also houses part of the Liechtenstein family's magnificent collection of two thousand firearms, some of which date from the sixteenth and seventeenth centuries.

Princess Gina—merry, more extroverted than her husband, and dressed as often as possible in slacks and a pullover—drives her own car and does errands in Vaduz like any other Liechtenstein housewife. She buys most of her wardrobe in Zurich, the closest metropolis, and prefers high-quality ready-to-wear clothes to haute couture, eliminating the need for time-consuming fittings.

In contrast to her husband, Gina loves modern art—particularly the painters Soulages and Poliakoff—as well as contemporary Italian furniture, which she uses extensively in her favorite retreat, an isolated mountain chalet not far from the castle with a spectacular view.

Deeply involved in numerous projects—the Liechtenstein Red

Cross, of which she is president, a school and workshop for re-
tarded children, an old-age home, and a program for prisoner re-
habilitation—the princess still finds time for an active social life
with her husband. The prince and princess occasionally invite a few
members of the English royal family, with whom they have cordial
relations, to a hunting party or to ski runs down nearby snowy
trails. They rarely, however, give parties or receptions in the castle
at Vaduz. When they do entertain on a grand scale it is usually in
Austria. Every year they spend a month in their residence in Vienna
—Liechtenstein Palace—which faces the Grand Theater. There,
they hold an annual reception for several hundred guests and from
time to time give a grand ball. Also on their Vienna agenda are
concerts and operas, two of their favorite pastimes while they were
courting. Movies are generally out since the prince is not a big fan,
although he does enjoy documentaries; even with all the available
space, he has never installed a private screening room in the castle
at Vaduz.

In the summer the royal family travels to the seashore, either in
Italy or by the North Sea. It is often their only annual trip; the
prince says he hardly has time to travel.

In 1967, breaking with their normal policy of low-profile living,
the prince and princess of Liechtenstein provided a lavish wedding
for their son, Crown Prince Hans-Adam, when he married Countess Marie-Aglaé Kinsky. Hans-Adam was twenty-two years old
and had not yet completed his studies in political science at the
University of St. Gall. Countess Marie-Aglaé, from a fine, noble
Bohemian family, was twenty-seven and working quite successfully as a graphic designer. Marie-Aglaé had met the young prince
at Vaduz Castle, where she was a frequent guest of the family. The
prince was not quite nineteen years old when their friendship blos-
somed into romance. The young couple shared a taste for music
and traveled all over Germany to hear great operatic performances.

Shortly after their marriage, Hans-Adam and Marie-Aglaé
moved into a large wooden sixteenth-century chalet near the castle.
Formerly quarters for the domestics, it became available when the
head chef refused to live there. The ten low-ceilinged rooms of the
chalet were completely redecorated by Marie-Aglaé.

During the day, Hans-Adam prepares for his future role as reigning prince by managing the dynasty's estates and representing his
father at occasional official ceremonies. Marie-Aglaé is involved

with the arts and educational programs. At home, the crown princess has two in help—a nanny for the children and a young woman
who keeps house. There is no chef. At noon Hans-Adam and
Marie-Aglaé lunch with Prince Franz-Josef and Princess Gina. In
the evening they have a simple dinner at home, often a fondue
accompanied by a bit of air-dried beef from nearby Grisons. Bordeaux or local wines usually accompany dinner. Occasionally,
Marie-Aglaé prepares a lavish meal. A specialist in French cuisine,
she is a fine cook whose grilled meats and sauces are renowned
throughout the princely family.

Marie-Aglaé and Hans-Adam have four children, the eldest of
whom, Aloïs, will be the fourteenth reigning prince of Liechtenstein. A blond child who bears a striking resemblance to Princess
Gina, Aloïs was baptized in a dress of sheer dotted swiss, with his
godfather, Hans-Adam's brother Phillippe, by his side. Conform-
ing to the princely tradition of the Liechtenstein family, the child
has no godmother. Aloïs has two brothers, the Princes Maximilian
and Constantin, and a sister, Tatjana, the baby of the family, born
in 1973. All four attend school in Vaduz. Several years ago, when
they outgrew the cozy chalet, the crown prince and his family
moved into the east wing of the castle, which was redecorated to
Marie-Aglaé's specifications.

THE PRINCIPALITY OF LIECHTENSTEIN is a constitutional
monarchy. The prince's hereditary position is passed on exclusive
of the people's will, while the people's right to govern themselves
exists independent of the prince, to whom nothing is owed. In
theory, according to the Liechtenstein Constitution, the prince has
absolutely all powers. Officially, he is the supreme authority of the
state. He can rule by emergency decree, he represents the state in
his relations with foreign powers, and he names high officials upon
recommendation from the Landtag, Liechtenstein's Parliament. In
practice, however, the power is in the hands of the people. Fifteen
deputies sit in the Landtag, elected by the people of Liechtenstein,
who can participate directly in political decisions through their constitutional rights of initiative and referendum. Switzerland also
benefits from these two tools of popular expression, but in tiny
Liechtenstein, where everybody knows everybody else and where
the financial resources of the state are limited, the size of the coun-

Crown Prince Hans-Adam and his family outgrew their cozy chalet and now live in the east wing of the castle at Vaduz. (Press and Information Office of the Government)

The monarchs surrounded by children and grandchildren. (Press and Information Office of the Government)

try gives a rare power and acuity to the expression of the people's will. All parliamentary decisions involving a new annual expense of 20,000 francs or more or a single expense of at least 50,000 francs must be submitted to popular vote whenever it is called for either by the Landtag or by a petition of six hundred citizens.

In principle, the prince signs everything that the five members of government—the prime minister and four councillors—submit to him. And his sanction is required to enact any new law. The Constitution also confers on the prince the power of veto, but he has used this right only once, on an issue concerning new hunting laws, a subject he takes very much to heart. Justice is rendered in the prince's name, but the only serious offenses that occur from time to time concern the tens of thousands of foreign corporations in and around Vaduz. The police force is unarmed and maintains a blind eye toward the source of capital held by the private companies.

Between 1923 and 1928, the Liechtenstein government developed and promoted tax laws and fiscal privileges that were extremely beneficial to foreign companies domiciled in the country. At this same time Liechtenstein citizenship was easily obtainable at a reasonable price. However, in 1953, when the International Court of The Hague refused to recognize any nationality so easily obtained, the practice diminished. Today it is practically impossible to obtain Liechtenstein nationality, even for Austrian or Swiss residents living on the border with close family ties to Liechtenstein. It is said that many exiled kings at one time or another solicited their "cousin" Prince Franz-Josef for a new identity under a Liechtenstein passport, all to no avail. To one of them, the prince is said to have responded phlegmatically, "It is so difficult that you would do better to give up the idea. Get some other nationality."

In his castle overlooking the city of Vaduz, the prince usually remains above—both figuratively and literally—the affairs of state. He has, however, taken a stance in favor of stricter controls over the foreign companies operating in his country. In a recent interview in the London *Sunday Telegraph,* he came out in favor of revising legislation to implement much stricter controls over the activities of foreign companies, not only in Liechtenstein but also abroad: "Our laws should be as strict as those in Switzerland, or even more strict. Certain corporations established in Liechtenstein would leave the country, but others, on the other hand, would be drawn here because of our improved reputation." The industrialization of the country, he affirms, is much more profitable than the artificial money generated by phantom companies. The prince is an advocate of modernization: he supports the women's vote, which still does not exist in the principality, various social reforms, and close international cooperation.

Franz-Josef travels abroad occasionally, but only on private visits, never official ones. "It would be ridiculous," he maintains, "for the sovereign of a country as small as mine to travel on an official visit and, upon arriving, to find an honor guard larger than the population of Liechtenstein."

He does receive foreign envoys at home, and also names representatives from his own country to go abroad. Liechtenstein has only one foreign ambassador—Prince Henri de Liechtenstein, the youngest of Franz-Josef's seven brothers and sisters—who is posted in Berne, Switzerland. Almost all ambassadors posted in the Swiss capital are automatically accredited in Liechtenstein. In the past, the princely house of Liechtenstein, whose power and prestige far surpassed the reputation of the country, conducted all of the principality's foreign affairs. Today foreign politics, such as they are, are in the domain of the government, which rarely has the opportunity to follow up any kind of diplomatic initiative or controversy, given that Liechtenstein is neutral and is surrounded by two equally neutral countries, Switzerland and Austria. Aside from its customs and postal agreements with Switzerland, Liechtenstein has no alliances, either political or military, and the prince, a descendant of one of the most illustrious lines of military marshals of the Holy Roman Empire, possesses neither armed forces nor armaments, not even an honor guard to deploy on special occasions.

In 1984, Franz-Josef, while remaining head of state, will turn over most of his duties to the heir-apparent, Crown Prince Hans-Adam. There is no doubt that when Hans-Adam assumes a more active political role he will be a strong supporter, following his father's lead, of one particular issue that has always interested him —that of giving women the right to vote. (Twice during Franz-Josef's reign, proposals to grant women the vote were turned down in a plebiscite.) The crown prince also favors a gradual pulling away of his country from its ties with Switzerland. Addressing a youth group in the city of Triesen, he declared that Liechtenstein "traveled for two centuries in the knapsack of Austria, and it is

Crown Prince Hans-Adam represents his father at many official ceremonies, while Marie-Aglaé is involved in educational programs and in the arts. (Press and Information Office of the Government)

now in the knapsack of Switzerland. Sooner or later, either we begin to travel on our own or we will be forced to give up a larger and larger part of our independence. Economically we are very active, but politically we are Sleeping Beauty." To some people, Hans-Adam is no more than his father's mouthpiece, instructed to make declarations which Franz-Josef promotes but which, as sovereign, he does not want to assume responsibility for. The crown prince's declarations have caused mild irritation in Berne among federal officials. Switzerland observes these verbal machinations with extreme distrust, believing that Liechtenstein has an ulterior motive: to one day become an independent member of the Common Market with the same rights and under the same conditions as Luxembourg.

By the same token, normally discreet Liechtenstein is becoming openly and increasingly irritated with its big sister and neighbor Switzerland. Many Liechtensteiners feel that Switzerland, by means of various contractual agreements, is inhibiting their banking development. The irritation is exacerbated by frequent incursions of Swiss police who illegally cross the border in pursuit of traffic violators.

These bones of contention, which occasionally border on the burlesque, serve to strengthen the deep reciprocal bonds between Liechtenstein and its prince. The royal family would not exist today if its ancestors had not, centuries back, bought this little valley lost in an Alpine hollow. But without the monarchy, Liechtensteiners would have long ago lost their independence; without a doubt they would now be citizens of a twenty-third Swiss canton. Today, however, even if Switzerland wanted to admit them against their will, the effort would pose almost insurmountable problems. As one Swiss council member states, "How would we admit a principality among all our bourgeois cantons?" Thus it is that Prince Franz-Josef, a reserved and modest old gentleman, remains the best shield minuscule Liechtenstein could brandish against its greedy neighbors, a noble and venerable defense guaranteeing the country's independence and sovereignty.